Praise for *The Conspiracists*

"Insightful, nuanced, and thoughtful, *The Conspiracists* offers a refreshing take on the complex and often misunderstood world of conspirituality. It expertly blends empathy and honesty with captivating storytelling."
—**Eviane Leidig**, author of *The Women of the Far Right*

"For anyone who has wondered how so many women went down the QAnon rabbit hole, Cook's deep dive into two women's stories is a must-read. A compelling, eye-opening account of the vulnerabilities and vitriol that have dragged so many women into unimaginable beliefs."
—**Dr. Cynthia Miller-Idriss**, author of *Man Up: The New Misogyny and the Rise of Violent Extremism* and professor and founding director of Polarization & Extremism Research & Innovation Lab (PERIL), American University

"As conspiracy theory belief becomes more mainstream and acceptable, it becomes that much more important to understand what it offers believers. Through empathy and curiosity, *The Conspiracists* reveals how two women sought community, personal success, meaning, and a higher purpose to their many traumas in the delusions of QAnon and the false promises of gurus—leading to them going to prison for storming the Capitol. This is a deeply reported and highly compelling examination of a problem we are only just starting to grasp."
—**Mike Rothschild**, journalist, conspiracy theory expert, and author of *The Storm Is Upon Us* and *Jewish Space Lasers*

"*The Conspiracists* is a thought-provoking and timely look into the complexities of the emotional lives of women who participated in the Capitol insurrection. Through deep analysis of real-life cases, Cook explores the human side of misinformation, the trauma behind those stories, and what drew some people away from their conspiracy theories. This powerful study illuminates the common danger of conspiracy theories."
—**Dr. Christine Sarteschi**, LCSW, professor of social work and criminology

The Conspiracists

Women, Extremism,
and the Lure of Belonging

The Conspiracists

Noelle Cook

BROADLEAF BOOKS
MINNEAPOLIS

THE CONSPIRACISTS
Women, Extremism, and the Lure of Belonging

31   30   29   28   27   26   25   1   2   3   4   5   6   7   8   9

Library of Congress Control Number: 2025938523 (print)

Cover design: James Jacobelli
Cover image: © 2025 iStock / Getty Images Plus; Princess Mask by CSA_Plastock

Print ISBN: 979-8-8898-3242-3
eBook ISBN: 979-8-8898-3243-0

Printed in India.

For my grandma, my person,
Lorraine F. Robison (1927–2019),
a writer who dreamed of being published.
She would be so proud of me.

Contents

CHAPTER 1

Capitol Conspiracies

We left the federal courthouse in Washington, DC, in a hurry. Yvonne St. Cyr and her husband, Troy, were anxious to reach their car, parked near Union Station, so they could get out of town. They were driving to their son's house in Ohio and then back home to Idaho the next day.

It was drizzling, and the wetness was starting to flatten the long brown hair Yvonne was letting go gray. She had stopped coloring it during the pandemic, which had brought massive changes to her life and worldview. Yvonne is an attractive, charismatic woman in her mid-fifties, with an energetic presence and an expressive face. Today she was speaking in her usual impassioned tone, but she was talking quickly without many pauses. She was complaining about a trial that has just happened: denouncing the verdict, the prosecutor, the judge, and then the verdict again.

Our quick pace had less to do with the bad weather and more to do with Yvonne being rattled by the courtroom verdict. It was March 10, 2023, and a jury had just convicted her of four misdemeanors and two felonies for storming the US Capitol Building on January 6, 2021.

Yvonne had been hoping for an acquittal. Over the course of the trial, her husband had reported receiving nods from a male juror. He thought they had an ally. Perhaps this juror felt bad after learning about Yvonne's abuse-filled childhood, her decorated service in the Marines, or the fact that she was a mother of five and grandmother of eleven. "It only takes one heart to change," Yvonne had said many times during the trial.

The problem for Yvonne was that the evidence against her would likely overwhelm any sympathy jurors might have felt. From the start, the public defenders representing her had called the case "indefensible," she told me. They had begged her to take the plea deal the government had offered, which would have scaled back the charges to two misdemeanors. Judging by sentencing in similar cases, Yvonne probably would have spent less than sixty days in prison. By rejecting the plea, she now faced four misdemeanors—and two felonies.

Those felony charges carried extra weight, given that Yvonne had already spent time in prison for possession and distribution of cocaine. That was back in 2003, when Yvonne was a Marine drill instructor stationed in South Carolina. She had built a successful career breaking down recruits and building them into Marines. It all came crashing down after a court-martial, four months in the brig, and a dishonorable discharge. If found guilty on the January 6 felony charges, Yvonne's prior conviction would undoubtedly hurt her at sentencing.

Yvonne's lawyers warned her that a conviction was practically guaranteed because all the January 6 crimes she was charged with had been captured on camera. Yvonne's trial was mostly a long string of video clips accompanied by testimony from FBI agents and police officers. Prosecutors had scoured hours of footage from security cameras, social media accounts, and the huge bank of cell phone video collected during the January 6 investigations. Seemingly every move Yvonne made was captured from several different angles, including from her own cell phone. You can see her everywhere on videos from that day, dressed in a white winter coat, blue hat, and pink backpack. At her trial, prosecutors presented video clips and then witness testimony from Capitol and Metro Police officers who had told Yvonne numerous times to leave the grounds. The prosecution also presented lots of damning evidence from the videos Yvonne had recorded and posted to social media while the insurrection was going on.

Yvonne had gone to Washington that day to be part of history. She and her husband had driven across the country from Idaho to attend Donald Trump's Stop the Steal rally because Trump had announced the protest would be "wild." The rally was a product of a conspiracy theory perpetuated by Trump that the 2020 presidential election had been stolen by Joe Biden, a claim for which there was no credible evidence. Yvonne wanted to be present for what she believed would be a historic event. After the rally, they had both marched to the Capitol with the crowd. Yvonne got separated from Troy as she pushed her way to the frontlines, eventually reaching the perimeter of interlocking bike racks that surrounded the building.

When she got to the racks, the crowd was already pushing against them, and Capitol Police officers were trying to restore the line to keep the barricade from buckling. The former Marine gunnery sergeant turned her back to a rack, planted her feet, and pushed the full weight of her body against the metal frame, using her leverage to hold the line against the police on the other side. A shot of pepper spray to the face didn't deter her, nor did police officers begging her to move off the racks before she got hurt. Yvonne's response was to bark out orders to her fellow protestors: "Tear it down! Let's go! Push it! Don't be scared! Push it! . . . There are millions of us! Push it! They can't stop us all! This is our house! Let's go!"

When the line broke, Yvonne was one of the first people into the tunnels that led to the ground-level entrances on the Capitol's west front. She climbed a ledge in the tunnel behind the crowd that was trying to force its way through thick glass security doors. "We need fresh bodies! We need fresh bodies!" she shouted from the tunnel opening. When the crowd started rhythmically rocking, using their collective mass to "heave-ho" open the doors, Yvonne called the cadence. "Push! Push! Push!" she repeated fifteen times.

When the police reclaimed the tunnel, an officer had to prod her with a flagpole to make her leave. But she re-entered the Capitol Building through a broken window, combat crawling over shattered safety glass to get through. Once inside, Yvonne walked around and recorded several live stream videos. "Patriots are in our house!" Yvonne proclaimed triumphantly in an early one. In the next, a fog of pepper spray hangs in the air and sirens blare as she announces: "Americans are being beaten for wanting to save their country!" In the last video that she live streamed from the Capitol grounds, she says that it's too chaotic inside and that she's leaving the building to charge her phone and find Troy.

Sitting in the courtroom as an observer on that March day, I was surprised the prosecutors hadn't used the video montage Yvonne had put together herself shortly after January 6. That montage collected all her photos and live streams from the day in one place. The video's text banner reads "No regrets" and "I would do it again and again." Yvonne set the violent imagery of January 6 to a lighthearted, uplifting musical track, like you might do if you were making a video celebrating a high school graduation or a fun family vacation.

Yvonne's fate with the jury was likely sealed when she took the stand in her own defense. Her testimony had been the subject of a long and heated debate with her attorneys. Yvonne wanted to take the stand. Her lawyers told her that testifying would guarantee a conviction. But Yvonne was so insistent about testifying that she told me on several occasions that she was considering firing her attorneys. One plan was to let them handle the case until the very end and then fire them so that she could present her own closing argument. She was still debating with her lawyers the night before the trial started.

Yvonne and Troy wanted the lawyers to help them expose the "truth" that the 2020 presidential election had been stolen by a cabal of elites they believed were plotting against freedom. "Are you willing to risk your licenses for the truth?" Troy had asked his wife's lawyers. No, the attorneys said; they were not.

Yvonne was going to deliver the message regardless of what her attorneys advised. Speaking her truth was why she had demanded a jury trial in the first place, and why she had insisted on taking the stand. Yvonne's lawyers worked with her to tone down the language and remove references to January 6 as the start of an apocalyptic end to an old, corrupt order and the dawn of a new age. The full message Yvonne had wanted to deliver included talk of an impending spiritual transformation across the earth, in which some people would ascend to a higher level of consciousness and others would be left behind. Yvonne wanted to announce that she was an ascended being, one who would help lead the righteous in a spiritual conflict that she believes will soon engulf the planet—a conflict that, according to her, large numbers of people will not survive.

Even the watered-down version that Yvonne delivered was unsettling. "This is war . . . We are at war," Yvonne repeatedly testified. "I have eleven grandkids. I want to ensure that freedom remains for our country. I took an oath to support and defend our Constitution. That meant something to me." Her voice was tinged with something between determination and anger. "I will stand for truth and freedom for my brothers and sisters. I believe with all my being in all my soul that we are in a spiritual war between good and evil right now. And I stand with the light."

This was Yvonne's defense: She was innocent because she was an American citizen who had been called to the Capitol Building by Donald Trump to fulfill her spiritual destiny.

"I'm a divine sovereign being, and I believe that my right is given to me by the creator of this universe," she said. "It is the right to life, liberty, and the pursuit of happiness, that is my birth right. And if any law or anyone stands in the way, I will stand up for truth and liberty, that is my sole purpose. That is why I'm here."

"There are no limitations to the rights given to me by God," she said. "I believe I had the right to be inside the Capitol Building at that time because our liberty is at risk, and I stand for truth and freedom and liberty, and I'll do it until my last dying breath." Yvonne said she would fight for liberty "for as long as it took." "I would die for freedom," she said.

The jury didn't take long to reach a unanimous guilty verdict on all six counts. The judge ordered Yvonne to return to Washington for sentencing during the summer.

At a final meeting with counsel that March afternoon, Yvonne's attorneys told her to keep a low profile between then and her sentencing. Stay off social media, they advised, warning her that anything she did or said between then and the sentencing hearing could affect how long she would have to stay in federal prison. The lawyers told Yvonne she was probably looking at anywhere between eighteen months and five years, depending on how they factored in her prior conviction. They reiterated that speaking out on social media like she had already done during the trial, talking disparagingly about the trial or judge or jury—any of that—could result in a longer sentence.

Now, about fifteen minutes after that meeting, we were walking from the courthouse to her car, with Yvonne telling me what her lawyers had said about staying off social media. Then, in mid-stride, she whipped out her cell phone, turned on her camera, and started live streaming on Facebook.

"I have been advised to not talk about their corrupt system," Yvonne announced, "but you know me: I'm not afraid of anything. And if there's consequences for telling the truth, then I'll take the consequences, 'cause God's got my back, and I'm protected." She then launched into an utterly unrepentant rant condemning the trial and vowing that "we will bring this system down."

I said goodbye to Yvonne and Troy near Union Station, where I was heading to catch a train. She told me she was grateful that I had been with her through the trial. I said I planned to be there for her sentencing hearing as well. We agreed to talk the following week when she was back home.

You are likely wondering how I knew Yvonne, and why I was attending her trial and speaking to her in the way a friend would. Sometimes I wonder the same thing. Defining our relationship is not easy. I don't agree with Yvonne about a lot of things—politics most of all. We come from different worlds in many ways. But our unexpected and unintended association, connection, friendship—whatever you ultimately want to call it—stands at the heart of this book. Yvonne has long known I have been writing a book about the women who stormed the US Capitol Building. She knows she will be part of it. And that's just fine by her.

Yvonne wants her story told because she believes she is at the center of a much larger fight than this court case. Her fight is larger than Donald Trump's "stolen election" or the Capitol insurrection, or even the QAnon conspiracy about child trafficking, blood-drinking elites. It started long before January 6 and even brought her away from evangelical Christianity. Yvonne believes she is fighting a spiritual war with real-world consequences and that the fate of humanity rests on its outcome.

Yvonne's new religion comes from the realm of what some scholars have called *conspirituality*, which is a blend of New Age religion, anti-vaccination advocacy, and anti-government extremism, all mixed with various right-wing conspiracy theories and heaping spoonfuls of antisemitism and white supremacy. Conspirituality is "a means by which political cynicism is tempered with spiritual optimism," according to academics Charlotte Ward and David Voas, who coined the term. This spiritual movement is quickly growing via the internet, creating what Ward and Voas call "a broad politico-spiritual philosophy based on two core convictions, the first traditional to conspiracy theory, the second rooted in the New Age: 1) a secret group covertly controls, or is trying to control, the political and social order, and 2) humanity is undergoing a 'paradigm shift' in consciousness."

Since the pandemic, the number of adherents to conspirituality has been increasing at frightening rates, as has the spread of conspiracy theories and the ranks of those who believe them as truth.

Yvonne has made it clear that she will keep fighting in the spiritual war that brought her to the Capitol even if she gets a long prison sentence. "I'll just teach people in prison," the former Marine drill instructor told me, already making plans to train an army of spiritual warriors among the other inmates while she is behind bars.

Yvonne has told me that just before someone ascends to the highest level of consciousness, right before their "third eye" is about to open, they start to have visions of themselves saving the world through their own sacrifice.

Yvonne told me she feels like her third eye is about to open.

✦

When I started the research that has ended up as this book, getting to know these women personally was the last thing I intended. I began from a place of academic objectivity—a distance from my subjects that I never planned to abandon. At that time, I was in a graduate program in women's and gender studies, and I had been trained to approach subjects with as much analytical distance as possible. At one point, my graduate advisor cautioned me about the pitfalls of getting too close to my participants.

I didn't go to Washington, DC, on January 6, 2021, looking for subjects to interview. I went in search of a new project for my graduate thesis after COVID-19 destroyed my original one. On March 9, 2020, I had arrived in New Delhi, India, for a two-month stay to film a documentary on women rideshare drivers. Two days later, the World Health Organization declared a global pandemic. A week after the announcement, I was on one of the last flights out of India before the airports closed.

When it became clear I would not be returning to that research any time soon, I reluctantly scrapped the project and started looking for a new one. I was interested in visual anthropology, and I had been fascinated by the different protests I had attended as a participant during the first Trump administration: the Women's March, the March for Science, the People's Climate March, and several others, including a Black Lives Matter protest in Baltimore. I had taken extensive photographs at each one. I was interested in the visual comparisons between protests on the left and right. So I went to Washington on January 6 to photograph the Stop the Steal rally, hoping my photographs could form the basis of a new thesis project.

You could say that I got more than I bargained for.

I drove to DC from my then-home in Maryland that day, arriving just as the crowd was breaching the Capitol Building. I spent most of my time on the east front, which was far less combative than the west front, which faces the National Mall. On the east front, most of the fighting happened at the entrance doors at the top of the steps.

My view of the doors was blocked by the tightly packed crowd, and when I moved to get a better angle, one woman nearby warned me, "Don't go that way, hon; they're gassing the patriots." As I walked further, I saw people sitting on curbs, hunched over and trying to flush pepper spray out their eyes. One man rubbing his eyes was wearing a Duke University alumni sweater.

Through the course of the afternoon, I was shaken by the violence I witnessed. The most chilling part was the casual discussions of extreme acts of violence that I overheard. Lots of people were talking about the execution of "traitors" in offhanded ways, as if it were a highly anticipated sporting event. I remember thinking that if Nancy Pelosi or Mike Pence had been outside, they would have been brought to the gallows on the lawn and there would have been loud cheers for them to swing.

Many of the people around me were calling January 6 "Our 1776," and it was clear that they imagined their intended revolution to be a violent one. I am still haunted by the angry joy I saw all around me, the many people I heard saying, "This is just the beginning."

When I got home, I couldn't stop staring at my photographs. The whole next week I sat on the floor, leaning against the couch in front of the television screen, my laptop on the coffee table, listening to the news and staring at my photos from the day. For hours at a time, I flipped through my photographs, trying to make some sense of what I had seen.

I spent most of that time studying the group shots I had taken of the densely packed crowds on the central stairs leading to the rotunda. I found myself trying to figure out the different groupings of people. I tried to determine who seemed to be together, and what entity they represented. Was it the Proud Boys? Oath Keepers? Three Percenters? Patriot Front? Veterans for Trump? I looked at the different shots for so long that soon I could easily identify the same people and groups in numerous photos as they moved between locations over time.

I was struck by how many people looked like they could have been my aunt, uncle, cousin, or neighbor. Most of the people in the photos were white and middle-aged like me. The whole scene looked like a Gen X or Boomer high school reunion—at least if that high school was in a town that was almost entirely white.

I also noticed that while most of the people in the crowd were men, a surprising number of women populated my photographs. There were plenty of women who looked working class, at least as far as I could tell. But I was surprised by how many looked like older versions of the middle- to upper-middle-class women I used to volunteer with, during the three years I spent as president of the PTA when my kids were in elementary school. In fact, the east front steps of the Capitol were filled with middle-aged bleached blond women, without a lot of gray roots showing. There were North Face ski jackets and fashionable coats, often with matching gloves and hats, coordinated around color and style. They accessorized with earrings and scarves. Zooming in on faces, you could see more than a few signs of plastic surgery: severely taut faces, unusually pronounced cheeks, swollen Botoxed foreheads.

Women were a far greater presence at the Capitol insurrection than you might expect, given that just 13 percent of federal arrests for January 6 were women. Women were all over the Capitol grounds that day. And that fact, in and of itself, should be concerning. As Cynthia Miller-Idriss, a scholar of right-wing extremism, puts it: "When women get involved, a movement becomes a serious threat."

Much of that white, middle-aged crowd clearly embraced conspiracism. Many people in my photos wore clothing or carried signs and flags that signaled their belief in the QAnon conspiracy theories. There were also signs alleging that Joe Biden was a secret member of the Chinese Communist Party. Many people were protesting the COVID lockdowns and masking requirements with shirts, hats, signs, and banners that claimed the virus was a hoax. Many of them called it a "Plandemic."

On my way to the Capitol, I had passed a separate protest at the Senate Park against government pandemic restrictions. The man on the stage when I walked by claimed that COVID was part of a globalist plot. He wanted the government's leading pandemic expert, Dr. Anthony Fauci, to be tried and executed for crimes against humanity for his support of lockdowns and having people mask in public. Many people that day held signs condemning vaccine mandates. My biggest worry that day, personally, was being singled out for wearing a mask in the almost entirely maskless crowd. The winter wave of COVID outbreaks was cresting, and I didn't want to catch the virus among a group of people who considered the pandemic a hoax or a nefarious plot.

Since January 6, journalists and scholars have traced the strong connection between conspiracism and the Capitol insurrection. In early 2024, 69 percent of Republicans and more than a third of all Americans continued to believe that Joe Biden had stolen the 2020 election. More generally, research has confirmed that January 6 drew together a wide range of people—as Jaclyn Fox and Carolyn Gallaher write, "allowing groups that are operationally independent and ideologically suspicious of one another to bang the same rhetorical drum." They identify the Capitol insurrection as the kind of "conspiracy-based coalition that brings far-right and mainstream operators together," by espousing multiple patently false, easily debunked, or wildly absurd conspiratorial beliefs.

Research has also shown a disturbing link between conspiracism and political violence. People prone to believe conspiracy theories are more likely to act based on those beliefs, including resorting to violence. One study revealed that "QAnon-adhering militia members . . . cited a belief in widespread government corruption as justification for violence against political figures leading up to and on January 6th."

Although many scholars show that male conspiracists are typically more likely to embrace violence than female ones, researchers are only beginning to understand the gendered nature of conspiracism. Many older studies found that men were more likely than women to believe conspiracy theories. The most recent research reveals that men and women are attracted to different kinds of conspiracies and that some theories attract far more women than men. Conspiracies involving children, health, and education are especially appealing to women. Those findings suggest that we have likely underestimated the potential for women to express their conspiracism through violence, a trend that appears to be growing more common.

Like most people, I was initially surprised by the staying power of the conspiracy theories surrounding January 6. I expected most conspiracists to start returning to reality when the outlandish predictions they had believed failed to come true. Many of those who stormed the Capitol had imagined Donald Trump would expose the cabal and bring the perpetrators to justice on January 6. When that didn't happen, the retribution date shifted to Biden's inauguration. Then it was moved to a day during the summer. Like before, that day came and went, without the promised big reveal and mass arrests.

But instead of petering out, the conspiracies just kept going and evolving online. New ones emerged, and subgroups formed around them. For example, many "Anons" believed that on November 2, 2021, John F. Kennedy Jr., who had died in a plane crash in 1999, would appear at the site of his father's 1963 assassination in Dallas, Texas, and reveal that he was still alive. They were convinced that JFK Jr. would become Trump's running mate in the 2024 presidential election and that together they would overthrow the cabal. Many of these people also believed that a 104-year-old JFK himself would also come out of hiding to support his son and Trump. This was but one among many new conspiracies that drew-in parts of the larger conspiracist community.

As I write this, conspiracy theories continue to germinate, spread, and evolve. By the time you read these words, who knows which conspiracy theories will hold sway? Mass conspiracism has become a perpetual-motion machine, generating an endless supply of new conspiracies to keep the attention of the faithful.

When older conspiracies fail, the conspiracists simply gravitate to new ones or revive old conspiracies in new guises. The ideas spread in viral ways across mainstream platforms like Facebook, Instagram, and TikTok. The theories are fungible, and so are the beliefs of the faithful. People are capable of shifting entire conspiratorial belief systems as the conspiracies evolve in new directions. That flexibility is what has allowed thousands—and perhaps millions—of women to head down distinct paths like conspirituality. As we will see in the pages of this book, ordinary people are radicalizing each other. They are even self-radicalizing through material they find on the internet.

The enduring strength of conspiracism and its continuous evolution raise a lot of important questions. Why are people drawn to conspiracy theories? What do people get out of conspiratorial thinking? Why have so many recent conspiracy theories—and especially ones based in QAnon and conspirituality—disproportionately attracted middle-aged white women? What makes these conspiracies stick? Why do people continue to believe in outlandish theories when none of the predictions ever come true? Why is the hold so strong? And how do you bring conspiracists back to reality?

These were not questions I started out trying to answer. I didn't set out to study conspiracism. I was led to it by the women I studied and the communities to which they were connected.

After January 6, I began to study what I thought of as the "gendered pathways of radicalization" that had brought so many middle-aged white women to Washington, DC, on January 6. That approach now strikes me as superficial and profoundly limited in what it can tell us. I started by compiling as much information as I could about the women who had been arrested for their actions at the Capitol. I put together a spreadsheet, entered the data, and looked for patterns in demographic factors. I scoured their social media accounts and searched public records. I was hypervigilant about maintaining distance from my subjects; my work was all about collecting a solid dataset on the first hundred or so women arrested.

I immersed myself in their worlds. I started with the arrest records and tracked down social media accounts across different platforms. I read their blogs, Facebook entries, and Instagram posts. I watched their TikTok and YouTube videos. I started hanging out in the online spaces they frequented. I joined the same online groups they belonged to and let the algorithms bring me friend requests from people who believed the same things they did. Meanwhile, I dug around in newspapers and public records and found court cases, domestic disputes, and past brushes with the law. I even reconstructed a few family trees.

I learned a lot this way, but I still had only a remote understanding of what I was seeing. I was hovering too high above it. I was summarizing people and their beliefs based on a few key facts about them. From that height, it all looked simple and clear. It was easy to put people in well-defined, predetermined boxes.

But summarizing lives based on short personal sketches and a handful of demographic markers can make the actual individuals disappear. Human agency and contingency fell to the background. Actions and beliefs became expressions of demographic factors, as did identity. This approach tended to reaffirm the broad stereotypes and labels we put on people, and it can obscure as much as it reveals.

This all started to change when I got to know the women personally. I wasn't intending to do interviews; I simply reached out to women because I was confused about beliefs they expressed in their public social media posts. I messaged Yvonne on Facebook to ask about spiritual concepts I didn't understand. She messaged back with her phone number and said, "Call me."

We talked for an hour. And then another hour the next day. And then off and on for the next three years.

It was the same pattern with several other "J6" women I contacted, including a woman named Tammy Butry, who was among the first women arrested for entering the Capitol. More than any "J6er" I have gotten to know, Tammy has changed my thinking about the people who were drawn to the Capitol by conspiracy theories. Regardless of my own feelings about her political and spiritual beliefs, I believe that Tammy, like Yvonne, is a sincere person. Over the last three years, she has told me many conspiracy theories that are blatantly false, but she has yet to lie to me. Just the opposite: Tammy talks about herself and her life with refreshing and sometimes shocking candor. Her honesty is why she joins Yvonne at the center of this book. I could not have attained my understanding of why people are drawn to conspiracism, what holds them in place, and how difficult it is to bring conspiracists back to reality, without the insights I got from my relationship with her.

Unfortunately, that relationship started with a suicide.

✦

News of the suicide came across my Twitter (now X) feed. I recognized the name immediately: Mark Aungst. He was Tammy's codefendant in their January 6 case.

I had been following Tammy online after her arrest in early February 2021 for entering the Capitol Building on January 6. Tammy and Mark had sat together on the chartered bus that had taken them from the Wilkes-Barre region of central Pennsylvania to Washington, DC, on the morning of January 6. Tammy and Mark were both middle-aged. She was fifty and divorced, with four adult children and numerous grandchildren; Mark was in his late forties and was also divorced with a daughter.

The criminal complaint included photographs of Mark and Tammy from the day. One showed Mark on the bus wearing a Trump cap and a black sweatshirt with a line drawing of an assault rifle across the chest. A picture of Tammy from inside the Capitol showed her wearing a white winter coat, a Trump ski cap, and a blue Trump flag tied around her neck like a cape. The charging documents reported that they had stood beside one another at the rally and marched together to the Capitol when Trump's speech finished. They briefly entered the building, walked around with the crowd, and swigged from a bottle of Jack Daniel's whiskey that someone had handed them, taking souvenir selfies of the moment. Less than ten minutes after entering the building, they walked back out.

On the bus trip back home, Mark bragged to others about going in the building and showed pictures of himself and Tammy inside the Capitol.

The person who organized the charter bus and several of the passengers later called the FBI to report them. Tammy and Mark were arrested and charged together.

They were both unrepentant about their actions at the Capitol. Days after Tammy got home, she posted on social media that January 6 was "the best day of my life." After her arrest, she posted photos of her charging papers calling them "FAKE NEWS" and saying that "Whomever wrote this should be sued," signing the post, "Pissed off Patriot!"

Two months after her arrest, Tammy posted a meme with a red, white, and blue skull with the caption "WHEN DO WE MOUNT UP AND FIGHT FOR OUR COUNTRY." Tammy replied, "Ready."

She posted another meme featuring a realistic cartoon of Donald Trump holding a long, high-powered automatic rifle, dressed in a navy-blue suit and red tie, wearing a long dress coat and standing in front of the Capitol Building. There were camouflage stripes across Trump's face and belts of high-caliber ammo draped over his shoulders. The caption reads, "I've Got Some Shit To Take Care Of! YOU COMING?" to which Tammy replied, "Sure am" and Mark responded, "Fuck yeah . . . let's roll."

Tammy's violent language was fueled by the far-right QAnon conspiracy theories. As you may remember, QAnon started in 2017 with posts by an anonymous account on the 4Chan message boards that claimed to be a top-level insider with "Q clearance" that gave access to highly classified information. Q sent out cryptic messages on 4Chan, warning the public about an alleged global cabal of satanic pedophiles who ran a child sex trafficking ring and drank the blood of children. The members of the cabal allegedly included Hillary Clinton and a host of world leaders and Hollywood celebrities. QAnon spread rapidly via the internet, breaking out of the 4Chan message boards and infecting mainstream social media platforms like Twitter, Facebook, and YouTube.

As QAnon evolved, it rapidly became a clearinghouse for all kinds of far-right conspiracy theories, absorbing existing conspiracies and adding new ones of its own invention. Over time, the message drops from "Q" mattered less than users creating QAnon lore from the bottom-up, branding it with their own conspiratorial concerns and fears. As more people on the right participated in its creation, QAnon messaging became riddled with anti-government, antisemitic, and often racist imagery. In QAnon's belief system, Donald Trump is a hero working to defeat the cabal. Most QAnon followers,

Tammy included, believed that Trump had called them to the Capitol on January 6 to expose the leaders of the cabal in the US government and bring them to justice. Many of those who went to the Capitol expected to see public executions that day.

Tammy wasn't discouraged when QAnon's prophecies about January 6 didn't come true. She continued to believe that a violent showdown to defeat the cabal was just around the corner. In spring 2021, she posted memes announcing that "Pedophilia will bring down: The Royal Family, The CIA, The Deep State, The Vatican, Hollywood, and Politicians." Another post announced that people in other nations were rising up in "THE GREAT AWAKENING Worldwide" against the cabal. In the comment section, Tammy lamented that, instead of standing up, Americans were "wearing double masks outside" against a virus.

Tammy fully believed the QAnon conspiracy claim that the pandemic was a hoax designed to enslave the public through vaccine injections. Later Tammy reposted the image of a calendar purported to be the timeline of the official secret "New World Order Plan" for using COVID-19 vaccinations to turn Americans into slaves.

For the rest of the year, Tammy kept reposting numerous memes that proclaimed her enduring faith in the QAnon conspiracy theories, despite the fact that their prophecies never panned out. One showed the far-right character Pepe the Frog dressed in a Revolutionary War–era tricorne hat and smoking a cigar. The caption reads, "WHEN ALL YOUR FRIENDS AND FAMILY CALL YOU CRAZY AND THEN FIND OUT YOU WERE RIGHT ALL ALONG." At the bottom of the image, the meme promised, "You'll have the last laugh. I guarantee it. Hang tight." Tammy replied, "Yep." Mark responded, "I like being crazy . . . doing the sane shit for 45 years . . . time to turn up the crazy and have some fun . . . look the fuck out, feelings are 100 points per hit." That last line was a reference to the popular right-wing slogan, "fuck your feelings," aimed at liberals, with the "hits" being insults designed to induce "liberal tears."

I lost track of Tammy in early 2022. Back then social media platforms like Facebook and Twitter were banning accounts that routinely posted conspiracies and disinformation about COVID-19. Like many QAnon followers, Tammy had multiple accounts shut down. She'd make new ones, post more conspiracy material, and get banned again. It was easy enough for me to find the new ones by searching for her name.

But then in early 2022, the trail ran cold. Tammy had left the mainstream platforms and switched to far-right ones like Telegram and Rumble, temporarily falling off my radar. I knew from news reports that she had taken the government's plea deal, but I didn't know what she was up to. All I knew was that she and Mark were waiting for their sentencing hearing. That's when Mark's suicide in July 2022 came across my Twitter news feed.

In the wake of his death, I decided to track down Tammy again and reach out to her. Up to this point I had only observed her from afar. My prior research into Tammy's background gave me concerns about how she might react to Mark's suicide, given what seemed like their close relationship. Public records revealed a woman with a hard life who had experienced numerous emotional breakdowns in the past. Based on social media posts, I didn't get the sense that she had any kind of reliable network of friends or family to help her deal with traumatic news like this. I felt enough concern that I reached out to ask if she was okay.

When I messaged Tammy, she replied that she was glad I had gotten in touch. She hadn't heard about Mark's death, even though she had recently been staying in an apartment he owned until she could find a place to live. Tammy said she was grateful to have someone to process the news with. She gave me her phone number and asked me to call her.

Months later, Tammy told me I was the only person who ever asked her how she felt about Mark's suicide. She told her family what had happened to him, but no one said anything about it or ever checked in to see how she was doing. Tammy said that was a normal response in her world.

When I finally acquainted myself with Tammy's new social media accounts, I noticed something was different. There were still the same old QAnon and anti-vaccination posts and memes. But I noticed her postings had taken a New Age spiritual turn. Prior to this, Tammy had presented herself as a devout Christian. The profile for one the accounts she created after January 6 had read: "Jesus is my Savior, Trump is my President. Pissed off patriot fighting for my country." Now her posts referenced her devotion to spirit-guides. She reposted memes about how the Second Coming would not be the return of Jesus but, instead, "an alien arrival."

The tipping point for me was Tammy's use of the word "Kryon," an odd name I recalled from some of Yvonne's posts. I looked it up. Kryon turned out to be a mystical entity "from beyond the veil" who allegedly spreads his messages to humanity by channeling through a medium named Lee Carroll, a Californian who worked as an audio technician for thirty years before he says Kryon contacted him back in 1989. Carroll has written nearly two dozen books, more than half of which are purported to be messages from Kryon. Carroll claims Kryon is an angelic being from the "magnetic service" who has come to earth to prepare it for an impending spiritual and evolutionary transformation that will bring humanity to a higher level of consciousness. Kryon apparently sends messages through Carroll to help prepare humanity for the transition into a new spiritual dimension.

I had never heard of Kryon before. And now here were two women who had stormed the Capitol who didn't know each other, both using the same obscure spiritual language and belief system. They were even referencing the same apocalyptic transformation involving extraterrestrials partly based on the purported channelings of a retired sound engineer from San Diego.

This wasn't an isolated incident. I was seeing a lot of this kind of thing filtering into the social media posts of many of the other January 6 women I had been following. It was also happening within the different online political communities to which they belonged. It wasn't all Kryon; there were lots of different variations and individuals. But all were New Age, and all were dealing in an array of conspiracies. The believers have the flexible logic typical of conspiracism, one that tolerates all kinds of wild inconsistencies and contradictions. Like QAnon, conspirituality can absorb other conspiracies into its vortex—including QAnon itself.

I was watching thousands of women who supported January 6, some of whom had participated in it, getting sucked into that vortex in real time, right before my eyes, mostly independently of one another, being drawn in from different directions.

I was watching a new evolution within conspiracism: the massive and rapid growth of New Age conspirituality. I was witnessing conspirituality take its place in the center of the conspiratorial mainstream, alongside the other main threads of conspiracism, with which it easily blended and merged.

✦

"There are no accidents" is a phrase from the world of conspiracism that Tammy and Yvonne both frequently repeat when I am chatting with them. They don't think coincidences exist. To them, everything that happens is part of a master plan that remains mostly secret, even to the faithful. They believe that the people who come into their lives do so as part of this larger plan.

That's how they each view me: that our relationship is part of a divinely inspired greater purpose. They aren't surprised at all that I was at the Capitol on January 6, 2021, a liberal from the political "other side" who found herself in the wrong place at the wrong time. To them, I was in the right place, and the right time, to fulfill the destiny that brought our life pathways together.

Tammy and Yvonne believe I was sent to share their stories. This is why they have both been so forthcoming with me, why they were determined to tell me their hard truths, and why no subject has been off limits in our conversations. As they see it, my research and this book were meant to be.

On one hand, their need to believe in conspiracies, and to be a part of a community of people who share their conspiratorial faith, makes sense to me. I can deeply appreciate the need for hope and faith. At some level, and especially at difficult moments in our lives, we all grasp for stories that lend meaning to our lives and purpose to our suffering. Nothing is more human than the need to make sense of the senseless and to explain the great unknowns about our existence. As we will see in chapter 8, conspiracy theories become what some anthropologists call a "method of hope." Knowing these women as I do now, I understand a bit more about how and why they chose this path and why they remain on it when it has brought so much additional suffering to their lives. I appreciate their need to believe that their lives are unfolding according to a divine plan, that their hardships are part of a journey toward a new age that will be created by a mass spiritual awakening.

Yet I have always been far less certain about the role that fate played in bringing us together. Where they see patterns, I see creative, wishful thinking. Where they see conspiracy, I see falsehood. Where they find certainty, I find elaborate coping strategies for handling life's disappointments, hardships, uncertainty, chaos, and cruelty. I would like to imagine the divine at work, but I have seen too much of what humanity is capable of to believe that this is all part of some scripted plan.

Over the last three years, I have logged hundreds of hours of phone calls talking with J6ers about their lives and beliefs. Although my conversations with Yvonne and Tammy form the core of this book, their embrace of conspiracism follows a similar path to many of the women I have studied.

This book is my attempt to understand how so many white, middle-aged women have gotten sucked into conspiracism. The book examines the factors that drew women in and explains how conspiratorial thinking came to dominate their worldview over a period of years. I show why many of these women have gone even deeper-in over time, and I trace the different paths that have led so many of them to conspirituality. We will journey to a small town in Idaho, a trailer in Pennsylvania, and a New Age trade show in Los Angeles, where many of the convention-goers believe they are extraterrestrials here to save humanity. We'll travel back to the nineteenth century, to meet the Russian-American woman whose mystical beliefs birthed the New Age movement, and into a federal women's prison where a children's book by a *New York Times* bestselling author was passed around to "awaken" the inmates to the idea that, before they were born, their souls chose to experience incarceration, in an agreement called a "soul contract."

This is not an academic inquiry into women and radicalization. Nor is it a comprehensive or data-driven portrait of the women who stormed the Capitol on January 6. Instead, it's a vivid and intimate look into the lives of two women as they travel along the same kinds of paths to conspiracism that have led millions of people "down the rabbit hole."

I see myself as a guide into a world you will probably find strange and unsettling. Think of me as someone who is not from this place but who knows the culture, speaks the language, and is on good terms with the locals (or at least some of them). I've tried to view this place like an anthropologist would. I wanted to understand the culture I was witnessing and the meanings they attached to the actions and beliefs I was observing. The point was not to judge people who live a different reality than my own or attempt to change their values and ways of thinking. I was there to observe and learn from them, on their own terms. The women in this book were not "my subjects." They were people I got to know. Our relationships developed organically as our conversations deepened over time and as we shared more about our lives as middle-aged women and experienced things together in real time.

This means the book is also about my relationships with Yvonne and Tammy. It is about how our views of each other have changed over the years, along with what we mean to one another. My hope is that you will join me in trying to understand them, how they view the world, and how and why they ended up in this place. There are a lot of valuable things to learn about the challenges we face in a society riddled with conspiracism. My experiences with these women show that the road back to a shared reality is long, hard, and uncertain. Their stories also show that any solution will require something that has been in short supply in our deeply fractured and politically polarized present: true curiosity about, and empathy for, people on "the other side."

Finally, this book is a trip through recent research on conspiracism and political polarization. In trying to understand Tammy and Yvonne's belief in conspiracies, I turned to psychologists, sociologists, political scientists, and other scholars to see how what I was finding fit with the latest research. The study of conspiracism is relatively new, and there was surprisingly little scholarship to turn to as I was working on this project. The publication floodgates have opened in the last two years, and, when consulting the research, I found a perfect match between the new things scholars were discovering about conspiracism and what I had already observed with Tammy, Yvonne, and other women I have been following. These women personify the trends in the latest scholarship on a variety of important topics: the reasons people turn to conspiracism, why conspiratorial beliefs have such incredible staying power, and what works—and doesn't—when it comes to getting people back to a semblance of consensus about what constitutes truth and fact and a shared reality.

By witnessing Yvonne and Tammy's lives in up close and intimate ways, we can see how conspiratorial thinking takes root and why it has such a powerful grip on people. Conspiracism's power comes from its versatility. Conspiracy theories are a coping mechanism for trauma, powerlessness, and dislocation in times of great stress or change. They provide answers for those anxious about life's uncertainties and who need a belief system to anchor their craving for faith. Conspiracies offer a more hopeful alternate reality where all the world's complex problems have simple causes and can be solved in an instant. They provide ideologies—and even theologies—and communities that sustain conspiratorial beliefs, shielding them from facts, and reason, and their own failings and internal contradictions. Conspiracism works on such a fundamental level, and has so many self-reinforcing elements, that there are no easy ways out of it. It is so powerful that the only way to counter its force are approaches based in empathy and the rebuilding of basic levels of trust across embittered political divides.

We start our journey of understanding by turning back the clock to meet Tammy and Yvonne in their childhoods. Here we witness one of the primary factors that drive people to conspiratorial thinking: deep and chronic traumas, which often start in childhood and follow people into adulthood.

CHAPTER 2

Trauma

One afternoon as I was doing research for this book, I found myself reading about the personality profile of a conspiracist. A massive 2023 study of "The Conspiratorial Mind" by the American Psychological Association (APA) summarizes all the available research on the personality traits most common among conspiracists. According to the APA, conspiracists are "insecure, paranoid, emotionally volatile, impulsive, suspicious, withdrawn." Conspiracists tend to believe the world is a dangerous place and display cynicism, powerlessness, anxiety, a sense of alienation, and depression.

Reading that list of descriptors, I felt a strange sensation of creeping familiarity. It was not unlike the feeling you get when an internet search of your aches and pains returns a list of catastrophic diseases. You don't *really* think you have meningitis, stage-4 cancer, or a rare-but-fatal skin disorder . . . but what is that rash, anyway? And why do I have lower back pain, a persistent headache, *and* dry mouth?

I couldn't ignore the fit. Insecure, emotionally volatile, impulsive, cynical, anxious: the traits identified with the psychology of conspiracy theorists described me, with some accuracy, three years after COVID shut down the world. Even now that things had opened back up, the symptoms of my emotional hangover from the pandemic lingered. I saw the same symptoms among many of my friends and family members as well. We were all still feeling powerless, and paranoid, and suspicious, and withdrawn.

And yet, I do not believe in conspiracy theories, nor do any of my close friends or family. I don't believe that pedophile Satanists secretly run the world, or that COVID vaccinations implant mind-controlling nanochips. So,

I started to wonder: What separates non-conspiracists like me, who can tick the boxes on "The Conspiratorial Mind" checklist, from those who fall prey to conspiracy theories? Tammy, Yvonne, and the other women I study have fallen deeply into worlds of conspiracism. Why have I rejected conspiracy theories while they ended up refashioning their lives around them?

The reason that some people believe conspiracy theories is not entirely rooted in the information sources to which they turn. While misinformation is more likely to circulate on right-wing media, it's also not the case that everyone who watches Fox News or One America News Network is a dyed-in-the-wool conspiracist. In most cases, other factors are at work, many of them dealing with personal traits and experiences that drive certain people to believe in conspiracies.

Most scholarship on conspiracism focuses on the questions of *who* adopts conspiracy theories and *why* they turn to them. Initially, many researchers thought conspiracism was a neurological disorder. Early studies targeted the strong correlation between belief in conspiracy theories and schizophrenia, bipolar disorder, and other illnesses rooted in brain chemistry.

That link is real, but it only accounts for a subset of those who turn to conspiracies. Chemical imbalances in the brain cannot explain why a significant portion of the US population believes in QAnon or conspirituality. The neurological theory does not explain why so many Republicans think the 2020 presidential election was stolen and the COVID pandemic was a hoax. Something else is clearly at work.

Moving beyond neurological explanations, researchers tried to identify conspiracists based on demographic factors and the role played by things like age, race, sex, income, education, and political affiliation. The findings were mixed and often contradictory. Some studies showed that older women were more prone to conspiracism, others found that sex and age made no difference, and another batch found that younger men were more likely to fall into conspiracies. One of the few constants seems to be the strong correlation between conspiracism and lower levels of income and education. Early studies also showed that ethnic and racial minorities were more prone to believe conspiracy theories related to systemic racism, like the belief held by many African Americans that the government created HIV/AIDS to kill Black people.

Newer research suggests that falling into conspiracism is a dynamic process. Recent studies have shown that personality traits alone do not make conspiracists. What matters is how those traits interact with other factors. The biggest difference maker between conspiracists and non-conspiracists is lived experience. It's not so much that people have certain personality traits that automatically make them into conspiracists; it's that certain kinds of life experiences tend to drive people with those traits into conspiratorial thinking.

In considering why people turn to conspiracism, recent scholarship tends to focus on the role played by life stressors, especially deep and chronic trauma. Over time, heavy life stressors can create a sense of powerlessness, insecurity, and anxiety that can lead people into conspiratorial thinking. That's especially true in cases of post-traumatic stress disorder (PTSD) and complex PTSD, which is essentially the repeated and prolonged version. When life stressors become intense, people with long histories of trauma often turn to extreme beliefs like conspiracy theories to make sense of what they are going through. It's easier for some people to explain the things happening to them as part of a grand nefarious plot than to accept the inherent chaos, structural inequity, systemic cruelty, or indifference that characterizes much of life.

In these cases, researchers suggest that conspiracism is a method for enduring the complexity and pain of life—*Conspiracy Beliefs as Coping Behavior*, as the title of one recent book puts it. For those who experience chronic "anxiety, loneliness, and a sense of powerlessness," research finds that embracing conspiracy theories "may in some way offer them relief from their stressors," write authors Helen Hendy and Pamela Black. That seems to be especially true when intense new life stressors fall on top of existing PTSD or complex PTSD symptoms. Their research suggests a sequence where "individuals who face intense *life stressors* (health, money, loneliness), and who experience symptoms of *powerlessness*, become at increased risk for adoption of *extreme beliefs* as cognitive coping mechanisms that might restore their sense of power and community."

All this suggests that we need to approach conspiracism with a measure of care and understanding. If you're a non-believer, it's easy to dismiss conspiracy theories as outlandish crazy talk and the conspiracists themselves as xenophobic, antisemitic, or racist dupes. That is true in certain cases, and nothing excuses dehumanizing rhetoric. But the massive wave of conspiracism currently spreading across the globe defies easy analysis. Understanding the scope and depth of the problem—and finding effective solutions—requires that we come to terms with the ways that people turn to conspiracy theories to cope with their pain and anguish.

In the end, the big difference between me and Yvonne and Tammy might be that they experienced intense life stressors and PTSD events going back to childhood. We may share certain markers of "the conspiratorial mind," but part of what separates us is that they experienced an unusual level of trauma in their childhoods that carried over into adulthood and I did not. I have found this to be a common pattern among the January 6 women I have gotten to know who embrace various strains of conspiracism. Nearly all of them cite traumatic childhoods and significant life traumas as formative experiences in their lives. Their history of personal trauma is always one of the first things they mention when we talk.

Trauma histories abound, for so many people, and reading about other people's trauma can enliven memories of our own. I present Tammy's and Yvonne's histories of trauma not to intrude on their privacy or to surface anyone else's traumatic memories but simply to offer a fuller picture of how childhood trauma interacts with conspiracism. For Tammy and Yvonne, it wasn't just one or two traumatic incidents. Their paths to conspiracism were blasted-out by a constant firehose of trauma that began in childhood and kept blowing open new pathways deep into adulthood. Researchers continue to explore the links between trauma and conspiracism, and much work remains to be done. But it doesn't take a lot of data to see the ways in which conspiratorial thinking, at root, dissociates someone from reality, allowing them to live in an alternate world of possibility and illusion where they are better able to handle what life has handed them. In this chapter, we'll look at some of the ways that conspiratorial thinking can serve as a coping mechanism for survivors of trauma.

For Tammy, the trauma began while she was still in her mother's womb.

✦

"I was raised by Jesus and a brother who was in prison for murder," Tammy tells me when we're chatting on the phone. It's one of our earliest conversations. "I don't remember having dreams like most kids do. I loved ice skating, wanted to take dance class, but my dad wouldn't let me. I would go with my friends and watch."

Tammy tells me she has always struggled with self-doubt and defeatism, often blaming herself for everything in her life. She says she has to remind herself that she never had much support. "I wasn't set up for success. No way," she tells me, like she's still trying to convince herself. "I would often lay in bed wondering if I just turned out this way because of all my choices. I concluded that I didn't. I had absolutely zero guidance from the age of eight up."

"It took a long time to get over a lot of it. But I spent most of my life depressed," she says and then starts laughing at the thought. "I'm laughing so I don't cry," she tells me. "I feel like I've cried enough for five lifetimes."

Tammy's first suicide attempt occurred when she was eleven years old and she took a bottle of aspirin. There's a picture of that little girl just a few months before she took those pills. Tammy's mother had taken out an ad in the "Happy Birthday" section of the local newspaper. In the photograph in that birthday ad, Tammy is wearing a white blouse and smiling for the camera. Exactly one month later, Tammy's childhood effectively ended.

Even then the smile in the newspaper was more a pose for the moment than a snapshot of Tammy's reality. Her childhood prior to that photo was generally not a happy one. While pregnant, Tammy's mother had developed a serious illness that didn't respond to treatment. The symptoms continued after Tammy was born. The ultimate diagnosis was lupus, a disorder in which the immune system attacks healthy body parts and causes inflammation and extreme pain. Tammy's mother had a particularly serious case.

Some of the family blamed her mother's poor health on the pregnancy itself. "My uncle said that if it wasn't for me, my mother would still be alive," Tammy tells me. "The story is that she had rheumatic fever and couldn't take antibiotics because she was pregnant with me, which led to lupus. I was told that the lupus ate her brain. I was devastated for a very long time. I believed it, of course." Only years later, when Tammy talked to her aunt, did someone assure her that she was not to blame for her mother's ill health. Her aunt explained to Tammy that her mother probably had lupus for a long time before it was diagnosed.

While Tammy's mother struggled with a difficult pregnancy, Tammy's father was having an affair. Two months after Tammy was born, her father's mistress announced she was pregnant. Tammy isn't sure whether her father asked for a divorce, or her mother threw him out. "I was a baby when my parents split up. I think he left her," she tells me now. "I hated him for that. Because he knew she was sick. Since my mom was so sick she couldn't take care of us, so my dad had custody of the three of us."

Tammy's father remarried almost immediately, and her pregnant step-mother took over raising her as an infant along with her two brothers, Harry, age four, and Frank, who was eight. Soon there would be a fourth child, a baby boy who was a half-brother to the three siblings. Tammy's oldest brother rebelled against his new stepmother and was sent to live with his grandparents. Tammy said it was probably the best thing to ever happen to him. "At my grandparents' house, he had guidance and support growing up. Harry and I didn't. He did really good for himself. Retired from the Navy, married his high school sweetheart. They have two boys that have good heads on their shoulders. So I call him the Golden Child."

Tammy's mother was so sick during those years that her children would not see her for long stretches of time. That meant her stepmother was the dominant figure for the first eight years of her life. "Because my stepmom was always there for me, I was confused about who my mom was when I was little. I thought that because we lived with my stepmom, and I called her Mom, that she was my real mom," Tammy recalls to me now. "We used to visit my real mom on weekends. One night I remember when my mom and stepdad were bringing us home, I thought they were kidnapping us from our parents. I told my mom that and she cried. I never questioned it again."

Tammy describes her first eight years as the closest she came to a typical childhood. Her stepmother was a Brownie leader for Tammy's troop. She worked with the kids on their 4-H projects. When Tammy was eight, her pin cushion took third place in the craft competition at the annual 4-H "Moo-In" festival. That same year Tammy took home the "Best Camper" award at 4-H summer camp, winning the honor over one hundred other children. "My stepmother was great. I know that now," Tammy tells me, with appreciation and remorse. "She treated me like her own. I was always dressed pretty, hair always done. She took me to Brownies and 4-H Club. She let me go to 4-H summer camp. That was the only time I went to camp. She was a good mom."

That stability ended abruptly when Tammy's father left her stepmother while she was pregnant with the couple's second child. "The years with my stepmom were the only time I really had normalcy. After they split up, no more normal childhood. After that I was pretty much on my own." She rarely saw her stepmother or half-brother after that.

Following the separation, Tammy, her brother Harry, and her father moved in with Tammy's grandparents. Although she was reunited with her oldest brother Frank, Tammy doesn't have fond memories of that year. Tammy's grandparents were determined to enjoy their retirement. Frank was seventeen and on his way to the military after graduation. They had no interest in raising two more of their son's children. So they mostly left Tammy, now nine, alone or in the care of Harry.

"When I lived with my grandparents, I was always alone," she told me one day on the phone. "They knew I was always alone but never came by to check on me. My grandmother was always at bingo. My grandfather was always out. And my dad worked third shift at the time, so he was gone all night and slept during the day."

Tammy always felt like her grandparents looked down on her. In her eyes, her grandparents had achieved the American dream. Although they had working-class jobs, her father's parents had attained a degree of middle-class respectability. They owned a home in a nice neighborhood. They traveled for pleasure. When they died, they left each adult child a relatively sizable inheritance. Tammy's father's share was large enough that he gave Tammy $10,000 from it, the single largest sum of money she had ever received. "My grandparents had some money. I wouldn't say they were wealthy, but very comfortable. Vacations, anything they wanted. My father's sisters were like that, too. They were dental assistants, but they married well. One is married to a now-retired lawyer. The other one's husband owns a tombstone business."

She always felt like her grandparents treated her as if she wasn't up to their standards. "My grandparents were terrible. Where I grew up, there were lots of Black people. But when a Black boy called me when I was living with my grandparents, my grandmother picked up the phone and had a fit," Tammy tells me, indignant about their racism. "I could imagine what they would say today if they saw that four of their great-great grandchildren are mixed-race!"

Tammy doesn't remember when the abuse started, but, at some point in her childhood, a teenaged relative began making Tammy do sexual things to him. She says she doesn't think her earliest memory of it was the first time it happened. Tammy has never discussed the topic with her molester. Eventually she told her mother, and it never happened again.

At the time, Tammy was also being sexually abused by the uncle of a friend. He would take her and her friend into a dark room to abuse them while the girl's little brother played with matchbox cars in the hallway. Tammy never told anyone.

These kinds of traumas are the root of Tammy's conspiracism. Her childhood was filled with what medical professionals call adverse childhood experiences (ACEs). These are extremely traumatic events like violence, abuse, neglect, substance abuse, or mental illness that children experience directly or witness in their homes. ACEs play a direct role in negative outcomes and health problems later in life. Researchers have linked ACEs to nine out of ten of the top causes of death in the United States. According to the Centers for Disease Control and Prevention (CDC), preventing ACEs could avoid as many as 1.9 million cases of heart disease and 21 million cases of depression. It could cut persistent feelings of sadness or hopelessness by as much as 66 percent, prescription pain medication misuse by 84 percent, and suicide attempts by high school students by 89 percent.

Those numbers are so large because far more children experience ACEs than you might expect. The CDC reports that about 64 percent of US adults "reported they had experienced at least one type of ACE before age 18. Nearly one in six adults (17.3%) reported they had experienced four or more types of ACEs."

Tammy had hit four types of adverse child experiences before she turned ten—and she was just getting started. I recount these childhood and early adult traumas of Tammy's not to be gratuitous but because you can't understand Tammy's conspiracism without appreciating how a never-ending chain of extreme experiences defined her childhood and young adulthood, how it shattered her trust in other people and stunted her views of herself and what she thought was possible.

The biggest trauma was yet to come. A year after moving into her grandparents' house, Tammy's mother started to deteriorate rapidly, and no one knew how much time she had left. Tammy's father decided that it was important for the kids to spend as much time with their mom as they could before she died, so they moved into an apartment in the house where she lived. The house was owned by Tammy's mother's longtime boyfriend, who Tammy and her brother referred to as their stepfather. Tammy's mother and stepfather lived in the first-floor apartment, and her father and Tammy and Harry moved into the second-floor apartment.

Tammy was ten and happy to be living just upstairs from her mother, even as the lupus got worse, and she had to be hospitalized repeatedly. Tammy watched her mother's body wither and deteriorate before her eyes. She was thirty but was sometimes mistaken for being Tammy's grandmother. She had procedures that took out chunks of her body that Tammy describes as looking like "shark bites." Tammy recalls watching a neighbor regularly dress her wounds.

Meanwhile, Tammy's stepfather, who she describes as a "raging alcoholic," would have violent episodes during which he would scream at everyone. Tammy recalled one episode when he was on the front porch yelling at the neighbors. Her mom tried to make light of it. Tammy says she thinks her mom was scared for herself and her kids and tried to defuse the situation by laughing it off.

Tammy's stepfather had a long criminal history and had been incarcerated numerous times for stealing cars, breaking and entering, and parole violations. He had even planned an elaborate prison break that ended with him trying to scale a wall in the prison yard and breaking his ankle. While in prison, he petitioned a judge to deport him to Italy, citing abuse by prison guards, saying he was taking his case to the United Nations. Another petition asked to be released so he could travel to Europe and "plead his case before the World Court at the Hague, Netherlands."

Tammy says her stepfather pushed her mother the night she died. She had had a stroke, and he refused to call an ambulance, insisting on driving her to the hospital. Tammy told me that some of her mother's last words to him were, "Slow down. I don't think I'm going to make it this time."

Following her mother's death, things went downhill quickly for eleven-year-old Tammy. Her father seemed to forget he was a parent. "After my mom died my father was never home," Tammy explained to me, sadness filling her voice. "He worked and he went out often. I was either alone or with my brother, Harry. But usually, I was alone. I felt lonely, bored, and unloved."

She especially remembers her father forgetting to shop, so the house never had any food in it. "I remember my father cooking occasionally but not often. I mostly ate at my friend's house. I am sure my friend's parents noticed, but they never said anything," she said.

With her father gone, a bored, lonely, and hungry Tammy sometimes visited her stepfather downstairs, who quickly took advantage of the situation. "When I was home alone, my stepfather would give me beer, cigarettes, and pot. I was eleven," she tells me in disbelief. "He knew my father was never home. He would also take me to Burger King a lot. He used to let me drink and then we would go driving. He always let me drive," she said with a measure of disgust. "I think he started doing those things right before he started to molest me."

"Most times I would get beer from him, I would drink, smoke, and party by myself," Tammy explains without much emotion. "But I also partied with him in the basement. I don't remember how long after Mom passed that he started. I remember the first time like it was yesterday," she says with cold and calm certainty. "I had a Lowenbrau beer, cigarette, and weed. The table-cloth was red with flowers. I was sitting at the kitchen table. The song *Sexual Healing* was playing on the radio when he started to rub my leg and tell me I was going to be a woman soon. He carried me to the bed and proceeded to molest me. I don't remember what I was thinking. It went on for about a year."

On at least one occasion Tammy's stepfather sexually abused her friends as well. She recalled a night she had two friends over, and he took them driving and gave each girl a chance behind the wheel. He let Tammy drive most of the time because she was the most experienced. While Tammy was driving, he assaulted the other two girls in the back seat.

Then suddenly, one day when Tammy was twelve years old, her stepfather was gone. She knocked on his door one day, hoping for a cigarette, and he never answered. She didn't see him again until she was sixteen. After he left town, Tammy spent most of her time alone or hanging out with her brother, Harry, who was now sixteen. "He would have friends over, drinking and doing whatever. A few of his friends let me drink," she says, her voice hinting at what was going to happen next. One of her brother's friends who was eighteen or nineteen said he was making a Burger King run and asked Tammy to go with them. "But he took me to the woods instead," she says with a note of sarcasm before she tells me how he raped her. When her brothers found out what happened, one of them tracked the guy down and, as Tammy put it, "kicked his ass."

Things bottomed out emotionally for Tammy when the twelve-year-old found herself alone on Christmas. Harry celebrated the holiday with a friend, and her father had made other plans for himself. There were no invitations from her grandparents or other family members. "The last Christmas I was with my father, he spent it with his girlfriend," she tells me. "I didn't see him. He told me where my one Christmas present was and that was it. It was a hair dryer shaped like a gun," she says and takes a pause. I ask if she's okay. "That brought tears to my eyes, remembering that," Tammy says, in a voice that suggests the full weight of all she just told me had caught her off guard.

When Tammy turned thirteen, she started acting out. Her father had no tolerance for it. "He punched me in the face once, right before he threw me out. I was thirteen. I was skipping school. The truant officer had called him and I didn't know, so I lied to him. So he punched me in the face. I think he just didn't want to be responsible for me. Not like he ever was. It took me a long time to forgive my father. Was just last year he said he was sorry for not being a better father to us but especially me. Now I forgive him." Tammy went to live with her mother's sister, feeling like an outcast that no one wanted.

Tammy's childhood was like an ACE spreadsheet. Her mother was dead, and she was estranged from her father. Her kindly stepmother was years gone. Her abusive, criminal stepfather was gone, too. She had been sexually abused by multiple men, and she could rely on no one in her life in any meaningful way. Her teenaged years and young adulthood would only add more columns.

Meanwhile, 2,400 miles away in Idaho, Yvonne's childhood was compiling an ACE spreadsheet of its own.

Yvonne was born in Mountain Home, Idaho, a mostly white community of under ten thousand residents near an Air Force base about an hour outside Boise. She spent some of her early years in Japan, while her father was stationed there, but she lived most of her childhood in Mountain Home.

Yvonne describes her parents in unflinching terms. "My mom was a bitch," she tells me directly, as if describing an innate trait like hair or eye color. "She was mean to me. I don't think she even realized how mean she was."

"There were times, I remember when I was little, like when I peed my pants when I was seven years old, that she could be *very* mean," she says flatly and definitively. "She didn't know how to control her words. She didn't know that her words mattered. . . . She'd get so mad. She'd say, 'I hate you.' Like, she would actually say, 'I hate you.'"

Yvonne says this like she's still coming to terms with it. "Those kinds of things do not just hurt, they become part of who you are." At the time Yvonne told me this, she was working through her feelings. It was hard to be a little kid with a mother like this, Yvonne told me, but now as an adult, she understood why her mother acted this way. "Mom was from Spain and her parents both died in the Spanish Civil War when she was very young, so she didn't have a mom or dad her whole life," Yvonne says with empathy in her voice. "I'm sure she was molested. I know that everything comes from the pedophilia stuff."

Yvonne's mother had a daughter prior to meeting her father, and the marriage and move to the United States only seemed to make things worse. "My dad was in the Air Force and came to Spain, and she thought that she could give my sister a better life by coming to America," Yvonne tells me. So her mother came to the United States, not realizing that she was marrying an alcoholic, abusive man. "My father adopted my sister and then threatened my mom by saying he would keep my sister if my mom tried to leave him and take her back to Spain. So my mom stayed," Yvonne says, as if the rest is self-explanatory.

When Yvonne was five years old, her parents divorced. She lived with her mother, along with her older sister, who was eleven, and a younger sister who was two. Life was rough. Yvonne's mother spoke little English and cleaned houses for a living. They ended up on government assistance. Barely able to look after herself, Yvonne's mother leaned heavily on her eleven-year-old, who became the family caretaker. Yvonne's older sister would later confirm the dynamics. She told me their mother took out her anger and frustrations on Yvonne.

Both Yvonne and her sister say that their mother saved most of her affection for men. As Yvonne saw it, her mother tried to get ahead by using her good looks to find a man who would marry her. "She didn't know how to love. Her way of love was all about money. It was all about security," Yvonne says with certainty. "That's what love was to her: security."

"My mom was very promiscuous," Yvonne says without judgment. "She was very beautiful, and she was Spanish, and she didn't have anything. Her body was all she had. She didn't know any better. . . . She didn't have a mom to raise her. She didn't have anyone to tell her anything different. All she had was her beauty."

When Yvonne was in fourth grade, her mom remarried, and things went from bad to worse. "She married a pedophile," Yvonne says directly. "My stepdad molested my little sister when she was probably in first- or second grade. I have no memory of being molested. But I don't have a lot of memories of my childhood, so I don't know. There were things that he did that were inappropriate, but I don't think he did mess with me. I really don't. I think I'd remember," she tells me, genuinely unable to recall. Every time I have asked Yvonne about those years, she is unable to remember much. "I have a lot of memory loss," she tells me each time. Yvonne's older sister says she doesn't know what, if anything, happened with the stepfather, but that Yvonne has always been unable to remember much about that period of her life.

It's worth noting that these kinds of "black holes" in memory are common among the survivors of childhood sexual abuse. They are especially strong when it comes to the kinds of autobiographical details that Yvonne is unable to recall. Research shows the rates of amnesia like this increase with the severity of abuse, or its frequency. It is particularly prevalent in children molested by family members, especially where the child is reliant on their abuser for basic survival. In one study of known victims of sexual abuse, 59 percent of respondents experienced autobiographical memory loss of the kind that Yvonne describes.

Whatever happened, Yvonne's situation at her mother's house made her idealize her father, even as she saw his shortcomings. "I loved my dad," Yvonne said with affection in her voice. "My mom and sister hated him because he was an alcoholic. But my dad was also very kind. He would always pick up hitchhikers and he would always help people in the town," Yvonne says, clearly identifying with him. "I would never say this in front of my sister, because my sister hates my dad, but my dad was probably where I got my heart from. I think I got a lot of empathy and compassion from him. He was very, very kind."

She quickly amends the statement: "Very drunk, but very kind." Yvonne feels compelled to explain her father's behavior. "He had a horrible childhood and didn't know how to deal with it. His dad had died young, and he suffered as a child," she says softly. "He was just a very broken soul and turned to alcohol. He was never abusive to me."

The mistreatment by her mother eventually drove Yvonne back to her father. After the divorce, Yvonne's father relocated to Boise. When he moved back to Mountain Home, Yvonne fled from her mother's house to live with him. "I ran away from home in seventh grade, which really wasn't running away. I ran about four blocks to my dad's house. He had a trailer. So I stayed with my dad."

When her father went on drinking binges, he would send Yvonne into foster care. She increasingly refused to live by the rules of the foster households and eventually got bounced from one living situation to another. In eighth grade, she was put into a foster home. By ninth grade, Yvonne's misbehavior had exhausted the foster system in the small town of Mountain Home, and she was placed in a group home in Boise. "That was really bad," Yvonne recounts. "It was a bunch of girls, and I was learning more bad things than I was already doing. I was the only virgin in the group home in Boise."

The situation grew so untenable that Yvonne's mother eventually intervened and petitioned the state to allow her daughter to return to Mountain

Home to live with her. Fearing her stepfather, Yvonne stayed away as much as she could. "At that point, I just kind of finished out school on my own. I was pretty much on my own. I stayed at my dad's when he was sober. . . . I stayed at my boyfriend's house, who ended up finally being my husband. I stayed at whoever's couch I could sleep on. I look back now and I think, how the fuck did I do that?"

While Yvonne was moving from couch to couch, her younger sister, who was now in high school, informed her mother that she had been molested since she was little. Yvonne's mother filed charges against the abuser. The fallout from the situation was too much for Yvonne's younger sister, who ran away from home at age fifteen, making her way to Seattle, Washington, where she lived on the streets for years. Yvonne tells me, with regret, that she was far from a supportive and loving older sister. "I just cut her out of my life," she says. "We were so different, and I was so broken. We just didn't have a relationship as kids or anything, so it was easy for me to cut her out. It was shitty. I mean, that will probably be part of my life review," Yvonne tells me. She is referring to a spiritual concept in which a soul is evaluated after death on the progress it made toward enlightenment during its latest lifetime. "I'm sure my younger sister is probably the one person I treated the worst out of my whole life."

Soon Yvonne had other things to worry about: She discovered she was pregnant. "I got married in my senior year in high school. I got pregnant at seventeen, and I got married at eighteen. I graduated pregnant. I had no idea how to be a parent. I had no idea what that meant."

Yvonne felt lost. She was a recent high school graduate with a new husband and baby and no plans or direction. She tried to begin a career but quickly squandered the opportunity. "I started cosmetology school and, from lack of having a healthy foundation, I didn't do very well with money. That's never been my forte. And so I blew through my student loan, and I found myself at a crossroads. I was headed down a dark road. I wasn't making good choices. Definitely not good choices for my son."

Back in Pennsylvania, Tammy was heading down a dark road of her own.

✦

Nineteen-year-old Tammy showed up at her grandmother's wake with a black eye. She told everyone she had gotten hit by a softball. "Of course, they knew

I was lying," she tells me. "That was bad. Really bad," she says, shaking her head at the memory. "My ex did that. He was twenty-one at the time. He was my high school sweetheart. I had three children with him. Had my first child at sixteen and my third at nineteen."

"We were so young," she says, recalling decades back. "He was very abusive, didn't keep a job, and was a cheater." Tammy had already fled numerous times to escape physical abuse from the man she called her childhood sweetheart. At one point she went to a shelter. The relationship ended with the children in temporary foster care and Tammy spiraling her way into her next relationship with a roofer named Dave. She married him with high hopes—which were quickly dashed. "Dave was an alcoholic," she says, like it was his defining feature. "When I found out I was pregnant on our first wedding anniversary, he went out to celebrate," she tells me like she's setting up a joke. "He didn't come back for days," she says as if delivering the punchline.

"He did that often after that," she says in a more serious voice. "Much later on, I found out he was using drugs. Back then, I had no idea. I thought he was getting drunk and passing out and waking up and doing it all over again. I was so naive."

I asked her if there was any physical violence. "He abused me pretty often, more than my ex even. Probably that was because Dave was usually drunk," she says lightly. "But I kept staying and then leaving and going back with both him and my ex. I didn't deserve a lot of what they did to me. I did my fair share of fucked-up things. Believe me, I was no angel. Far from it. But I didn't deserve the beatings. I know that," she says. It sounds to me as if she's still trying to convince herself.

Dave was also being emotionally abusive toward the three children Tammy had brought into the marriage. Tammy says Dave hated her children and would pick on them relentlessly. One by one, they each went to live with Tammy's ex to avoid their abusive, drunken stepfather.

Like many women, Tammy experienced intimate partner violence at the hands of multiple men. Over 35 percent of women report experiencing physical violence from an intimate partner. In Tammy's age cohort, 77 percent of female victims of intimate partner violence report repeated physical abuse from the same partner. About 81 percent of victims of such violence report significant impacts on their lives, like injuries or PTSD. Survivors are three times more likely to meet PTSD criteria and to develop a major depressive disorder. They are six times more likely to develop a substance use disorder and four times more likely to attempt suicide.

Meanwhile, Dave's drinking and disappearances left Tammy scrambling to pay the bills. The family received cash assistance and food stamps. Dave worked for irregular stretches and often drank his wages. Due to his fluctuating and uncertain income (and him not telling her what he earned), Tammy failed to update the family income with social services, and she was charged with welfare fraud since she was the one who handled the paperwork. She pled guilty.

A few years later, Tammy finally left Dave for good. Months afterward, she started a relationship with a man who was a corrections officer, and they were soon engaged. The night before their wedding, Dave was picked up by the Wilkes-Barre police for public drunkenness along with an outstanding warrant and a parole violation. When the police put Dave in the cell, he was screaming Tammy's name and saying he couldn't believe that she was doing this to him, according to a newspaper article about the incident. Fifteen minutes later, the guards went back to check on him and found Dave hanging in the cell, already dead. He had made his socks into a noose and tied them to the cell cross bars.

Tammy's new husband helped her and her daughter through the suicide, taking on the role of father for Dave and Tammy's child. "I always thought of myself as a single mother until him," she says of her corrections officer husband. The other kids were living with their father, who had stepped up his parenting. "It was really his wife that made the difference," Tammy explained to me. "He was a truck driver, always on the road, so his wife took care of them, really."

Not long into the marriage, Tammy's new husband started to change. "He thinks he treated me like a queen, because he bought me whatever I wanted. But he was so controlling, especially after we got married. I used to have to hide my cigarettes. He was always threatening to divorce me for dumb shit like reading a horoscope or watching *General Hospital*. Sometimes he made worse threats. A bruise goes away; words sting for a long time."

Her husband's controlling ways led to Tammy losing her job. He had helped Tammy apply for a job at the prison. Tammy loved it. She even wanted to go to school to become a prison counselor. Then, eight months into the job, she got fired. When she had filled out the application, her husband had given her explicit instructions not to include a minor charge related to improper trash disposal on the form. Prison administrators discovered the omission and fired her for not including it.

Getting fired sent Tammy into depression and led her to consider leaving her husband. When I ask if physical abuse played any role in her wanting to leave, Tammy initially denies that there had been any. I ask her about a newspaper account I had read of him being arrested for violence against her. She pauses to remember the incident and then tells me about it. After thinking for a moment, Tammy adds, "I guess I minimize the abuse."

Tammy tried to take her life a year into the marriage. A doctor had pre-scribed her Wellbutrin for depression and to help her quit smoking. She wasn't taking the pills, so she had a few bottles worth on hand. She took fifty-two Wellbutrin. "I was feeling guilty about my children not living with me," she reflects now. "My husband hated my three oldest kids. I felt a lot of guilt. My husband said the EMTs brought me back. I spent five days in the psych ward." She was diagnosed with severe PTSD and put on disability.

Eventually, after a decade of marriage, Tammy couldn't take her husband's controlling ways and left him. He filed for divorce in 2010, and the court required him to pay Tammy $1,000 a month in spousal support due to her disability. He dropped the petition and reunited with Tammy, insisting that she sign a binding document saying that she would not claim spousal support if they ended the marriage after their reconciliation. After a year, he filed for divorce again and thus got out of paying Tammy any support.

By now Tammy's children were grown and mostly on their own. Depressed, hopeless, and lonely, Tammy started using meth. During this period, Tammy was in and out of relationships with men, the longest being with a fellow meth addict. She eventually switched to crack, spending two years as a crack addict. When Tammy cashed her disability checks, her dealer would hold the amount of money she needed for rent so that she didn't get kicked out of her apartment.

Tammy looks back on this as an act of kindness. It's more likely that he was only protecting the safehouse for his deals. That was probably a good idea given that she was frequently out of control. The worst episode ended with Tammy running around the neighborhood naked and high. She kicked the officers when they tried to handcuff her.

"I was still on my crack addiction, and I was partying for five days," she says like she's talking about someone else. "Well, partying for three days, four days, when somebody thought it would be a good idea to get a half gallon bottle of spiced rum," she says with an ironic laugh. "Well, it wasn't a good idea for me. By day five, I don't have much memory of it. But I do remember I woke up in a jail cell in the county jail after they arrested me naked. Took me to the magistrate naked," she says with emphasis.

"Got out of jail five days later," she says, shaking her head at her past behavior. "I slept most of the time, which was a plus. . . . They had to give me state-issued sweatpants and shoes and everything to leave."

Tammy eventually quit when she got tired of living in crack-induced poverty, despite craving the refuge it provided from real life. "I loved smoking crack. I lost two apartments, a car, and a lot of other stuff. One day I was sick of not having money, using coffee filters for toilet paper. I was just done."

Tammy was not yet done, however, with suicide attempts. "I took a bunch of Xanax when I was forty-something. Another broken relationship. Then it was over-the-counter sleeping pills. That almost did it. I was in the critical care unit for four days then to a psych ward. I tried to hang myself in 2018. I was so depressed. Was always crying and sobbing all the time. I had something around my neck, I was wrapping it around the shower rod. As I was standing there on the bathtub, I thought about how much I missed my mom. And how the only thing worse than being alive would be to see my children crying for me or thinking I hated my life because of them."

By the time Tammy turned to conspiracy theories, she had already tried, in a variety of ways, to cope with a life filled with trauma. It was cigarettes, alcohol, and marijuana when she was a child. It was alcohol through her marriages. After divorcing her second husband, it was meth, crack, and sex. When none of that eased her pain, Tammy tried suicide.

By the time the pandemic hit, Tammy was ready to believe in anything that promised to change her life. She was longing for something—anything, really—to give her some hope and some company.

CHAPTER 3

Something to Believe In

Like many people drawn to conspiracism, Tammy is constantly on the lookout for messages from the divine. She believes these messages come to her in the form of signs that seem, to others, like coincidences.

For the last several years, she occasionally wears a baseball cap adorned with bird feathers. Whenever she finds a new feather while out on walks in her rural Pennsylvania neighborhood, she takes it home and adds it to the hat. She sees those feathers as signs from beyond the veil. "We live in a spiritual world. We are supposed to be in the world, not of the world. I think that's me," she says when we are chatting one day.

Tammy tells me about how the feather messages started. One day in 2019 she found a black feather outside her door. "I said to my then-boyfriend, 'The Angel of Death left this for you.' A day or two later, I was reading this thing I get in my email, kinda like a horoscope, but from 'Guardian Angel.' It said, 'When you find feathers of any color, it's a sign that your angel is close.'"

Just about every time Tammy went for a walk after that, she says, she would find a feather. She started calling them "angel hairs" and collecting them.

A few months later, there was a Donald Trump rally in her area. She wanted to attend, but she didn't have a car, and so she didn't know how she could get there. It was a Saturday evening in October, and she was reading the Bible and listening to worship music. "I got a thought to put a feather in my cap," she tells me. "So I got my collection and put an angel hair in every hole. Then I read Psalm 91." She paraphrases Psalm 91:4: "He will cover you in his feathers; under his wing you shall trust. His truth is your shield and buckler."

When it turned out that Tammy was able to attend the rally after all, she saw it as a miraculous intervention. She interpreted her urge to wear the feather hat and the biblical passage as signs that God wanted her at that Trump rally. Helping Trump must be part of God's plan for her, she thought.

After that experience, Tammy was on the lookout for anything having to do with feathers and hats with feathers. She saw any reference to feathers as another divine message to be decoded. When a meme of Dr. Seuss's Cat in the Hat wearing a red MAGA hat with a feather in it came across her Facebook feed, she interpreted it as a message sent directly to her from the spirit world. Tammy interpreted the meme as a message that her support for Donald Trump was following God's will.

Months later, Tammy encountered QAnon conspiracy theories, which we'll look at a bit more later in this chapter and elsewhere. By that time, her flexible spiritual beliefs in the supernatural could easily incorporate Q's various prophecies. As we'll see, prophecies and ideas and rhetoric from a wide range of sources—charismatic Christianity, conservative Catholicism, New Age spirituality, wellness culture, pseudopsychology, and various far-right ideologies—can coexist in the realms of conspirituality. They easily mix and merge in a vast and dizzying array of patterns.

For many conspiracy-minded believers like Tammy, all these religious and spiritual raw materials combined with the 2020 presidential election and then were filtered through internet chat board posts, memes, and videos. The bizarre results can be seen in a video that Tammy recorded of a dream she had one night. That dream was so vivid she talked about it for days afterward. Tammy still references that dream sometimes; she sees it as a moment when she received a prophecy.

Dreams and visions are standard fare in QAnon circles. They are the kind of conspiratorial prophecy you can find all over the internet if you understand what you're seeing. Here's Tammy talking on the video she posted about her dream and vision:

> I had a dream a few nights ago that my grandson and I were walking from the store. I was holding Angel Soft toilet paper in my hand. I don't know why that's significant, but for some reason I believe it is. We were walking up a hill and at the top of the hill we were walking up, there was a wall . . .

As we were walking, I looked up, and in the clouds, it appeared to be, like, a stairway. And I said to my grandson, I said, "Look, a stairway to heaven." And as I was looking, a trumpet appeared. . . . Then it blew and it blew like three times really loud. And then I heard . . . a woman . . . say, "The savior is coming! The savior is coming!". . .

There was a man walking towards the woman with a megaphone. The man had one of those hats on that the Jewish people wear, I don't know what they're called, but he was wearing one of them. And he had on a black robe, lined in red. He was yelling through the megaphone, "Don't worry about the Savior, go to the New World Order." And he was walking towards her like he was gathering people to go somewhere else.

And, that's when I woke up, shaken. It shook me up. I woke up. And I was up for a few hours after that.

A couple nights before that, I wasn't sleeping, but I had a vision that in the city where I live there's a bridge that connects the cities. Over the bridge were coming Army tanks of Antifa. I knew it was Antifa. I don't know how I knew. I just knew it was Antifa. And they had Biden signs on the tanks. And that's all. That's all.

I think these dreams are connected. Like I said, that first one wasn't a dream. I was awake. I was fully awake when I saw this happening. In the town where I live . . . there are multiple, multiple buildings with Illuminati symbols all over them. I took pictures of them. They're on my Facebook. "If you, you know."

I'm just continuing to pray, you know, for our safety when we go to vote, for the corruption to keep being exposed as it's being exposed. I know that the Lord has our backs and our fronts. He's our refuge and he's our saving grace. I just want to thank him for loving us, for saving us. And I pray that he continues to keep his followers, his children, safe.

And for those that aren't saved, I pray in the name of Jesus that they do become saved before it's too late. Thank you. And God bless.

Tammy genuinely doesn't want people to suffer and die in the apocalypse she believes is coming. She hopes for mass salvation and that people can live in harmony. But she is also convinced, based on what she's heard, that there are Jewish people at the center of all this. Tammy is also certain about the grave threat posed by Antifa, the "globalists," and the Illuminati.

She thinks Hollywood stars and most national leaders are reptilian, blood-drinking pedophiles. She thinks McDonalds sells human meat and that Hillary Clinton and the Obamas engage in satanic rituals. She wants them all defeated as the prelude to the people of the world coming together for a new golden age, which she believes Donald Trump will help create.

If you haven't heard the particulars of a conspiracist's beliefs, just reading about them can be jarring. It's tempting to dismiss all of it as delusional thinking. It's easy to focus on the strangeness of the conspiratorial beliefs, their inherent contradictions, and deeply embedded bigotry. But the same criticism could be applied to varying extents to any religious belief system. In fact, it's important to understand the way in which conspiracies work as a kind of religion. Like other religions, conspiracism is a belief system based on faith. Conspiracism hardly has the market cornered on the supernatural. Most religions include some form of angels and demons, signs and portents, and people who claim to have had direct communication with the divine. In the worlds in which Tammy and Yvonne move, those messages come via feathers, dreams, visions of stairways to heaven, and symbols of the Illuminati.

Understanding conspiracism as a spiritual belief system and appreciating the ways it acts—and doesn't act—like a religion can give us a better sense of how conspiracism works. It can illuminate why people are drawn to it, and why it's so resistant to criticism based on facts and logic.

This perspective—that conspiracism is proximal to religious belief—can also help us better understand our own religious or spiritual identities. In fact, I was surprised at how thinking about conspiracism as a religion made me rethink my own vision of faith.

✳

I did not grow up in a religious household. My social worker mother raised my brother and me with a clear sense of values but not with an overriding theological explanation of the universe. We never went to church. In high school, I joined in the activities of Young Life, a Christian ministry, mostly because the group did fun things, and my friends invited me along. I kept coming back because Cyndi and Glenn, the young couple running the program, were kind people who gave me comfort and support during the most difficult period of my teenage years. For a few months, they even opened their home to me to stay with them. I always thought they embodied the best of Christianity, and I am beyond grateful for their presence in my life. They remain friends to this day. But I do not follow their faith. I have always remained skeptical about the active presence of the divine on earth given the constant awful things that happen on this planet.

The closest I have come to any kind of spiritual awakening occurred in India at the start of the pandemic. The ancient holy places I visited in India would normally have been packed shoulder-to-shoulder with pilgrims and tourists. After the World Health Organization declared a global pandemic, the sites started to clear out, and no one arrived to take their place as India locked down. In a near-empty Rishikesh, I watched the evening Ganga Aarti ceremony by the Vedic priests. I sat directly across from the giant statue of the Hindu god Shiva, which stands in the middle of the Ganges River, with my feet dangling in its sacred headwaters. This intimacy would have been impossible at most any other time in the city's history. It was as if Shiva, the god of destruction and rebirth, had summoned me for a personal audience to warn about the impending calamity ahead. It was almost as if he were assigning me some special role in the drama to come. Shiva destroys lies and injustice and rebuilds with truth and fairness. I could get behind that concept.

During the height of the pandemic, I embraced the idea of Shiva at work in my life. Looking back now, I see this as a method of hope, which we'll look at in chapter 8. As I was waiting for the car to rush me to the airport six hours away, I purchased figurines in a market in Haridwar, where I was one of the only Westerners remaining in the holy city. They were representations of Shiva, his wife Parvati, and their son Ganesha, the trickster elephant-headed god who places obstacles in life pathways and removes them in accordance with a greater divine plan.

When I finally got home, I put the figurines on the mantle. For several months, at the same time each day, I made chai from scratch, in my own little tea ceremony. The pandemic was worsening, and millions of people were dying. Yet I let myself feel comforted by the idea that maybe this was happening as part of Shiva's plan. Maybe I could play a special role in creating the new world that would come out of the destruction.

I didn't truly believe that's what was happening. I'm not Hindu. I don't really think Shiva had summoned me to Rishikesh for a private audience or had given me marching orders. I had always realized that I was self-consciously creating a fable to escape my fear and anxiety. I was intentionally finding solace in a fantastical idea, which helped me cope during a desolate time.

Mostly, I think the comfort came because I loved my short time in India, most of which was spent at its first national park in the foothills of the Himalayas with warm and friendly people. I spent each day exploring a place filled with Bengal tigers, wild elephants, exotic birds, and all kinds of unfamiliar wildlife in its natural habitat. My daily chai ceremonies back home were an attempt to recapture the joy I felt when the driver named Bablu parked the jeep at a scenic location and the naturalist guide, Rakesh, poured cups of hot chai from a thermos and told stories about the incredible scenes he had witnessed at this very spot during past trips into the jungle. That feeling was what I wanted to keep alive through my "belief" in Shiva and my little rituals. I wanted to be transported to those wonderful moments I had experienced on the eve of destruction. I longed to believe that a new and better world awaited on the other side of these chaotic and uncertain years.

Thinking about my own beliefs alongside those of Tammy and Yvonne has helped me better appreciate the ways that conspiracism, like religion, can bring a sense of meaning, purpose, and belonging. Whether it's my own flirtation with Hindu rituals, my neighbor's Presbyterian tradition, or someone else's religious commitments, faith provides a sense of comfort, solace, beauty, an ability to cope with suffering, and the prospect of a new and better world that awaits us all.

For Tammy, and especially for Yvonne, as we will see, faith and belief occupy a far more central place in their lives than they do in mine. They arrived at conspiracism via a variety of spiritual and religious traditions. They aren't alone in starting out in an established organized religion and ending up putting their faith in conspiracy theories. Research has shown that people who have a strong need to believe in something, who don't handle uncertainty well, and who need definitive answers to complex and unknowable questions are often drawn to conspiratorial thinking. So are people who put faith in their own intuition above verifiable facts.

That simple certainty, an unwavering faith, is something Yvonne has yearned for her entire life. It is the impulse that drives her above all others. In the search for answers, Yvonne trusts her gut over everything. "I trust myself and my intuition," she says all the time, even on the stand during her trial for her actions on January 6. These views are what brought her to conspiracism and delivered her into the realm of conspirituality.

Organized religion plays a role as well. There is a strong link between believing in conspiracies and attending charismatic churches, the kind that preach modern miracles, prophecies, and channel spirits by speaking in tongues. Most religious beliefs have no clear correlation with conspiracism. But there is a correlative link between conspiratorial thinking and charismatic traditions like Pentecostalism and nondenominational apostolic churches, which are the fastest growing organized faith movement in the world. Every other organized religion is losing membership. The charismatic ones are recruiting new followers at a rapid pace.

At different times throughout their lives, both Tammy and Yvonne have engaged with charismatic Christian faith. It's where they both got their spiritual start. For Yvonne, faith began by getting on a bus by herself at the age of eight.

⁎

"I spent my whole life seeking, on and off," Yvonne tells me one day when we are talking on the phone. When it comes to her childhood and her journey of faith, Yvonne is remarkably consistent, often using the same words and phrasing each time she tells the tale. She has told this story many times before. It's part of the personal salvation story that Yvonne has reworked for each of her spiritual awakenings over the years. There's even a joke she frequently repeats: She has been saved so many times by so many different churches that she's got it down pretty well.

That narrative always begins with the story of her attending church by herself as a child. "I was the little kid that would get on the bus and go to Pentecostal churches by myself," Yvonne says. "My mother was Catholic, and Christianity was all I was introduced to. I went to my first communion and all that. I loved God, but I wasn't finding it in the Catholic church."

A young child getting herself to church on her own might seem surprising but remember that Yvonne was essentially on her own at a very young age. It was also the 1970s, a time with much looser parenting norms, and Yvonne's mother seemed to have few rules. "My mom was busy partying and sleeping with guys, you know, partying every weekend. So I would get on the bus and go to a bunch of different churches all by myself as a kid. The charismatic stuff. I think it's because you could feel it, it was in your body. Definitely more charismatic than evangelical. I mean, the evangelicals are charismatic too. It just depends on which denomination you pick."

As Yvonne's childhood became more chaotic, she stopped going to church. She lost her faith bouncing between the homes of her divorced parents and in and out of foster care. By the time Yvonne graduated from high school, she had started to lose hope, despite having a new baby and husband. When the young marriage fell apart, she started engaging in self-destructive behavior. "I was so desperate for money. I was starting to do things that I wouldn't have done before that. I was starting to get into drugs, starting to dabble with stuff stronger than marijuana."

Yvonne's craving for direction and purpose led her to the Marines. It was the 1980s, and the idea of a woman joining the Marine Corps was still strange to many people. "Everyone told me I couldn't do it, so I had to prove them all wrong," Yvonne says. Each time she tells this story she emphasizes her strong-willed defiance of conventional wisdom, her stubborn refusal to accept social norms.

All these years later, Yvonne still describes the Marines in reverential tones that seem almost religious. Yvonne wouldn't dispute that depiction. Although the unofficial motto of the Marine Corps is "God, Country, Corps," for her, the Marines became number one on the list:

> I needed the Marine Corps. I needed that. When I first joined the Marine Corps, God wasn't necessarily at the top of my list. The Marine Corps gave me discipline. It gave me guidance. It gave me a family. It gave me a brotherhood that I'd never experienced. It changed my life. It changed who I was. It changed my trajectory. It gave me something that was bigger than myself. It was the first time I had purpose.
>
> I loved my service in the military. I spent my whole life alone. Only me fighting for myself. And in the Marine Corps, I was not alone anymore. I was surrounded. I always wanted a brother, and I was surrounded by brothers. And camaraderie is real. I don't know how to explain it to civilians, but it's real and it's powerful. And it was life giving. Life changing.

The Marine Corps recognized Yvonne's talent and promoted her through the enlisted ranks. She was ultimately entrusted with a series of high-profile, public-facing jobs that showcased her intelligence, charisma, and broad array of skills. She began her work with the Marines as an air traffic controller.

Then she moved into administrative work until 1991, when the Gulf War happened. Then she moved into public affairs.

As she rose through the ranks, Yvonne was also dealing with a growing family. During her sixteen years in the Marines she gave birth to four children, each with a different man, all of whom were Marines. She struggled as a mother with unstable and volatile personal relationships. Moving around to different bases and assignments didn't make it any easier. "When I was a young corporal in Okinawa, Japan, I was a struggling single mom. I was living off base and, you know, didn't have money. I did that so I could bring my kids, and we wouldn't be separated. Living off base, I didn't get all the benefits that I should have had. I had to pay a lot of stuff out of pocket. It was expensive to live out in town. So I was struggling and always broke."

Yvonne's family responsibilities faced their greatest strain with her promotion to drill instructor, the most time-consuming assignment of her career. Drill instructors are the Marines who train new recruits, breaking them down and building them into the image of the Corps by instilling the values that all Marines hold sacred. "At the time I went to the drill field, I had four kids and my youngest was only two. I was breastfeeding, and I did not want to go to the drill field. So many females in the Marines were parents. They tried to keep us at ninety hours a week. That never happened. We usually worked well over a hundred to a hundred and twenty hours, I would say, especially for the beginning of training. It does ease up a little bit towards the end, but it's still a hundred hours a week."

Apart from the hours, Yvonne loved everything about the job. She loved the sense of purpose, the responsibility she had, the authority she commanded, and the respect she got. "As a drill instructor, I was an example of what honor was supposed to stand for." She speaks in the past tense. The foreboding in her voice comes from the terrible end of her time as a role model and a Marine. That ending followed her marriage to Troy St. Cyr, a fellow drill instructor, and the birth of a baby, Yvonne's fifth child. After giving birth, Yvonne struggled to lose weight. When a mother in the Marines is six months postpartum, she has to "make weight." With the deadline approaching, Yvonne was still eight pounds over, even after being on a weight-control diet issued by the Marines.

One day she was lamenting about her weight loss struggles to a female friend, who was dating a guy on the base. The woman said her boyfriend had the solution. "She's like, 'Yvonne, I could get you some coke,'" Yvonne recounts now. "Prior to that I had never bought from anyone on base or done drugs on base."

Yvonne and Troy had "dabbled" with recreational drugs with friends off base a few times prior to deciding to have a child. "We would go to parties and stuff, but we had never done anything on base, never done anything around any other Marines." They tried cocaine and ecstasy, which Yvonne said "are easy to get out of your system" to elude any drug testing. But the day she bought the cocaine from her friend's boyfriend was different:

> The NCIS [Naval Criminal Investigative Service] had been trailing these guys for like six months and the day that I buy it was the day that they busted them. And then he gave my name. They showed up at our house in the middle of the night. I had a half an ounce of cocaine, and they never found the cocaine. They found a little baggy with residue and that made all three of us have to go take urinalysis. And of course, we were positive. I ended up going to jail. They charged me with distribution. And I took a plea agreement. It's like, really? I distributed it to my own husband. I've always been the kind of person to own my shit. If I fuck up, I own it. Because that's just who I've been. And so I agreed to the plea agreement. I went to jail for four months with a six-month-old. Well, by the time we went to court-martial my son was a year old.

Yvonne spent three weeks in a jail in Beaufort County, South Carolina before they transferred her to Norfolk, Virginia. "I was away from my children, and I was ashamed of the discharge," she reflects now.

Those of us not from military families may have a hard time understanding the deep impact that a court-martial and a dishonorable discharge has on someone like Yvonne, a Marine for sixteen years who had risen to one of the highest enlisted ranks. I recently talked to a friend of mine, a proud Marine who had faced a court-martial for being gay during the "don't ask, don't tell" era when homosexuality was forbidden in the armed forces. He successfully defended himself and earned an honorable discharge, but the experience and sense of loss still haunts him. I asked him how Yvonne would have likely experienced her court-martial and discharge. His answers were revealing. "Imagine being fired from your job for criminal conduct and not being able to hide it from anyone in the future," he told me. "'Have you served in the United States military?' is a question on almost every job application, followed by 'Were you honorably discharged?' Sixteen years is a big gap that has to be explained."

Beyond the practical impact, he added, there's an emotional one. "You aren't just *in* the Marines like other services; you *are* a Marine. No other branch identifies in that way. Losing that at all—but especially after sixteen years—would be devastating. You know the expression 'once a Marine, always a Marine?' She lost that. There are no *former* Marines. But there are ex-Marines."

.✦.

Like Yvonne, Tammy was raised as a Catholic. And like Yvonne, Tammy also had a powerful experience at a Pentecostal church at a young age. It helped to convince her that supernatural, otherworldly interventions were regular occurrences, if one is paying attention. Tammy now believes that her spirituality is distinct from any particular organized religion and its doctrine.

When Tammy was ten years old, she accompanied her dying mother to a healing service at a Pentecostal church close to their house. Her mother was on a desperate quest for a cure for the lupus that was not responding to treatment. The revival finished with an altar call, and her mother stepped forward. "There was a guy with his hands on my mom's shoulders, hers on his, and I was in the middle," Tammy tells me. "They started speaking in tongues. I laughed. I had no idea what was going on. Then she fell—'slain in the Spirit,' they say."

After Tammy's mother died, she questioned God a lot but ultimately found a way to explain the lack of intervention. "I concluded that He healed her by taking her life. God saved her and my brothers and I from a lot of pain and suffering. I realized it would have been worse to watch her suffer."

After the death of her mother, Tammy did not return to that church, or any other, with regularity. It's not that she abandoned Christianity. It's more that she developed her own understanding of it outside of any organized denomination. And those beliefs seem to draw heavily from the charismatic style, prophecies, and miracles of charismatics, a stream of Christianity that emphasizes gifts of the Spirit such as speaking in tongues, prophecy, and faith healings.

Tammy's beliefs in the supernatural realm and her ideas about the divine are exceedingly flexible and syncretic. To her, good and evil are always fighting it out in the real world. Jesus Christ is the savior, but he exists in a spiritual realm of angels and demons, visions and prophecies, signs and omens that don't necessarily require knowledge of the Bible or any other kind of doctrine to decode. Tammy incorporates her own dreams and visions into the mix, along with her attempts to connect with the spirit world. Christianity meets the occult and whatever else she adds—which, in the last several years, has included alien beings and entire new dimensions and universes. While less needful of a clear and certain faith than Yvonne, Tammy is driven by her spiritual understanding of the world. "We don't see half of what is going on around us," she tells me firmly.

Tammy believes that demons and spirits are real and tells me that she has a photograph of one. I say I'd love to see it. She sends me a link to the Facebook page of a relative who had taken the photo. The camera is positioned at the bottom of a staircase, looking up the stairs at a child about to reach the top landing. Tammy tells me the spirit is on the landing. I see what she's talking about. It looks to me like a child holding onto the rail and doing a pose for the camera. The details are washed out by a harsh hall light or bright sunlight shining through a second-story window in the hallway. My guess is that the image Tammy was calling a spirit was the shadow of another kid standing just outside the camera frame.

On Facebook, Tammy's relative captioned the photo: "This is a beautiful lost soul roaming the earth." The first commenter asks skeptically, "Are you sure?" and then says it looks like the older sister of the girl climbing the stairs. A second person guessed that it was the older sister's shadow projected onto the wall.

Tammy thinks they're wrong. Despite the questions and the photographer's history of making up wild stories, Tammy is convinced the image at the top of the stairs is not a child but a genuine spirit captured with a cellphone camera. This is the nature of her faith: She chooses what is real and what is illusion, which stories and images are wishful thinking, and which are the real deal.

For Tammy, the porous nature between the natural and the supernatural worlds is a strong conviction. And more than once, that conviction has landed her in jail—and on a few occasions, in the psych ward:

> The first time—this is going to really sound crazy—but the first time I was with this girl I would smoke weed with and play with a Ouija board. One night we went for a ride in her car, smoked a joint, and I

started seeing and hearing things that were evil. She was hearing and seeing them too. But I lost it. I punched her in the face and took her car. The cops were chasing me. I honestly thought, and still do, demons were chasing me. I asked for hospital treatment, and that's what happened. I had a priest come in. It was terrible. They insisted I took more than weed, but I didn't, and the bloodwork proved it. That's when they diagnosed me with schizophrenia. I didn't accept that. When I was seen by the disability doctor, she confirmed that I'm not schizophrenic. She said PTSD. I say something else.

Tammy easily incorporated QAnon into her spiritual worldview, blending its apocalyptic vision with her own beliefs. Tammy's dream and vision that I recounted early in the chapter shows how seamlessly it all fits together. QAnon could be seen as a millennialist religion that parallels the book of Revelation with a different storyline and without Jesus. It is based on the belief that, in a soon-to-arrive apocalypse, evildoers, who are not actually human, will be vanquished by the forces of good. QAnon's conspiratorial world is so broad and accepting of divergent ideas that there is lots of room for people to put their own spin on its end-of-days prophecies, just as Tammy has done.

Tammy has been drawn to a particular branch of QAnon that sees the bad guys as nonhuman reptilian people, many of whom are Jewish. The main QAnon narrative focuses on a "cabal" of elites who control most everything through a "New World Order" than runs a "deep state" within national governments. Parts of the QAnon conspiracy theories are deeply antisemitic, using old tropes, some of which go back to the medieval era. The strain of QAnon that Tammy follows is especially antisemitic. It also sees the bad guys trying to create a New World Order run by the Illuminati, a secret society formed around the time of the American Revolution that has been the lead actor in numerous conspiracy theories ever since. For people like Tammy, the Illuminati serves as a stand-in for every real and imagined secret society. To her, masonic symbols are signs of the Illuminati, as are virtually every other symbolic reference she sees but doesn't understand.

QAnon's close alignment with the political right has always portrayed those on the left as the evildoers in the conspiracy. This is how QAnon lore turned people identifying as anti-fascists, shortened to Antifa, into the "army of the New World Order." In recent years, the standard-enemies list also includes Hollywood elites, public health officials, and members of the Democratic Party.

And of course, QAnon's great hero is Donald Trump, who took full advantage of his place as the savior in its secular theology. By repeating QAnon talking points, displaying its symbols, and liking and reposting content produced by its social media influencers, Trump recruited Anons into the MAGA fold and deepened the faith of existing supporters like Tammy.

Trump did not hypnotize QAnon followers into some "cult of Trump." He merely exploited a network of people who had self-radicalized online by skillfully signaling that he was on their side. Trump's way of couching his support—never openly embracing QAnon and often denying knowledge of it—only strengthened the connection. The strategy played right into QAnon's game-like culture of cryptic messages, which followers believe are puzzles waiting to be decoded. Anons think the puzzles will unlock secret knowledge needed to win the war against evil. Trump's coy refusal to confirm or deny his belief in Q must itself be a sign, conspiracists believed.

Tammy saw Donald Trump as the only politician who understood her plight and the danger she believes threatens the world. She was not political before Trump came on the scene. She didn't vote. But Trump's depictions of an America in decline spoke to her. He captured her sense that things have gone off the rails in a profound and existential way, which can only be explained by evil spiritual forces at work. Critics scoffed at Trump's dire language about "American carnage" in his 2017 inaugural address, with his talk of "rusted-out factories, scattered like tombstones across the landscape" and "millions and millions of American workers that were left behind" in places now riddled with "crime and gangs and drugs." Tammy wasn't offended. She felt seen. She and her family *were* American carnage.

Tammy felt inspired by Trump's promise to bring an instant cure to all her problems. Trump sold hope to people like her who had given up on the idea of positive change. The appeal wasn't just his open embrace of popular grievances against "the elites" and a government many Americans have come to distrust and dislike. It was how Trump expressed those grievances in a spiritual register: a good vs. evil framing, which fit with Tammy's worldview. The more righteously bombastic Trump's claims have become, the more his followers are sure of his commitment to vanquishing evil. The more harsh and certain Trump's proposed solutions, the stronger his appeal has grown. Their faith is buttressed by his embrace of conspiracism and insistence that all the naysayers will be proven wrong. That's exactly what they want: to have their beliefs validated by an authority figure who seems to understand the threat the world faces and who knows what to do about it.

Tammy was also drawn in by Trump's constant promises of immediate relief from all the evils. He gave Tammy and millions of others hope that their struggles would soon be over. He convinced them that he would defeat evil and that, afterward, all the personal and financial troubles that plague their world, all the things that frighten them and cause great worry, would be gone in an instant.

Tammy's vision of victory can be surprisingly inclusive. Her ideal future, in many ways, is painted on the side of a collection of buildings in downtown Williamsport, Pennsylvania. It's a mural called "Inspiration: Lycoming County," painted by the artist Michael Pilato, and it currently holds the world record for largest outdoor portrait mural. The 3D mural spans across a collection of old brick buildings, most of which date to the nineteenth century. It depicts the region's history through portraits painted on walls and in windows, Pilato using the natural features of the buildings to display his subjects in imaginative ways. It's a positive, civic-boosting scene that includes historical figures in little tableaux. The mural depicts people of different races and religions all sharing the same space.

Tammy imagines that the new age to come will be an inclusive place like in the mural. Several of her grandchildren are mixed-race with skin colors that range from white to brown to black. In the mural, the brown, black, and white faces are smiling and happy together, like Tammy hopes her own family could be one day.

Two days after the 2020 presidential election, with the results still in doubt, she recorded a video of herself standing in front of Pilato's mural, holding it out as the world she hopes Donald Trump would usher in, if re-elected. "This is what America is about," Tammy announces. She pauses and corrects herself, sinking into a more cynical tone. "What it's supposed to be about, anyway." After a pause, her voice lifts into hopeful confidence. "And it will be again. Under the leadership of Donald Trump, being led by the Lord."

That's what Tammy thought she was doing on January 6: helping Donald Trump defeat real-world predators and supernatural evils that she believes are trying to make life into hell on earth. She thinks Trump will usher in the dawn of a new age of peace and harmony. Trump convinced Tammy that the scene from the mural could pop off the walls and windows and doorways and become a reality. Tammy believes this because she wants and needs to believe it.

There is a utopianism in the kind of conspiracism that has attracted Tammy and Yvonne and many other middle-aged women. Both Tammy and Yvonne are desperate to be positive people, to maintain a hopeful outlook in the face of crushing disappointments and despair. They refuse to give into the darkness they feel, as both have come close to doing in the past. Their beliefs share a sense of hope for the triumph of goodness and light, which they want to be shared by as many people as possible.

Or so the idealized version of their beliefs goes. As we will see, in practice, things are less inclusive and a lot more complicated.

✦ ✦ ✦

Yvonne reached her version of a utopian vision from a different spiritual direction than Tammy did. She found her way to QAnon and conspirituality along a path that started in the Marines, traveled years through evangelical Christianity, and finally landed in a New Age health and wellness culture that would become the launching pad for her conspiracism. Tracing that path shows both the resiliency of Yvonne's faith and its remarkable adaptability.

After her fall from grace from the Marines, Yvonne turned to evangelical Christianity. The conversion was almost immediate. Her preteen daughter had been attending church with a friend and asked her mother to attend her baptism shortly after Yvonne's arrest. Yvonne had no intention of joining the church but went along. "Of *course* I went," she said when I asked. "I mean, I wasn't against God at that point. I just was, you know, flailing in my life. My whole life I'd been searching." Yvonne was so emotional at the baptism, given all that was going on, that she threw up. She joined the church soon after, bringing her husband, Troy, and the rest of her children along with her.

Their new community in the small church in South Carolina rallied around the family when both Yvonne and Troy had to serve staggered prison sentences. One church family looked after the older kids while Yvonne was in prison so Troy could concentrate on the baby. Yvonne was incarcerated in August 2003 and was out of prison in time for Christmas.

Not long after, Yvonne and Troy moved their family back to Idaho and found a small but growing evangelical Christian church that would be their home for the next decade. Yvonne refers to these years as a rest stop on her spiritual journey, a dormant phase when she fell into spiritual stasis. "I went to sleep," she says in a matter-of-fact tone about this era. "You know, and it's funny, even then Troy and I were talking about doing our own landscaping business, and we had all these dreams. But when we came home, we quickly did what everybody else did. We got stuck in corporate America and then I got fat, and I went to sleep."

At the time, Yvonne threw herself completely into the church—an embrace that grew even tighter after she and her husband had marital troubles. Yvonne decided to repair her marriage and poured herself into God and church. "I was very active in my church. It wasn't just to show up to put a check in the box and show up on a Sunday morning. Church was who I was," Yvonne says. She speaks with a sense of distance from the person she was at that time. Then she tries to explain her mindset back then and how it links to who she is now. "I believe all of us are here for a purpose. I want to make a difference. I want to serve my community, and for me, church was a way to do that," she says.

Yvonne concentrated her church work with the youth ministry. "After what I went through growing up, I have a heart for teens. So I went to the church camp whenever I could." She is proud of her dedication. "I used my vacations to go with the kids to camp. I helped with the teams. I went to retreat every year that they would let me. It was my way to give back to the kids, because I didn't have that support as a child and I didn't have a normal childhood, so I wanted to make a difference."

At the same time, Yvonne was also turning to food for comfort. Yvonne says she gained over a hundred pounds after she left the Marine Corps. "I was really overweight. I've lost 130 pounds since then. It was like I was in the sleepwalking, hypnotic state that everybody does." She talks about using food as a coping mechanism and her weight as a defense during what she now sees as a retreat from the world.

After more than a decade of being "asleep," Yvonne began a weight loss journey in 2017 that launched her on the path to conspiracism and conspirituality. She went to Mexico for gastric bypass surgery. Then she turned to the health and wellness community. Three years after the surgery, her weight had plateaued at 185 pounds, and she was growing frustrated. In January 2020, a friend from church suggested that they do a "Ten-Pound Takedown Challenge." The package included a nutrition coach, who required all her clients to watch three documentaries as part of the weight loss program.

The documentaries were about the unhealthy nature of processed foods and diets high in sugar.

One of the films, entitled *Fed Up*, discussed how the government had hidden the dangers of sugar from the public. "It was very eye-opening," Yvonne tells me. "I didn't realize that I had lacked so much information and knowledge about what we are given to eat in food and how our government and the organizations that monitor food, the FDA and things, have hidden things from us." There's a sense of outrage in her voice. Yvonne has told this story many times before, because she sees it as central to her spiritual journey. But each time she tells the story, the sense of shock about the news and sense of betrayal she felt from the government always seem fresh and raw.

That began what Yvonne calls her descent down the rabbit hole. "I started thinking, 'If they're not telling us the truth about sugar, then what else are they hiding from us?' And that set me up to start to consider everything to make sure that I was responsible for what I was putting into my body, what I was putting into my mind, and what my kids were consuming."

This was something of a new mindset for a woman accustomed to following orders and not questioning the chain of command in the Marines—and doing the same in her evangelical churches. "That shifted the whole way I looked at life because, for the longest time, I had trusted the people that I thought were put in place to govern us and to help us. And I realized they weren't here to help me. I had to help myself, and I had to help my brothers and sisters see the truth."

Yvonne started to doubt what she knew and things she had been told, not just about food and nutrition but on a wide range of matters. "It made me start to question everything," she says. That's when Yvonne really started questioning reality, discounting facts, and relying on her intuition. "I started to realize that there were things that I hadn't seen, and that I needed to start trusting myself and start researching for myself and start looking into things. Because I wasn't given the truth. I believe we're given bits and pieces of truth, but it's up to us to find the truth. And so I started looking, and a lot of truth started to come up. For me it was remembering things, researching, connecting dots, and listening."

Hungry for information about "truths" she believes have been hidden from her, Yvonne turned to the internet, especially YouTube and videos posted to Facebook. "I watched lots of videos," she says, in what is a true understatement of the effect the internet had on her spiritual beliefs and life course.

Yvonne was already in the mindset of seeking hidden "truths" when the pandemic began. COVID would turn her life upside down like it would do to people across the world. She would respond like millions of others who lived online during the pandemic. She dealt with the fear and uncertainty by losing herself in conspiracy theories and the online communities that promoted them.

Both Yvonne and Tammy identify the pandemic as the critical event in their embrace of conspiracy theories and their impending spiritual revolutions. Yvonne talks about the pandemic like it was an alarm clock that woke her out of her spiritual slumber. "When COVID happened, it really shook me," she tells me. "God said to me, 'Wake up Yvonne, this isn't about a virus. It's about control.'"

Not long after, Yvonne found herself as a new member of what many people were calling an online cult.

CHAPTER 4

Pandemic

Yvonne and Tammy have both told me, many times, that 2020 changed everything. So have most of the women I have spoken with for this project. "It all started with COVID," said one January 6 defendant, who served less than thirty days. Another woman said that 2020 was when she "woke up to what was *really* happening." A third woman said the pandemic shutdowns and masking requirements made her question the government. A fourth described herself as apolitical until the pandemic convinced her that the "deep state was behind a lot of this" and that "Donald Trump was the only one fighting against it." For all these women, COVID-19 was a shared trauma that disrupted life in ways that changed how they looked at the world.

In many ways the pandemic was an isolating event, confining us in our homes and alienating us even further from our neighbors and friends and family. Businesses closed, many never to reopen. Entire households started working and teaching and going to school at the same time in the same spaces, setting up makeshift offices and classrooms wherever some privacy could be found. People were losing jobs, and many women were halting their careers to look after kids, who were now perpetually at home. Hospitals were filling to capacity, and the sick and elderly were dying, as were people who seemed in the peak of health. The streets were empty and then filling again with protestors. People enraged on opposing sides of issues were gathering in the streets over masks, Confederate statues, and the killing of unarmed Black people by law enforcement officers. Many of those protests were led by a group called Black Lives Matter and were joined by people of different races and across different age groups, who saw themselves as confronting racial injustice.

But we also experienced the pandemic collectively, through television screens and social media apps on phones and computers. In a matter of months, social platforms were teeming with more people than ever before. The world went online. We were logging in everyday, looking for information and connection and something to do. And we found an internet rapidly filling with disinformation that flooded out solid facts, accurate news, and reliable public health information.

In this way, just as the coronavirus found a fertile new host in humanity, so did conspiracism. Conspiracy theories became a social pandemic, as potent and disruptive as the health crisis. They spread over the internet, infecting humans who could not resist clicking the links and watching conspiratorial videos. Conspiracy theories hooked into human brains like the protein spikes of a virus. As those infected with COVID filled doctors' offices, medical clinics, and hospitals, people infected with conspiracism collected in online forums, chat groups, and the new online communities they created. COVID claimed new victims with droplets, misted out in sneezes and coughs or just warm, moist breath. Conspiracies claimed their own victims, often in the form of people eager to learn more about how to keep their families safe and who inhaled Facebook posts and TikTok videos promoting disinformation. The algorithms took over and did the rest.

The pandemic ultimately served as a superspreader of conspiracy theories. It was like a massive social experiment gone wrong. All at once, millions of people found themselves trapped inside, isolated from family, friends, workplaces, churches, and social routines. They searched for news about the pandemic, and the algorithms introduced them to conspiracies. Conspiratorial videos warned that vaccinations cause autism, deformities, and death. They claimed that ivermectin could cure COVID and many other illnesses. Other posts claimed to reveal the secret intentions of the politicians and pharmaceutical companies pushing mass inoculation. Some said COVID vaccinations were part of a plan for world domination by globalist elites who wanted to poison the public or turn people into slaves. As soon as readers interacted with any of this content, or followed the accounts pushing it, the algorithms brought them even more. New followers appeared, and friend requests poured in from fellow conspiracists anxious to educate newbies and normies about what was *really* happening with the pandemic.

When discussion in open chat groups began to violate content moderation rules, the conspiracists formed private groups so they could speak more candidly about their theories. I found out through my research account on social media that it was easy to get invited to one of these private chat forums, which included hundreds and sometimes thousands of people. The forums spawned private groups on particular theories and assembled activists for real-world protests. The titles of the groups and forums changed constantly. They didn't advertise the conspiracies for fear of getting banned. Instead, they used informal codes like "Let's Go Brandon," a popular anti–Joe Biden phrase and signal to like-minded followers.

These online spaces radicalized quickly and decisively. A variety of right-wing activists entered the networks and inserted their content into memes and posts. The leading conspiratorial apostles converted new disciples. Those disciples spread the theories to their virtual friends and followers in different online communities. Many of the conversion experiences happened in regular conversations among small groups of new online friends, who discussed which conspiracies they believed and which ones they found to be far-fetched. Ordinary people were radicalizing each other. And the great volume of online conspiratorial content gave isolated people all the material they needed to self-radicalize.

As I continued my research, it seemed like entire online sectors began to embrace conspiracism overnight. The most dramatic changes appeared in the online health and wellness communities. In a matter of months, liberal-appearing New Age nutrition and yoga communities were remade into bastions of anti-government activism. Prior to the pandemic, most health and wellness influencers were largely apolitical, mainly focused on selling coaching services and non-FDA approved health supplements. Once COVID hit, however, they became vocal opponents of vaccinations, public masking rules, and business closures. Before long, many spiritualists and life coaches, whose main audience was organic-eating yoga moms, were now aligning themselves with right-wing conspiracy theories.

This blending of health and wellness/New Age spirituality and right-wing conspiracism fueled the conspirituality movement, which had been hanging around the New Age fringes for more than a decade. The pandemic super-charged it and brought it into the mainstream. Now, just a few years later, many of those once apolitical nutritionists and yoga instructors have become among the most influential thought leaders on the political right. We'll discuss this transformation and the role these influencers play in conspiracism and conspirituality in more detail in the coming chapters. That's where we will also meet the assortment of grifters who jumped into the fray, boosting conspiratorial outrage so they could milk it for as much money as possible. As we will see, given that most everyone was trying to profit from the pandemic, the line between charlatan and true believer wasn't always clear.

The central point for us to comprehend now, though, is that conspiracy groups became so formidable because they gave followers a supportive community during a frightening time. That was especially true for middle-aged women.

Women bore the brunt of the COVID restrictions. They often found themselves having to abandon jobs and community volunteering to focus on locked-down caregiving, with only television or the internet for companionship. Millions of women went online to search for COVID treatments and ways to boost their family's immunity to the virus. There they found other women dealing with the same problems who shared their fears, frustrations, and concerns. They complained together, learned together, and hoped together for better times. Online conspiratorial communities became their social lives and support networks. Women started referring to each other online as friends and even family.

All these changes can be seen in how Yvonne and Tammy experienced the pandemic. For Yvonne, the pandemic was a deeply radicalizing experience. She began the pandemic as the longtime youth leader of her evangelical Christian church and a recent follower of weight-loss advice from health and wellness coaches. By the time the pandemic's most intense phases were over, Yvonne had traced a path from COVID home remedies to New Age spiritualism, to the online religion Love Has Won, to the conspiracy clearinghouse that is QAnon. She also became an activist, starting with protesting COVID closures and masking restrictions to joining Ammon Bundy's far-right People's Rights Network, a rapid-response text-network to coordinate protests.

Meanwhile, the pandemic gave Tammy the thing she was most desperate for: friends and community. In many ways, the pandemic made the rest of the world like her: alone, socially isolated, lonely, and online. Suddenly she was not alone in her aloneness. Millions of others were catching up to what she already knew. They, too, were learning that the American story was one of carnage, desperation, and isolation, not merely endless improvement and limitless possibility.

Searching for news about COVID on social media brought lots of new people into Tammy's world. Most of them were mourning the loss of real-world friendships and hoping to fill the void. Tammy had been living with that void most of her life. In these many ways, conspiracism, and the QAnon conspiracy theories in particular, became Tammy's home.

Within a year, she would define her primary identity as a conspiracy theorist, saying it directly. "I am a conspiracy theorist," she tells me proudly all the time.

Tammy was thrilled to be introduced to a wide range of new people who, like her, were online all the time and kept strange hours. No matter the time of day or night, there was always someone to talk to.

✦

When the pandemic hit, Yvonne's identity was firmly planted in her evangelical church community. Facebook posts from the previous eight years showed Yvonne and Troy doing everything with their church friends: volunteering on Thanksgiving, sledding in the mountains, riding on a sailboat and snorkeling in the Caribbean, sharing cabins at a church leadership retreat.

Months after the COVID shutdowns started, however, Yvonne would leave it all behind. She describes the lockdown experience as an epiphany. "I started to receive 20/20 vision at the beginning of COVID. Something inside me screamed, 'Wake up!' I had no idea what that meant or where this journey was about to take me. COVID and masking happened, and right away I knew something was up. I had no idea what, but something in my soul started to really wake up and question everything."

Yvonne recounts that, at first, she didn't know what to make of pandemic restrictions, nor of what she saw as people's irrational fear of the virus. "I wasn't buying into or feeling the fear," she said of warnings about COVID's severity. "It was so weird to watch people literally turn into robotic beings that quit thinking for themselves. It was like whatever they heard, they followed, no questions asked," she tells me. "Nothing made sense, and I just couldn't wrap my head around what was happening."

Yvonne already distrusted most traditional media sources. "You watch one news station and then you watch another news station, and I can tell you: two *completely* different stories," she says emphatically, like this is all the proof anyone needed. "So I already knew that the media isn't trustworthy. But in 2020 I saw firsthand and really realized that you must go *find* the truth."

Her research led Yvonne to an online spiritual group called Love Has Won. Yvonne discovered Love Has Won through its daily live streams, in which two young, attractive followers remained on air for hours, connecting with viewers and fielding questions about COVID. They explained how the best protection could be found in the spiritual and health treatments that viewers could purchase through the Love Has Won online store.

Love Has Won was started by Amy Carlson, a former McDonald's manager who had abruptly gotten up from the dinner table one night in 2007 and left her family to join a man she had met on the internet who called himself WhiteEagle. WhiteEagle ran a group called the Galactic Federation of Light, which Carlson eventually took over. Carlson's theology cobbled together elements of other New Age spiritual movements, introducing Yvonne to many of the main concepts that would come to define her new religious worldview. Carlson said she was "Mother God," as well as the reincarnation of Marilyn Monroe and Jesus Christ. She also claimed to be able to channel a variety of angelic beings, including deceased comedian and actor Robin Williams. We'll look more at Love Has Won in all its strange and fascinating glory in coming chapters.

Love Has Won made national news in the spring of 2021, when police found Carlson's mummified body, with glitter sprinkled on her eyes. Several of her disciples were arrested for mishandling her remains. The actual cause of death was alcoholism, anorexia, and drinking colloidal silver, which poisoned her as it turned her skin blue. Since Carlson's death, Love Has Won has been the subject of multiple documentary films, news reports, and podcasts.

Amy Carlson's story resonated with Yvonne—"especially when they talked about her having to leave her kids," Yvonne says now. "She told them that an angel said to her, 'We need you to go help eight billion kids, or you can stay with your own.' I really felt like, if the angels came down, that I would be willing to do what she did."

Between watching the live streams from Love Has Won and a large archive of their videos, Yvonne was hooked. "I believe God is a woman. Whether or not Amy Carlson was reincarnated as Mother God, I don't know," Yvonne reflects now, as she looks back. "It is that Divine Feminine that I agree with. Anyone that's spiritual at all knows the Divine Feminine is vital and that the earth has been out of balance. That is what is missing."

Yvonne's voice turns pensive for a moment, as she remembers those days and the challenges she faced on her spiritual journey. "I was still dealing with my ego, so I still had a ton of judgments and programming I had to work through. But Amy ended up kind of helping expose the ego of the world. She had taken on a lot of the negative energy for the world, and she eventually ended up dying last spring of cancer as a result."

That's how Yvonne and the Love Has Won members explain Amy Carlson's drinking and erratic behavior: that Carlson took on the negativity of the world in order to restore balance to the earth. That burden became simply too much for her earthly mind and body to bear. In their view, Carlson had suffered like Christ did for the sins of the world, sacrificing herself for humanity.

Yvonne tells me to be cautious about drawing conclusions about Carlson and Love Has Won based on what I might hear from the mainstream media. "When they found her body and it was on the news, and they tried to go after Love Has Won, and they tried to call them a cult," she says with disgust. She warns me away from making snap judgments. "You'll have to do some research," she says. "But remember: Everything that you read on the news is going to make them look bad. I became friends with quite a few of them, and I love them dearly. They're all on their own journey, and they are good people."

Her voice changes. "And who am I to judge? I didn't live there. I didn't walk with Amy. I don't know her story. I didn't feel her energy the way they did, so I would never say to someone, you're crazy. . . . I've had people tell me that I'm crazy, and it's like: you have *no idea* what I've experienced. How *dare* you!" Yvonne says. She feels a kinship with a persecuted, misunderstood spiritual figure like Amy Carlson.

In early 2020, Yvonne followed Love Has Won to the QAnon conspiracy theories. Amy Carlson tried to piggyback off QAnon's growing popularity to gain more followers and donors. She took ideas from other New Age groups and influencers and claimed them as part of her own theology. After deciding to embrace QAnon, Carlson increasingly focused the daily live streams and her "Disclosure" videos on amplifying QAnon content. Once QAnon had the Love Has Won stamp of approval, Yvonne dove into it headfirst. She became an even more convinced Q devotee when she started encountering QAnon material in her real life.

One day, while waiting for an appointment with her chiropractor, Yvonne watched the QAnon recruitment video *Out of Shadows*, which was playing on the television in the waiting room. She watched most of it before the appointment, and then she rewatched it online when she got home. That led her to other influential QAnon videos, like *Fall of the Cabal*.

Yvonne started following a Q influencer whose style she liked—even though she admits she thought he was "off his rocker." Then she followed another QAnon influencer whose videos argued that Donald Trump was using international visits to signal that he was about to take down the global cabal of pedophiles. "Everything's very, very ceremonial," Yvonne explained to me, telling me what to look for in the memes and videos. "It's right out in the open with symbolism. They are out in plain sight." Over the years, Yvonne has given me an ongoing education in the various ceremonies and symbols of her conspiratorial and spiritual beliefs.

Yvonne was so convinced by the QAnon videos that she started sending links to church members to warn them about the global cabal of pedophiles. She was a volunteer with the youth group at the time. "We were doing Zoom calls every Wednesday with my youth group, and I had started to learn about the pedophilia," she tells me. "I had seen *Out of Shadows* at the chiropractor's office, and I shared it with my youth staff and my youth group. I just saw this video, and we were talking about sex trafficking prior to that. So I thought it was significant, since we had just been talking about sex trafficking."

At the same time, Yvonne got involved in local protests against COVID shutdowns and new public masking rules. In April 2020, a woman named Sarah Brady was arrested for defying COVID shutdowns by scheduling play-dates with a group of mothers at a park in Boise, Idaho. One of Yvonne's daughters had known Brady, who people were now calling "Park Mom," from anti-vaxxer circles before COVID. Brady recruited Yvonne to join a protest. That night Yvonne was featured on the local news, complaining about COVID restrictions with an angry expression on her face and wearing a shirt emblazoned with the name of her congregation.

Church leaders were not pleased with Yvonne's involvement with protests again public health mandates, and Yvonne heard about their displeasure. She took a reflective pause and considered her actions. "I went to that protest and I saw my face and I was like, I did not like the energy. I did not like who I'm becoming. So I stepped back a little bit, I'm like, 'God, what is going on?' I really started praying. It was like, 'God, something's wrong. What is happening? What is happening? What is happening?'"

In May 2020, Yvonne had to take a week-long work trip to Montana and refused to wear a mask in the airport. She recorded several videos of herself engaged in her own protest on the airplane and posted the videos on social media. In one of them, she pulls her mask down to expose her face, complains about the restrictions, and calls the flight attendant a "mask Nazi."

When church leaders heard about and saw the videos, they openly confronted her. "That's when I really said, 'God, I know I hear you and I know what is happening. I want the truth. Show me the truth,'" Yvonne says.

Alone in a Montana hotel room, Yvonne entered a full-on spiritual crisis. She was already upset by the church closing in-person services and moving all activities online. The negative reactions to her COVID protests by church leaders deepened her discontent and questioning. That night she searched for "the truth" in YouTube videos on QAnon. She reflects now on that time:

> I was very active in our church and was a youth staff volunteer. When the church closed, again that same spirit of wake-up came through and started having me question everything. We were doing youth group online via Zoom, and we were also attending church through live videos—all of which felt so wrong on a soul level. I didn't understand how the church could close. God isn't scared of a disease. I knew now more than ever the churches should be open and available, not closing their doors. The church closing was my biggest red flag and a monumental decision that really exposed to me to who was controlling the church. I saw that the God I had been searching for my entire life really wasn't the God I had learned about in the church.

Yvonne started messaging back and forth with church leaders, mostly by recording videos of herself that she posted to YouTube. She started sending them links to the videos that had her questioning her Christian faith. Her response to the concerns from church leaders was to watch even more videos about QAnon and spirituality that countered Christian teachings.

Looking back now, she sees that as a pivotal moment in her spiritual journey and even expresses a measure of gratitude. "That's when the Creator showed up in a big way and really started to dismantle my belief system as quickly and gently as It could without completely ruining me. I see that now," she wrote in a Facebook post directed to church leaders. "Thank you," she wrote directly to the youth minister, "for questioning my choice to not wear a mask on that flight. If I wouldn't have experienced that, I am not sure I would have seen the obvious truth about the church and the people who are serving in it," she wrote.

As the pandemic leveled Yvonne's Christian views, she headed back online to learn more about the spiritualism she was finding in YouTube videos. "Once that had been exposed and unraveled," she said of her Christian beliefs, "I didn't know where or what to do." "So down the rabbit hole I went," she said, embracing the conspiracist metaphor, "mostly looking for truth on COVID and what was happening. But it was in the darkness of the rabbit hole that I started to find the light and consciousness of the planet."

She explains the progression to me step by step. "First, I had to realize everything I knew was a lie. Everything! . . . All I would pray for was for God to show me the truth," she says of the mindset she took into her online searches. "I don't care how ugly, how hard. I want the truth. If I am going to die on this planet for a reason, at least show me the reason I am here and what I am fighting for." She pauses for effect. "And so She did," Yvonne says, referring to God as the Divine Feminine. "And then slowly and painfully, my entire belief system came crumbling down."

Yvonne also believed her church was crumbling, along with all organized religion. She increasingly saw churches as limiting humanity and began to consider them a massive engine for creating division among people. "The church has created more division than anything else," she tells me. "And when the church falls, all those people will learn that the dogma wasn't true. They will learn the truth: That God is love. Period. End of story. Mike drop. Nothing else. Fuck all religion."

What Yvonne describes is a New Age version of "accelerationism." The ideal is typically associated with white supremacist and neo-Nazi groups who believe society is so broken that the only solution is to tear it all down and rebuild from scratch. That same basic goal is animating many different factions of the right, all of which have their own version of the new world they imagine rising from the ashes of the old. The one thing they have in common is the need to tear down the current American system and global order, a goal also shared by the tech lords of Silicon Valley and most Christian nationalist groups. These factions might disagree on what the new age will look like and who will be in charge. But they are cheering on the destruction that will bring the demise of the existing order of things.

For Tammy, as for so many of the rest of us, the pandemic brought fear and worry. But ironically, it also brought something she had been missing: a sense of community and belonging. Tammy talks about the pandemic as a positive experience. She credits it with giving her purpose and direction and providing the companionship and support she had been missing throughout her life. It marks the start of both her political journey and her spiritual one.

"When COVID came, everything felt different to me," she tells me over the phone from the trailer that she calls home in rural central Pennsylvania. Tammy spends most of her time alone. When she interacts with people, it's usually with one of a few adult family members or a grandchild. Tammy loves nature and living in the country, but she is the first to say that her world is small and isolated and boring. The pandemic brought her excitement, while it brought other people a sense of loss. Tammy used the pandemic to cut ties with a bad relationship and find new friends online. She discovered new things to do and to think about. "I'm thankful for what COVID has done for me," she tells me, almost as if the pandemic had been an answer to her prayers.

Prior to the pandemic, Tammy's social media feed was mostly a series of selfies accompanied by posts about how bored she was. She posted comments and videos in which she talked about being alone, and how she had nothing to do, and no one to do it with. There was a brief interlude with photos of her with her meth-addicted boyfriend in which they both look strung out. Soon after, Tammy was posting memes about bad boyfriends and toxic relationships and appealing to social media for leads about an apartment or room to rent. Then it was back to posts about being bored and lonely.

That started to change on the eve of the pandemic. Tammy was intrigued by Donald Trump's constant attacks on the mainstream media. "I never followed politics until I kept hearing Trump talk about fake news." An incident at the 2019 American Music Awards shattered whatever faith she had remaining in the news media. It had to do with her belief that the media had hidden the conflict between Taylor Swift and Shania Twain she believed she had witnessed while watching the broadcast. "Taylor Swift was giving Shania Twain an award. Taylor tried hugging her several times, Shania shunned her," Tammy explains to me what she thought she had seen. She recalls thinking, "Wow, that's a big deal. I wonder how they will spin this." The next morning she was watching *Good Morning America* and the video replay of the incident looked nothing like what she remembered. "They totally edited it!" Tammy practically shouts. "They showed them hugging!"

Tammy is convinced that this is definitive proof of a hoax. "Robin Roberts even made a statement about how Shania accepted her hug," Tammy says, like she has lost a trusted news source. "So I started paying more attention to what was going on. And *man*, was I shocked," she says, trying to capture her sense of disbelief. "Then I decided I will do whatever I can to be sure my grandchildren don't grow up in a communist country where the government controls what people see."

Distrust of conventional news sources is a hallmark of conspiracism. The deeper conspiracists dive into disinformation, the less they trust the legacy news media. Research has long shown that right-wing news sources, like Fox News, serve as a conduit into conspiracism for many viewers. That pipeline has long existed, tracing back to groups like the John Birch Society, pundits like Rush Limbaugh, and through to more recent sources like Alex Jones, Tucker Carlson, and new networks like One America News Network and Newsmax.

As the 2020 presidential election geared up, Tammy became a local activist for the Trump campaign. She says she got involved hoping to meet people, but that didn't really work out. Although she liked attending political events, she didn't really make any new friends. She went to a few Trump rallies by herself, and then she joined a group that stood on bridges over highways, holding up Trump signs for passing cars to see. Tammy often stood by herself when the other people didn't show up or when they left shortly after arriving. At one point, Tammy got on the local news for standing with a "Pissed Off Patriot" sign alone by the side of the highway. Now she had a cause, although not yet the companionship she craved.

That changed when she learned about QAnon. It happened while she was protesting by herself in front of the main regional office of Joe Biden's presidential campaign. "I found out about Q by accident," she recounts. "I was standing in front of Biden's headquarters in Wilkes Barre with my signs, and someone asked me about Q," Tammy says about a fellow Trump supporter who wanted to enlighten her about QAnon. "I had no idea what he was talking about, so I Googled it. I still didn't pay much attention until I watched the series *The Fall of the Cabal*. Wow! What an eye opener that was."

Tammy quickly embraced the QAnon conspiracy theories. She began watching QAnon videos on YouTube and following QAnon accounts on Facebook and other social media platforms. She reposted QAnon memes and added her own text to reveal her knowledge of its conspiracies and show her support. She tried to convince friends and family members. But like most QAnon followers, Tammy found that people in her real life thought the conspiracies were too far-fetched to believe. When she failed to convince her loved ones, she increased her interactions with other QAnon followers, to the point that she began referring to people online as her friends and family.

Tammy has gone all in on the full range of QAnon conspiracy theories. She believes most world leaders and Hollywood elites are blood-drinking reptilian pedophiles. She believes Donald Trump is leading the forces of good that will take down the cabal of satanic globalists. And she remains convinced that the day of justice is coming, even though all the other promised judgment days came and went without the bad guys getting punished.

Tammy also believes in a wide range of conspiracies that sound like an issue of the old supermarket tabloid *Weekly World News*. She has reposted memes saying: Jews had prior knowledge of 9/11 and profited from the fall of the Twin Towers. Major meat packing companies are replacing beef, chicken, and pork with crickets, mealworms, and grasshoppers. McDonald's serves human meat. Donald Trump has met with space aliens to discuss joint efforts to defeat the global cabal of pedophiles. Everyone born has a secret "birth certificate bond" that will make them rich if they know how to find it and cash it in. The US Supreme Court ruled that you don't need licenses or registrations to drive cars. Taxes are voluntary. The US is under secret military control. There are devices called "med beds" that can heal humans instantly of whatever is wrong with them. Ivermectin will end the pandemic. The earth is flat. Princess Diana, who might be JFK's daughter, is still alive and is Barron Trump's real mother. Elvis is still alive and so is Michael Jackson, and together with Tupak Shakur, they are all helping to take down the cabal.

"I'm a little of a conspiracy theorist," Tammy tells me the first time we talk, before she knew I understood her beliefs. "I see a lot of 'theories' that I believe and some that have come true," Tammy says. Now she routinely announces that she's a conspiracist as she forwards me the latest warning from her conspiracy communities. That doesn't happen very often these days, perhaps because she knows I'm a skeptic. But she feels like she owes it to me to let me know if something big is coming, so I have time to prepare. Saying "I'm a conspiracist" is her way of telling me that she knows I won't believe what she's sending me, but she wants me to look at it anyway.

Ultimately, however, Tammy doesn't think any of this is real. That might seem incongruous, but it's true—because she doesn't think life itself is real. She thinks humans are enslaved in a computer simulation and that the 1999 blockbuster thriller *The Matrix* is actually a documentary. In this dystopian science fiction film, far in the future, all of humanity is plugged into a giant computer system, such that everything they experience is a simulation. The heroes of the story are the humans who wake up in a grim reality where humanity has been enslaved. Faced with the truth, they are given the choice to take a blue pill, which will send them back into enslaved ignorance, or a red pill, which will reveal the whole truth and enlist them in the war to break the Matrix and free humanity from enslavement.

Tammy believes that people like her, who know the truth, can learn to control time, space, and matter like the lead character Neo does in *The Matrix*. Tammy doesn't want to destroy the Matrix; she wants to learn to control it across its different dimensions. "You don't want to escape the Matrix; you want to master the Matrix. So that's what I'm here to do," she tells me. "I'm going to master the Matrix in 3D, 5D, 6D. Come and join me if you want. If you feel like you have the abilities, and we all do."

Tammy is not alone in these beliefs. Many conspiracists believe life is a computer simulation or a movie—that it's not real. They think human beings have been enslaved in a grim reality and that they are here to help.

Yvonne, too, thinks she is one of the heroes who is going to save the day. But unlike Tammy, she doesn't want to control the Matrix. Yvonne wants to destroy it.

✦

After Yvonne left her church in Boise, Idaho, she let her newfound spirituality take over her life. She began preaching her New Age faith, along with the QAnon conspiracy theories, to friends and family members, hoping others would join in her awakening. Most of them rejected the beliefs and expressed concern to Yvonne. "Do you know how many people I've had tell me that I'm following evil?" she asks me, her voice animated. "Do you know how many of my church friends have said, 'I'm so concerned about you, what you're doing? Who are you?' I started losing friends, but I just kept going. I didn't care. I really got to a point where it was like, I don't fucking care. I know something isn't right. I may not know all the answers. All I know is I started sharing spiritual stuff and losing friends."

Yvonne pauses for a moment. "But I'm not stopping until I figure out why I'm here," she says, her cadence picking up along with her volume. "You can either love me and join me or I will let you go, but *no one* is going to stop me from going where I'm supposed to go because I know with all my being—and I don't know how to explain it to anyone—but I know what I know, and I know that there's more!"

At the time Yvonne had a corporate job at a national lawn care company that also employed Troy and one of her daughters. Yvonne started questioning her own corporate mindset when the company began instituting COVID restrictions. She was critical of the company's pandemic policies and started questioning how it did business.

By the summer of 2020, Yvonne's "question everything" mentality had shapeshifted into a belief that she and every other human on earth had been brainwashed. "One day I was listening to a video, and it said, "We do what we're told. We go to school, we get married, we have children, and we never question." And I thought, 'Oh my God. I never questioned it.'"

Another day she came home from work for lunch and watched a video of "a team of doctors in DC about COVID, and they talked about having the cure and everything." I'm not sure what video Yvonne is referring to. She might have misunderstood a press conference projecting vaccine availability. More likely, she was watching a conspiracy video from one of the anti-vaccination groups like the one led by Los Angeles doctor Simone Gold, who lost her medical license for telling people the virus was no worse than the common cold.

Yvonne tells me what happened next. "I went into work, so excited, and started to share what I saw. All I got in return was the deer-in-the-headlights look," Yvonne says, like she was talking to idiots. "And it hit me then. I thought, 'Oh, that's the programming they keep talking about. WE ARE PROGRAMMED! How did I not see it sooner?'"

Yvonne said this was the moment that a conspiracy theory mindset truly sunk in. "It really clicked for me because as a Marine, I understood brainwashing. It was the joke of Marines, right? That we would come home from bootcamp, and we were these brainwashed little beings," she says, mimicking the voice of a brainwashed person. "It was a joke, and then it clicked that this is how humanity works. We absolutely *are* brainwashed—and so is each and every human being. They start programming us the minute we are in the womb. Everything we learn comes from another human being. Everything!"

She pauses and speaks directly to me. "Stop for just a moment and consider that." She waits a beat. "We are going around regurgitating someone else's beliefs."

Yvonne pauses again to let the news sink in. "In that instant everything changed for me," Yvonne says, concluding her conversion story. "That was really when my eyes opened, and I started to see things that I didn't understand."

Yvonne told me she went home and started meditating. Then she said she made a decision to end her programming. She was going to free herself from what she now described as the Matrix.

For Yvonne, the Matrix is modern life. It is corporate America, the forty-hour work week, mortgages, credit cards, shopping malls, car payments, and bills. It is individualism, selfishness, greed, jealousy, envy. It is isolation, division, ostracism, fear, and hate. Yvonne feels that to evolve, humans must opt out of the various systems of oppression and learn to live differently. That's what she means when she says humans need to be deprogrammed and leave the Matrix. Yvonne believes she has taken the red pill:

I got tired of being in the Matrix. Everything was about money, and I wasn't living because I was paying bills. That's what everybody does: They quit living because they want to buy. We became consumers. We think we need to buy shit. And then we're not going out and doing things with our families. We're not making memories. We're sitting behind TV, and we're sitting at jobs, and we're becoming robots. We're losing all our humanity. We're becoming their fucking artificial intelligence.

And they don't even see it. They don't even see. You can look in cars, you can see people. You can drive and watch, and you can see people that are so, so asleep. These are the ones that there is no hope for. They're not going to go to 5D with us. They are too far gone. It's going to be a big chunk of humanity that is that way.

And then there's the people like me that already know, that are conscious. And those that are maybe not quite as conscious as me, but the patriots that have been fighting. They're going to see even a different consciousness. There are also going to be people on the fence saying, "What's happening?" That's where I hope that the rise of consciousness will help many people go through the process quicker. Some of us have been doing the healing on our own. Some of them are going to get forced to it.

Yvonne believes a new world is coming, one in which none of the things people now value will matter anymore. When what she calls "Disclosure" happens, she thinks much of humanity will rise into a higher state of consciousness, one that transcends selfish individualism and the divisions that separate us. The world will move out of a "3D" mindset, focused on materialism and money, and jump dimensions into "5D," where everything is about community.

Yvonne tells me about a recent meditation exercise she did:

> The guide said, "I want you to close your eyes and think about where you are in five years." And at first it was really hard because I'm like, I don't even know if I'm going to be on this earth in five years. I may ascend as an angel as soon as Disclosure comes. I don't know. So, I started meditating. I closed my eyes and I really believe the future will be a commune. I really believe we're going to be in community living. We're going to live in villages where it's going to be about love. It's going to be families that take care of each other. There's not going to be jealousy.

Getting to that world means freeing herself from the programming of the existing world. It means detaching herself from the institutions and daily routines she sees as oppressive.

Yvonne's first act of liberation was quitting her job in July 2020. "You can only leave the Matrix if you are willing to step outside of work," she tells me about that decision, "if you're willing to say, 'You know what, you don't get to control me anymore. I don't buy into your systems anymore. I don't care.'" Yvonne explains the new attitude she took to the lawn care company with her the next day. "So I went in, and I didn't even call Troy that day," she explains to me with pride in her voice. "I literally went into work, and I said, 'I think I'm giving my notice.' It was a Thursday. I told them, 'I need to talk to my husband.' Although I knew he would let me. I knew Troy would. And he said, 'okay.'"

Yvonne next tried to free herself from material possessions and financial obligations. She was convinced that Disclosure was imminent and that she would ascend into 5D, where she wouldn't need money, credit, or possessions. Why worry about car payments, insurance, mortgages, money, or credit when that would all be gone soon? She also believed she needed to reject all those things because they represented an evil system of enslavement:

Literally, the universe told me to quit paying my bills, and I did. It's so bizarre. But that was a conscious decision. It was totally a conscious decision. I told Troy, "I feel like we're supposed to quit paying our bills and that I'm here to break the system down, that I'm not supposed to give any energy or put anything into it."

By the end of August, I basically quit paying our bills. I always struggled with money and credit. I'm very intelligent. But money was the one thing that I struggled with. I mean, I taught my daughter how to do her credit, and she bought a house at twenty. I taught my daughter how to manage her money, but I could never manage my own.

I quit registering my car. I didn't do insurance, we just added liability insurance back on when I got stopped for a ticket. I added the liability, because the police officer wouldn't let me drive away until I added it. And it was only $30. I thought, you know what, this is probably the right thing to do just to cover. I know I won't cause an accident because I know there are no accidents, and I'm conscious, and I know how to drive.

I told the police officer when he asked for my registration, I said, "Why do I have to register my car? It's my car." I said, "I'm sovereign." He goes, "Oh, sovereignty." I said, "I don't have any registration." I said, "The car's supposed to get repoed."

"Which it is getting, repoed," she tells me with a laugh, finishing the story, "because I quit paying the bill. It was supposed to be repoed in October of 2020. It only hasn't been repoed because of COVID. And the funny thing is the officer didn't give me a ticket for registration. He gave me a ticket for insurance. He didn't gimme a ticket for doing eighty in a twenty-five-mile-per-hour zone. He gave me a warning for that."

In speaking of sovereignty, Yvonne's is using concepts taken from the Sovereign Citizen movement, an ideology that claims people don't need to follow government rules because they are sovereign beings. Tammy also occasionally reposts "SovCit" memes. Neither are members of the movement, but they sometimes express support for a few of its concepts. This is an example of the pick-and-choose hodgepodge of ideas that form their eclectic belief systems.

When debt collectors called Yvonne to negotiate a settlement for the car before going to the expense of engaging a repo man, she saw it as a sign of society's corrupt value system. "The funny thing is, now they keep sending me offers, like, I just got one. So I owe about $17,000 on my car. The last offer they gave me was to pay $4,000 and to call it good. I'm learning that the system is corrupt. And that people can be free if they are willing to realize their credit score doesn't matter and that it's going to go away very quickly."

Yvonne took the same mindset to the mortgage payment on their trailer home. She thought Disclosure was imminent enough that she would not lose her home if she stopped paying the mortgage. She was pretty sure she had some control over the narrative of her life and could manifest staying in her home, so she had a place to stay until she ascended into 5D. But that's not how it turned out. Yvonne had been humiliated that she and Troy could only afford a trailer home when they came back to Boise after getting kicked out by the Marines. Now she embraced losing the mobile home as a spiritual step up, even though she had to borrow money from her sister to purchase a camping trailer that was a step down as far as comfort, space, and status.

> I quit paying our trailer payment. I honestly thought Disclosure was going to come a lot quicker. I realized then that we were writing our own stories and I was like, well, I won't lose my house. But I was okay with it down deep inside. I knew I was playing with fire. I knew that I was walking the path. And since losing our home, I've never been happier. I mean, I love that I will never live in a house again. I am inspired, and things are so expensive right now. I, we, really would like to live in a bus. That was ultimately our goal.

Increasingly isolated from family, friends, and former colleagues, Yvonne dove deeper into her spiritual beliefs and learned more about the QAnon conspiracy theories. "I spent the rest of the year doing everything I could to raise my consciousness and everyone else's, not even realizing that was what I was doing. I watched so many different videos. I read books. I was a sponge. I played with shrooms, had some crazy amazing experiences, and some super-scary experiences. I have used other plant medicine designed to raise consciousness, and I have experienced wild, supernatural, amazing things along the way."

Dedicating most of her days to studying spirituality and QAnon, Yvonne started to get what she calls "downloads": huge, immediate shifts in her beliefs. "It's been such a turbo-consciousness awakening," she tells me. "It must be downloads. I mean, it must be coming from somewhere else because, although

I am a sponge and I watch a lot of videos, there's knowledge that I get that I understand without having studied it."

Yvonne credits the downloads with helping her accept the more radical edges of New Age and QAnon beliefs. "Some things resonated right away; some things were just too much for my consciousness in that moment," she admits. "I would avoid so many hard topics: extraterrestrials, reptilians, spirituality, pedophilia." By reptilians, Yvonne was referring to the QAnon conspiracy in which the bad guys are all shape-shifting lizard people posing as humans.

"You know, it took me months to even look at reptilians," she says. "It took me months to unpack it and then think of all the lies and all the things that I had bought into and all the people and relationships. It was just like that whole dark night of the soul." Whether Yvonne knows it or not, she is referencing a concept that originates with the sixteenth-century Spanish mystic John of the Cross, who used "the dark night of the soul" to describe a season of painful purification, in which God seems absent. "But it just kept coming back up," she said of the reptilian memes and videos, "and slowly I started to look at those things and know I had to go deeper. I had to open my mind and heart. I think a key moment was [when] I really started to see and understand the programming we are under."

By late 2020, Yvonne felt like she had raised her consciousness to the point where she needed to back her beliefs with action. She had been reluctant to engage in protests because she worried about becoming the angry person she had seen on the television screen during the Park Mom protests at the start of the year. Yvonne wanted to follow the path of light and love, and that meant swallowing her anger and replacing it with positive energy. By year's end, Yvonne felt like she had the discipline to do that, even though she was still upset about mask mandates and was convinced Donald Trump had won the 2020 election.

At the end of 2020, the protests were happening, the election was stolen, and I knew with all my soul and being that it was stolen. I decided I needed to start experiencing life. We are here for the experiences, so it was time to stand for what I believe in. I knew I had evolved enough that I could go in and control my energy and anger and that I could be of more use than I felt like I would have been in the beginning when I was just angry at what was happening.

December 2020 comes around, and I decide to protest a mask mandate at our local Central District Health public meeting. The crazy thing is this was a very pivotal moment in my journey. I was learning about Spirit, I was meditating, I was learning about conscious breath. I knew we had higher selves, but I didn't really understand it until this night.

Yvonne views this anti-masking protest as another key moment in her spiritual development. She had joined Ammon Bundy's People's Rights organization, a kind of rapid-response protest team. Bundy is a far-right anti-government organizer, infamous for the standoff with authorities at a Federal Wildlife Refuge in Oregon in January 2016. Yvonne joined Bundy's anti-masking protest at the Idaho State Capitol Building. She believes that Spirit chose that moment to start speaking through her, giving her the words to say.

I went into the meeting ready to battle over this mask mandate and the control it was really about—only for things to shift. As I was trying to get in the meeting wearing their mask, all of a sudden my words changed. Everything I was saying to them was about the breath. In the moment I wasn't even aware, it wasn't until after I watched the video back I realized. I knew at my very soul level that our breath was sacred and that if we allowed them to take away our ability to breathe without a mask, they take away our ability to connect to Spirit and our higher selves.

When Yvonne was arrested for trespassing at the State Capitol Building in Idaho, she saw it as the work of a corrupt criminal justice system trying to stop her from expressing both her spiritual beliefs and her constitutional rights. Her rationale for her involvement in the event at the State Capitol Building foreshadows how she would eventually view her participation on January 6, 2021.

Yvonne explained to her friends and family on Facebook that her participation on January 6 was part of her spiritual journey. At times it reads like she was testifying at church or summarizing a conversion experience. She has said the same things to me in our conversations on the phone–using nearly identical language:

My next big event followed right behind the unconstitutional arrest. President Trump said come to DC, Stop the Steal. I knew beyond any doubt this election was stolen. I'd bet my life on it that's how confident I am. I knew it was going to be history in the making and I wanted to be a part of history. I had no idea how corrupt or evil these people really were until this moment.

I spent most days of Trump's first four years tolerating him. It wasn't until COVID, the rabbit holes, and a whole lot of truth did I see him for the LIGHT Worker he is! Someday you'll realize if it wasn't for him and the light helping, we'd have never figured out the depth of the corruption our world faces! When you know, you know!

The day of the rally happened and everything shifted. I had really thought up until that point that this was going to be easy and wouldn't require any work from me or humanity. Boy was I wrong. This was all about us doing the work. This is all about us finding out who we are and changing the future so we never go back to sleep again.

We are here for the Great Awakening. We come from all over the galaxy and we all have different journeys we are embarking on. The one thing I believe is that we come here to learn that LOVE is all that matters. We are not separate. We are all connected to Prime Source Creator. WE are brothers and sisters. We are energy. We are light and We are exposing the darkness.

I knew I had committed no crime and there was nowhere they would find me committing a crime, so I never believed they would come knocking at my door. Not only did they come knocking. I got arrested. It's after this that my life really started to take a turn.

Energy, awakening, love, changing the future: For Yvonne, January 6 became a spiritual event, and her arrest an inflection point. For both Yvonne and Tammy, the great spiritual awakening was only just beginning.

CHAPTER 5

Mama Bears

Tammy texted me shortly after the shocking news broke in December 2024. President Joe Biden had just commuted the sentence of one of the judges at the center of the Kids for Cash scandal in Luzerne County, Pennsylvania. For years, two Democratic judges had been taking kickbacks from the developers of for-profit detention facilities for underage offenders. The judges sentenced children to disproportionately long stays at the detention facilities based on minor charges. In return, the prison owners made secret cash payments to them. The prisons profited from the kids filling cell beds, and the judges got their cut for making it happen.

The story made national headlines starting in 2009. It became the subject of a book by a Pulitzer Prize–winning investigative journalist and a well-received full-length documentary film. The scandal breached popular culture by being featured in entertainment news programs, referenced in popular television shows like *Law and Order* and *CSI*, and included in the plotline in several crime-themed novels.

The idea of corrupt judges getting kickbacks for sending kids to a for-profit prison was horrifying to people regardless of their politics. Biden's commutation received widespread criticism from news outlets and social media platforms across the ideological spectrum. The text Tammy sent was a screenshot of a social media post from a right-wing account. It read: "Meet Judge Michael Conahan. He was sentenced to 17 years in prison for his role in the infamous Kids for Cash scandal, where he sent juveniles to for-profit prisons in exchange for millions of dollars in kickbacks. Today, Conahan was PARDONED by Biden!"

After sending the screenshot, Tammy texted me, "Crazy. SMH," internet shorthand for "shaking my head." I knew exactly what Tammy meant. She was incredulous, bewildered, but ultimately not surprised. We both knew the justice system wasn't always just. But for Tammy, Joe Biden letting Conahan out of jail early was just more proof that the QAnon conspiracy theories are accurate. As Tammy sees it, this is how the child trafficking cabal works. It protects itself by shielding members from the consequences of their actions. She thought the same thing when Biden pardoned his son, Hunter Biden, which Tammy viewed as a corrupt act to avoid a well-deserved prison sentence. She expects injustice like this from the government and courts, and especially from Democrats.

I couldn't deny how real life had mimicked the conspiracy theory. This kind of synchronicity is common in the world of conspiracism because the conspiracy theories are usually wrapped around a kernel of truth. The conspiracy about a cabal of reptilians working for the Illuminati might be unbelievable. But child sex trafficking is real. So was Jeffrey Epstein flying celebrities and world leaders to a private island in the Caribbean he populated with underage children. The corrupt judges scheming with a for-profit prison system were real, too, and their schemes destroyed the lives of children in ways that seemed to confirm the conspiracy theory's main premise.

Here is the other thing you need to know: two of Tammy's own children were victims of the Kids for Cash scandal. Those two children each spent years in for-profit juvenile prisons because of minor offenses. The experience had derailed their futures and probably helped ruin their lives. Neither child was the same after their time locked up in detention, an observation repeated by the families of other Kids for Cash victims. One of Tammy's children has been in and out of prison ever since. The other died by suicide after years of struggling with mental health issues, a tragic ending also not uncommon in the Kids for Cash saga.

Given how Michael Conahan's actions had directly harmed Tammy's children, it's hardly surprising she had a powerful reaction to Joe Biden commuting his sentence. This was personal for her. Biden's actions forced her to relive her Kids for Cash nightmare, a topic she and I have discussed many times over the years.

That nightmare began when Tammy's children received sentences of incarceration that seemed far beyond the scope of what they had done. The most egregious case involved Tammy's trans daughter Sabrina, who Tammy often refers to by her birth name Wayne (we will address Tammy's experience of having a trans child in the chapters ahead). Sabrina had been placed in special education classes for a variety of learning disabilities, including severe ADHD. The regular teacher had worked out a system by which Sabrina could excuse herself from the classroom when she felt agitated. She would walk the halls until she settled down and then return to class.

On the day of the incident, Sabrina's class had a substitute teacher who had not been informed of the procedure. Sabrina had an episode in the middle of a lesson and got up to leave the room as usual. The substitute told her to sit down. When Sabrina kept heading for the door, the substitute grabbed her arm. Sabrina swatted the substitute's hand away. That contact is what led to Sabrina being sent to juvenile court.

The judge handling both of Tammy's children's cases was Mark Ciavarella Jr., a Democrat who had run for office promising to get tough on juvenile justice. Tammy couldn't afford a lawyer. And each time, the same thing happened. Acting on Ciavarella's standing instructions, the clerk informed her that waiting for a public defender would drag out the proceedings and they would probably be sitting there all day. Tammy might even have to come back tomorrow and wait all day as well. The clerk suggested that if Tammy simply signed a waiver allowing the child to appear *without* an attorney, they would be in and out in about five minutes.

The clerks seemed sympathetic, like they were trying to help, so Tammy signed the forms. As soon as Tammy signed the waiver, Ciavarella immediately convicted each child and sentenced them to long terms at a juvenile detention facility.

Tammy was shocked by the harshness of the sentences, but she felt powerless to do anything about it. She wasn't the only parent alarmed by Judge Ciavarella's rulings. In 2007, lawyers with a children's rights organization called the Juvenile Law Center started an investigation after receiving multiple complaints about Ciavarella. The investigators noticed a pattern. When a child defendant showed up without a lawyer, Ciavarella's clerks would urge the parents to sign away their minor child's right to counsel, just like they had done with Tammy. After the parents signed the forms, Ciavarella would routinely convict the children and sentence them to long terms in one of two for-profit juvenile detention facilities, just like he had done with Tammy's children.

The deeper the investigators dug into Ciavarella's record, the more disturbing the pattern became. Ciavarella had convinced parents to sign away their child's right to counsel in more than half the cases that came before him. His rulings removed about 60 percent of defendants from their parents' homes, usually sending them to the for-profit juvenile detention facilities. The totals were staggering. From 2003 to 2008, Ciavarella incarcerated more than two thousand five hundred children in six thousand separate cases. Many children were sentenced to juvenile detention more than once.

The alarming patterns—and a series of whistleblower tips once the news started to go public—led to wider investigations by state and federal authorities that uncovered one of the biggest juvenile justice scandals in US history. It turned out that Ciavarella and the presiding judge of the county, Michael T. Conahan, had taken more than $2.6 million in kickbacks from the owners of the two for-profit juvenile prisons.

The criminal and civil cases against the judges dragged on for years but eventually ended with convictions for both and damages for the victims. Tammy's two children each eventually received a few thousand dollars from the initial settlement for their years of unjust incarceration. The last of the civil lawsuits ended in 2022 with Ciavarella and Conahan assessed over $200 million in damages. Newspaper accounts noted that the victims were unlikely to receive much of anything from the two judges because they had already liquidated most of their assets to pay their own attorneys.

A few thousand dollars was paltry compensation for the damage done to Tammy's children. The siblings would not talk about what happened in prison after their release. Tammy said neither was the same again.

Of the two, Sabrina held it together the best—at least it seemed like she did, until everything fell apart in 2022. By contrast, Tammy's son has had a hard time dealing with life outside prison ever since. He has spent so much time in and out of jail that Tammy now believes he feels more settled behind bars. Every time he's out, things start to spiral, he makes bad decisions, and then something terrible happens.

As you might imagine, there's a direct link between Kids for Cash and Tammy's embrace of the QAnon conspiracy theories. To appreciate the connection, you have to understand that Tammy blames herself for everything that happened to her children when they were growing up. As you will soon see, there's a long list. It doesn't matter that other people did the most serious damage to them, or that the institutions that were supposed to protect her children harmed them instead. Tammy feels responsible—for all of it. She faults herself for leaving them in a vulnerable situation and being unable to prevent the bad things that happened. "My children suffered because of deci-sions I made," she says with cold remorse.

The rise of QAnon was driven by women like Tammy. QAnon always had its fair share of male adherents, but women are the main reason it exploded during the pandemic. Women were the online superspreaders of the QAnon conspiracy theories. And they were more likely to act on their beliefs in the real world. Far more women than men who were arrested for January 6 traced their activism to QAnon—Tammy and Yvonne included.

It's not that the pandemic made women more conspiratorial than men. COVID drove both men and women to conspiracism. It's just that they took different paths and followed different conspiracies. Men were more likely than women to see COVID as a Chinese bioweapon, a byproduct of 5G technology, or a hoax cooked up to make Donald Trump look bad. Men were also more likely to believe that Bill Gates was funding vaccines to implant tracking devices that would enslave the public.

Meanwhile, women found conspiracism when answering QAnon's call to "Save the Children." Research has shown that women are attracted to con-spiracy theories that appeal to their roles as mothers and caretakers. QAnon catered to that mindset perfectly. Its basic premise is that a cabal of elites is running a global child sex trafficking network.

Now let's be clear: child trafficking *is* a real and serious problem, with an estimated 1.3 million children worldwide held in conditions of modern slavery. But QAnon gave that basic truth a wild conspiratorial backstory. It involved a cabal of pedophile politicians and famous people. Child murders and satanic blood-drinking rituals designed to give perpetual youth. Reptil-ian creatures in human form gradually amassing power all over the world.

QAnon appealed directly to women to step up to save the children of the world like they would defend their own kids. Women didn't need to buy into the full conspiracy about reptilians to get involved. It was easy enough to confirm that the child trafficking crisis was real. The rest was a pick-and-choose assortment of details, which could be believed or discarded as being too farfetched. Either way, you could feel good about sharing information that could *potentially* save children, even if you didn't quite believe all of it was true.

The more involved women became in QAnon communities, the deeper their belief in its different conspiracies grew. QAnon brought in more women when it absorbed various COVID conspiracies. It supercharged the anti-vaccination, anti-mask, and anti-shutdown opposition by appealing to women as mothers and caretakers. QAnon pushed women to advocate for their kids by refusing to get them vaccinated, protecting their right to breathe without a mask, and demanding school be held in person rather than remotely. And women jumped into the fray, becoming leaders of the protests against COVID restrictions and to open the schools.

In taking these actions, women were playing a well-worn traditional role as protectors of children that they have always assumed in far-right movements across time and around the world. In right-wing movements, women typically play a submissive role and maintain a public presence curated to soften extreme politics and messaging. Right-wing movements are usually patriarchal in structure, so women's public-facing voices tend to be muted. Despite being in the background, women have played essential roles in organizing these movements, a trend that extends to far-right groups like the National Socialist Women's Union and the Women's Ku Klux Klan.

However, when it comes to defending children, conservative women move to the forefront. They are afforded far greater latitude when acting out in their roles as mothers and caretakers. To protect kids, women can even act like men and resort to violence without being seen as challenging patriarchal norms. In the latest version, these women are said to be acting as "mama bears" or "mama grizzlies." That latitude also applies to women who are childless and older women whose children are grown. As the phrase goes on the right: "You don't need to be a mom to be a mama bear."

The recent increase in activism among conservative women comes out of this same defense of children and families. Many conservative women became activists during the pandemic because masking and vaccination requirements and school closings directly affected their domestic roles. Conservative women's groups like Moms for Liberty took the lead in attacking public education and inclusive and empathetic school curricula that emphasize things like social and emotional learning. They consider the things that their children learn and the values they are taught to be the purview of mothers, not educational bureaucrats and teacher unions.

These groups portrayed their defense of American history devoid of slavery and racial strife in the same way. They framed their counterprotests against Black Lives Matter and their attacks on the 1619 Project as preventing their children from being blamed for historical racism. They also claimed to be ensuring that their kids learned about the great accomplishments of American leaders—including Confederate generals, whose statues they wanted to keep in public places to honor the nation's "diverse heritage." In all these ways—and others we will explore in subsequent chapters—conservative women framed their activism as being frontline protectors of families and children.

Both Yvonne and Tammy see themselves as mama bears. Yvonne frequently references her children and grandchildren as important motivating factors in her activism. Tammy sees her support of QAnon and Donald Trump as an opportunity to succeed where she had failed in the past to protect her own children from sexual predators and institutions that victimized them.

.+*+.

The troubles for Tammy's children began not long after she went to her grandmother's funeral with a black eye. Her soon-to-be ex-boyfriend delivered something worse than a punch to the face when he called child protective services to punish Tammy for leaving him. He told the social workers that Tammy had been taking drugs. Tammy didn't use anything other than alcohol when her kids were little, and she passed all the drug tests. But the social workers concluded that the situation in the household was untenable.

Tammy was distraught. She told the social workers about her partner's violence and that she had been living on the streets periodically to escape it. She explained that he had gotten far behind on the rent and had left her without a means to pay. There wasn't enough money to keep the pantry and refrigerator stocked. He had shown up to one of the custody hearings, argued with the judge and the social workers, and then basically disappeared. The social workers concluded that Tammy was the only responsible parent. But she wasn't in a place to raise three children on her own. And while she might not be on drugs, there were strong signs of a drinking problem. "Children and Youth came; it was a Thursday," Tammy recalls. "They told me to get a Protection From Abuse order on my boyfriend, get the rent paid and everything caught up, and they will return the kids back home. Then I was told I had to go to a twenty-eight-day rehab program for my drinking. Their dad had stopped coming around. He had gone to one hearing and was belligerent to the court. Never came to any other hearings and never came to any visits. So the kids ended up in foster care."

The social workers concluded that Tammy needed time on her own to get herself together. They wanted her to get sober, pay the back rent, and figure out how to put food on the table. Since no other family members offered to take care of the kids, all three children went into the system until the social workers felt Tammy could be trusted with them on her own. They stayed in foster care for nearly two years.

Tammy still doesn't understand why it took so long to get them back. And she was furious when she learned what had happened to her children in the foster home. She was alerted to it by her youngest child at the time, Sabrina, who Tammy refers to here by her birth name, Wayne.

> Children and Youth wanted to bring one child back home at a time, kind of to "ease" me in and not overwhelm me. I was laying my youngest, Wayne, down for a nap. I read him a book and he said, "Do you want to have sex?" And started gyrating the air. I asked him some questions about why he was doing that, and he told me that the son of the foster family has sex with him. Turns out my three kids, and another little girl that was there, were all sexually abused by the foster parent's teenaged son.

That teenager was a deeply disturbed person, who several years later committed a gruesome murder during a botched home robbery. Tammy often thinks about what this person might have done to her children for two years other than just molesting them. She is still angry about the harm her kids endured. "I ended up completing twenty-eight-day rehab, all kinds of parenting classes, AA meetings. . . . I jumped through hoops of fire to get those kids back. And it took them getting molested for it to finally happen."

Tammy's anger and indignation also grow out of what happened next. The effects started to show in her son when he reached middle school. At the time, Tammy was married to Dave, the alcoholic roofer who already hated her children. When her son started acting out, the problem grew worse, and he went to live with his father. He came back to live with Tammy when he was about thirteen, but it didn't last. "I sent him back with his father," Tammy said. "He was out of control. Stealing, destroying my house, being disrespectful. Acting out bad."

The worst happened when Tammy's thirteen-year-old son went from being victim to victimizer. He would sometimes babysit a five-year-old boy, and on one visit he molested the child.

Years went by, including the ones Tammy's son spent in juvenile detention for his Kids for Cash conviction. Then in 2013, when he was twenty-five, he was overcome with remorse over what he had done to that five-year-old boy more than a decade before. Wracked with guilt, Tammy's son reached out on Facebook to apologize to his victim, who was now sixteen years old. He requested to speak on the phone so he could apologize in person. That apology would send Tammy's son to prison. The boy went to his parents after Tammy's son contacted him on Facebook, and the parents called the police. The police brought him in for questioning and he admitted everything.

The story of Tammy's son's arrest was front page news in her hometown. And because Tammy's son was now over eighteen, he was tried as an adult. The first trial resulted in a hung jury. On retrial he pled guilty and was given a sentence of between five and twenty-three months in prison, followed by two years of probation.

Tammy had a hard time coming to terms with what her son had done. "He isn't violent. He has a good heart, he really does," she tells me. "They had such a hard life. I'm not excusing their actions," she says in a blanket apology for her children, all of whom ended up in dark places. "But as we know, it does affect their adult lives," Tammy tells me; it's clear she's done some reading about childhood sexual abuse.

Nothing improved when Tammy's son was released from prison on the child sexual assault charges. He went through a series of short-lived, chaotic relationships. He developed a meth addiction and fathered three children with three different women. To Tammy's great dismay, he has almost no relationship with any of his children. The granddaughter with whom Tammy has her own relationship wants nothing to do with her father. Tammy talks often about this granddaughter, who has excelled in school against all odds. She hopes the child can salvage a relationship with her father, who has been incarcerated most of her life.

The rest of Tammy's adult children weren't doing much better. Her second oldest child, a daughter who had also been sexually abused while in foster care, followed her older brother into drugs. She went from shoplifting to a meth addiction and a variety of escalating drug charges. There were times when all she could bring herself to do was buy more meth. For these stretches, she stopped paying rent or buying food. She also turned over her two children to their respective fathers.

Meanwhile, Tammy's youngest daughter was starting to go off track. Tammy says she had never gotten over the death of her father, who had hung himself in prison. That was when she was five, and the suicide shaped how Tammy raised her daughter. "I was always really easy on her," Tammy said. "I felt bad that her father killed himself. And I think she blamed me for a very long time." Tammy says her daughter has a history of directing violent outbursts against her.

Tammy tells me things have improved, but she still worries about her daughter's anger and temper. "She's not as violent as she used to be," Tammy says like it's an accomplishment. Tammy is also concerned about how her daughter chooses much older men of questionable character as partners. In her late teenage years, Tammy's daughter started dating a "chef" in a world where a chef was a person who cooked meth. He was about Tammy's age. She left that relationship for another man who is older than Tammy by a year or so. Tammy has little respect for the boyfriend, other than that he's the father of a grandson she loves.

The couple's financial situation is not good, and Tammy moved in with them to provide childcare for her grandson when her daughter went back to work. Tammy continued to live there despite the tensions because she adores her grandson. "I was in the room when he was born, and the longest he has ever gone without seeing me is a month when I was visiting my father in Florida," Tammy tells me with pride. "I left there because I missed him so much."

Then her tone gets thoughtful. "I want to be the kind of grandmother I think my mom would have been. Now I can go back to that role instead of the mommy role." Ultimately, this role—protective grandmother—would finally convince Tammy to engage more actively with real-world challenges instead of conspiratorial ones.

The QAnon conspiracy theories make sense to Tammy because she feels like they explain her life. QAnon tells its followers that pedophiles are everywhere. That isn't news to Tammy. Everywhere you look in her world—no matter the stage of her life and the lives of her children and grandchildren—it seems populated by pedophiles and sexual predators.

Nor is it hard for her to believe that government officials would be involved in child sex trafficking. After all, the top two judges in the Luzerne County juvenile justice system were running a child trafficking ring for years, right under everyone's noses, and it took a decade of investigations and court cases to put a stop to it.

In all these ways, Tammy felt QAnon verified what she already knew. QAnon also gave her a broader framework for understanding why powerful people, mostly men, were being revealed as child predators and no one with authority seemed to be doing anything to stop it.

For Tammy and other conspiracist women who see themselves as mama bears, QAnon offered—and continues to offer—hope. It promised that the entire cabal would soon be exposed and brought to justice. Tammy's own desire for vengeance against pedophiles is fueled by a lifetime of pent-up rage over what predators have done to her and to her children. For most of her life she has felt helpless to stop it. Now she feels some agency, even a sense of power.

Tammy likes the idea of being part of the minority of true believers who will take down the global child sex trafficking network. She feels like she will be striking back for herself and her children and creating a better world for her grandchildren. She will do this now like she has done it for the last four years: by following conspiracies. She has also dedicated herself to the man QAnon has identified as the cabal's number one enemy: Donald Trump, the strong, tough-talking leader who she believes will get the job done.

✦

Like Tammy, Yvonne answered QAnon's call to save the children. She simply filtered it through her increasingly New Age spiritual beliefs.

Yvonne believes in reincarnation and that each human soul has lived out every possible life experience in past lives. She believes that each of our souls has cycled through all the possibilities. In past lives, we all were different people and played different roles. She thinks that prior to entering our new human bodies, each soul forgets everything it knows of its past lives so that it can experience the current life in the moment and learn the lessons that the present life has to teach. Part of that learning involves facing the choice to follow the path of light or darkness.

Yvonne sees QAnon and its attempt to stop child sex trafficking and government corruption as the center of the challenge for every soul in this lifetime. She believes we all must choose sides in the great spiritual war between light and dark. "The whole awakening is about the kids," she tells me. "It's about the child trafficking they've been doing. It's about the millions of children. We've all been victims of that child trafficking. We've been those kids in those cages in other lifetimes. We've been the perpetrators in other lifetimes."

Yvonne wants to make sure I understand. "That's what's going to rock the world: when people realize they've been the good and the bad," she says emphatically. "We're both. We are the duality. We are the ones that brought the bad. We're also angels. Even the fallen angels. And I am an angel."

That sense of divine agency and purpose is fundamental to Yvonne's New Age belief system. She sees herself as a key actor in the spiritual transformation she believes will sweep the globe and lead humanity into a higher stage of consciousness. Yvonne believes she was sent to help save the children. It is her mission on earth, and it is essential to the life lessons she believes her soul is here to learn. She sees herself as awakening to that purpose, which she envisions as her remembering the mission her soul selected for this lifetime.

Yvonne frames her mission as one that centers on the activism of other women. She believes that the world is out of whack because a damaged version of the Divine Masculine has taken over. The only thing that can restore peace and harmony is an assertion of the Divine Feminine. Women aren't subservient players in the spiritual drama she sees unfolding; they are the central actors, the heroes that the world needs. She believes women are the only ones who can really fix things.

She links all this directly to the rise in conservative activism by women on the right. "It is about the divine, and that's why so many women are waking up," Yvonne says with excitement. "That's why the Divine Feminine is waking up. It's the Marjorie Taylor Greens. It's me." Her voice gets more animated. "I'm surrounded by women that are waking up. I'm surrounded by the Divine Feminine and women stepping into their power!"

Yvonne believes Divine Feminine energy gives women special powers to protect children and their wellbeing. "I know something's wrong, but women are not really having a voice," she says of politics and society in general. "But when it comes to children, that's when they get their voice," she tells me. Yvonne sees the emphasis on motherhood and kids as a key to awakening conservative women as warriors in a battle between good and evil. "People that have enough compassion to see that will come over to this side. It's the kids that are going to make the difference. It's always about kids," she says definitively. "And that's why conservative women are stepping up to the school boards and all that."

Yvonne doesn't think most of these women, who tend to be evangelical Christians, fully understand why their souls are calling them into service. "They have no idea what they're doing. They have no idea," she says, shaking her head. "Most of the women on the right have no idea spiritually. But I do. I see them stepping into their power."

Her tone changes as she comes up with an example. "It's like my daughter: she has no idea who she is, but I see her. I know who she is." Yvonne describes her daughter like she's listing the qualities of the perfect tradwife. Short for "traditional wife," a tradwife is a woman who embraces an idealized image of womanhood from the past, centered on service and submission to her husband, domesticity, and child-rearing. The unofficial slogan is "femininity not feminism" and is associated with a range of right-wing groups, from evangelical Christians and traditionalist Catholics, to organic living communities and anti-modernity movements. Most stay-at-home moms are not tradwives. The women who use the term specifically tie their identity to reactionary beliefs that range from anti-feminism to Christian nationalism, to white supremacy.

Yvonne tells me more about her daughter. "She's the one with the seven kids. She's the one that's homeschooling. She's the one that's learning how to self-sustain. They're the ones that are going to live off the grid," Yvonne tells me with obvious pride. Yvonne admires her daughter for engaging in what she sees as sacred Divine Feminine behavior. But she's frustrated that her daughter doesn't get why the Divine Feminine is important. "I see her doing everything that she needs to be, and she has no idea why," Yvonne says. "But I do."

Yvonne blames her daughter's dogmatic Mormon beliefs for preventing her from seeing it. Yvonne shares most of her daughter's conservative and patriarchal religious values. But she doesn't believe that her daughter or her daughter's church understands the healing power of the Divine Feminine. "They've always been conservatives, and they're Christians," she says of her daughter and son-in-law.

In Yvonne's spiritual worldview, women have a complex role. On one hand, she believes that women need to fulfill their traditional gender roles by being mothers and caretakers; in that sense, she and her daughter agree. She is proud of her daughter for homeschooling her children. But Yvonne also believes that women need more earthly authority to express their spiritual power. She believes women need to assert that authority so that they can heal the Divine Masculine, which she believes has caused so many of the problems the world faces today.

Yvonne's basic views on spirituality are shared by many conservative middle-age white women whose religious beliefs have taken a New Age path. In recent years, and especially since the pandemic, conspirituality has grown significantly as a faith movement. It's one that primarily attracts women, and middle-age white women in particular. While New Age imagery is tradition-ally associated with left-leaning hippies and yoga instructors, the more recent versions are far more likely to be based on conservative values.

Middle-aged conservative women are attracted to conspirituality in part because of its gendered promises. It offers a sense of belonging and identity to women who no longer feel valued or even visible in popular culture. That's especially true on the political right, where traditional patriarchal ideals leave little place for older women. The ideal woman on the right is a young wife and mother who embodies an image of womanhood based in youth, purity, and subservience. The ideal is Yvonne's daughter, with her seven home-schooled children, who is preparing to live off the grid. It is not Yvonne, the outspoken fiftysomething with five adult children fathered by five different men who has worked outside the home for most of her life. Middle-aged women like Yvonne have no clear place in right-wing ideals or imagery.

Basically, there aren't any postmenopausal tradwives in the conservative imagination. There aren't any divorced ones either.

The lack of space for older conservative women in churches and popular culture helps explain the appeal of New Age conspirituality to this demo-graphic. The conspirituality movement is filled with older women, many of whom are divorced, who were reared in conservative Christian households but who no longer feel at home in the faith. In a sense, they have aged-out of evangelical Christianity as an identity that explains their life, offers meaning and purpose, and promises them a positive role in the community.

The push factors for middle-aged women who move from Christianity into conspirituality are many. Conservative denominations and networks often do not allow for women's ordination or leadership. The sexual abuse scandals that have rocked major denominations recently have caused many women to wonder how seriously the church takes women's voices. The push factors also include subtle and not-so-subtle age-related slights, like when Vice President JD Vance agreed with a podcast host who said that "the whole purpose of the postmenopausal female" was to help raise children. Clearly, many middle-aged women don't like being thought of as extraneous and want a greater role than the narrow one that many Christian churches allow them. New Age spiritualism has given these women a way to feel relevant in a culture where they are mostly invisible or intentionally marginalized. In turn, New

Age beliefs have changed to incorporate elements of the conservatism with which they grew up, developments we will trace in the next two chapters.

✦

Conspirituality is attracting not only conservative white women. The ranks of believers include many older liberal white women as well. These women might not share the full range of reactionary beliefs, as someone like Yvonne does. But they are finding common ground, having tacked in a more rightward direction since the pandemic, especially when it comes to skepticism of the government on health and wellness matters.

This speaks to a larger issue in Western culture that deserves more consideration: the invisibility and irrelevance that comes as women age, which is a feature on the political left as it is on the right. Liberal white women were horrified by JD Vance's comments too. But it's not like the brand of "choice feminism" (where women can choose a career, motherhood, or some combination of the two) treats middle-aged women much better. Like anti-feminist ideology on the right, second- and third-wave feminism often prioritizes youth and organizes itself around concerns of young white women. The dominant forms of feminism focus on reproductive rights, access to education and jobs, and childcare. Liberal feminist concern often stops at menopause, just like conservative anti-feminism does. It just doesn't broadcast the news. Instead, it pretends like there isn't a problem, because it treats older women like they don't exist.

These dynamics have made New Age spiritualism a landing place for women who live outside both the ideal patriarchal and feminist norms. A 2014 Pew Research survey revealed that the typical follower of New Age spirituality was a divorced or never-married Gen X or Boomer woman who has taken some college classes but didn't complete a four-year degree. In 2014 they were making less than $50,000 annually. Some 74 percent lived in households without children under eighteen. About 84 percent seldom if ever attended formal religious services.

That sense of being forgotten based on our age and gender was one of the few things that Yvonne, Tammy, and I had in common. My connections with them and the other January 6 women I spoke with were based largely on our shared experiences as white middle-aged women and the mothers of adult children. We had little in common politically. But we shared an understanding of the challenges faced by middle-aged women. We agreed about how our age and gender seemed to let us slip through society's cracks without anyone really noticing or caring. We shared a sense that America did not truly appreciate the work we had performed—and continue to perform—as mothers. We felt like we had sacrificed in terms of our personal and professional development and had gotten little to no substantive credit for the hard work of raising our kids.

In fact, we all felt like we had been punished by American society for having children and doing far more work than any of the men in our children's lives in terms of raising them. And now we were all struggling materially while the fathers of our children were doing fine. These men had been able to focus on jobs or careers without interruption. By contrast, we had all taken time off from work, or incurred expenses, or quit jobs, or bypassed opportunities so that we could be there for children or grandchildren. And now we were often having to look after our aging parents as well. However imperfect our efforts might have been—and continue to be—we showed up more than the men.

At points during our many conversations, I told Yvonne and Tammy about my own fall in status when I got divorced. During our marriage, my husband of twenty-two years and the father of my three children was a litigator with a top Los Angeles law firm. He worked crazy hours, made excellent money, and afforded us a comfortable lifestyle. I dropped out of college when we got married and started having kids.

As a child, I had longed for my working single mother to be a stay-at-home mom, to give me the parental attention I craved. I only saw my dad every other weekend, so my mom bore nearly all the parenting responsibility and had to work long hours. I wanted to be the mom I imagined I wanted her to be: the field trip chaperone or "class mom."

So I went overboard. I tried my best to be the perfect suburban, stay-at-home mother. I hired a nanny so I could have one-on-one time with each of my kids every week. I threw elaborate birthday parties. I was a Girl Scout leader. I ran the PTA. I got my kids involved in club sports (the path to college!) and drove my soon-to-be Division I athlete children to swimming and water polo practices and meets. At sporting events I shouted until my voice was hoarse. I built my life and identity around my kids and being the wife of an LA lawyer at a prominent firm. I even joined the Junior League. For years, I ran big charity events, and I made sure my auctions and fashion shows broke fundraising records.

Then it all fell apart. My then-husband and I got divorced, and I suddenly found the class rug pulled out from beneath me.

I learned very quickly just how much cultures, systems, and laws are stacked against divorced women. I went back to finish my college degree, but the spousal support I received wasn't enough to live on and pay tuition and books. I went from a PPO health insurance plan, where I could pick my doctor, to Medicaid. I used to lease a new car every few years; today, I still drive the same car I drove at the end of that marriage more than a decade ago. As a stay-at-home mom, I had accrued no Social Security credits of my own, and I discovered that I would only be eligible for half the payments through my ex-husband's account. I'd have to build to a full credit on my own—and I'd be starting in my mid-fifties, saddled with student loans.

I understand that I was—and am—living an unusually privileged life, and I'm not looking for sympathy. The point is that even women like me—a white woman living a comfortable upper-middle-class lifestyle—can fall down the economic ladder pretty quickly. Who is going to hire a fifty-something former stay-at-home mom with no resume of paid employment since 1992? It's surprisingly easy to reach a precarious financial place; a big medical bill or other financial setback, on top of student loans and a car payment, can cause you to slip below the poverty line. I'm not equating my circumstances or material hardships to those experienced by Tammy and Yvonne. I'm merely pointing out that as older women, we all feel largely invisible. We wonder whether society wouldn't notice or care if we ended up living in our cars.

In other words, Democrats are not offering an alternative for middle-aged conservative women who have slipped into conspiracism that might draw them out of it. Democrats appear not to understand this audience; in fact, they seem to have never really considered it. This also helps explain the growing number of white middle-aged women who once voted for Democratic candidates but who have fallen down the conspiratorial rabbit hole. Many of them now support Donald Trump or else don't vote at all. In the 2024 presidential election, support for Democrats dropped by 7 percent among middle-aged women, the steepest drop in any female age cohort. Part of the reason they have left the Democratic party is because they feel like the established systems have let them down.

Women like this, who feel forgotten, and find themselves alone and isolated, are more likely to engage in extreme forms of conspiracism, like conspirituality, that offer them a new role and identity. This conspiracy-based New Age faith is essentially a religion run by women, for women, and in it, women are the primary social influencers and entrepreneurs. As we will soon see, this theology envisions women guiding humanity into a hidden interdimensional universe of angelic alien beings, who will either allow humans to experience heaven on earth—or bring an apocalyptic end to their existence.

CHAPTER 6

Starseed Awakening

Are you a starseed? You've probably never considered the prospect or perhaps even heard the term. But if you go through one of the many checklists of starseed traits circulating on the internet, you might be surprised how many boxes you can tick. That's especially true if you're a middle-aged woman.

A starseed is an entity from a higher dimension that has taken human form to help lead the jump in evolution from the third dimension to the fifth, or what New Agers call 5D. These beings are said to be able to "astral travel" throughout the galaxy and between different spiritual dimensions. They have agreed to be born into a human vessel, forgetting everything about their alien origins and their great spiritual powers, so that they can better help serve humanity. Now that the time for the shift to 5D has come, they are awakening to their true selves and purposes and coming into their spiritual power. Maybe you're one of them.

If so, you have a lot of company—and your numbers are growing, having multiplied rapidly during the pandemic. There are now thousands, and probably more like millions, of starseeds out there. By early 2023, more than 570 thousand videos had been posted to the social media platform TikTok using the hashtag #starseed. Those videos had received over one billion views.

Starseeds are said to have a distinct set of characteristics. They possess a powerful sense of empathy and strong intuitive abilities. They feel out of place on this planet and are often isolated, alone, and lonely. Some checklists to determine if you are a starseed seem like they are assessing symptoms of depression, anxiety, ADHD, or unresolved trauma. Other checklists read like a roster of common complaints made by women over fifty.

After Yvonne's spiritual journey took its New Age turn, she started reposting checklists like these. Not long after, Tammy began doing the same. Both claimed their checklist scores were definitive proof that they are starseeds. One meme reposted by Yvonne announced, "You are a STARSEED when:

- You have a deep desire to be home, but you don't know where HOME is.
- You feel out of place—no one understands your cosmic MIND.
- You love being ALONE in solitude, peace, & nature and avoid places with a lot of people.
- You always felt that your life had a greater PURPOSE, but you weren't sure what it was.
- You have a highly INTUITIVE sense of mind and can sense the energy and emotions of other people, animals, places, and objects.
- You feel a great EVENT coming up in the near future that will change everything we know about Life and Humanity.
- You are SMILING right now as you read this because you know you are unusual and you are not alone."

"I am most definitely a starseed!" Yvonne proclaimed in response. "I see and understand things differently."

There are a variety of starseed checklists because there are numerous kinds of starseeds. Each one has its own set of characteristics. The checklist for "Indigo Children" includes: "headstrong, creative, prone to addictions, an 'old soul,' intuitive or psychic, tendency to isolate, independent and proud, possesses a deep desire to help the world in a big way, wavers between low self-esteem and grandiosity, easily bored, diagnosed with ADD, prone to insomnia or nightmares, history of depression, looks for real friendships only, and easily bonds with other non-human living things." If you check fourteen or more items from the list, then you are "in fact an indigo." The comments section for the meme was filled with people identifying themselves as Indigo Children based on their responses.

My favorite list is a meme Yvonne reposted on Facebook that describes common "Ascension Symptoms." In Yvonne's theology, "Ascension" or "Disclosure" is what happens when the world starts transitioning to 5D, a process that seems a lot like the biblical apocalypse from the book of Revelation. "Ascension Symptoms" are what you experience when the apocalypse gets rolling and you start transitioning into the higher dimension. I like it because it describes what I experienced going through menopause: headaches, anxiety, trouble sleeping, fatigue, perspiration, aches and pains. Yvonne reposted the list as confirmation that the shift to 5D had begun. "We are so close," she wrote above the meme.

Yvonne is also certain that she is the kind of starseed called a "Pleiadian." Pleiadians have ancient alien DNA from a species that originates in the Pleiades, a star cluster commonly called "The Seven Sisters" that's part of the constellation Taurus. Pleiadians are among the most advanced species of starseeds, and they will lead the way when Ascension comes.

Tammy isn't sure what kind of starseed she might be. She just feels certain that she's one of them. Tammy's convinced she will know more when the time is right, and her true identity and powers will be revealed.

Yvonne and Tammy both traced different paths to this fast-growing branch of New Age belief during the pandemic. The two women lived thousands of miles apart and, at the time, did not know each other. And yet they both started using the same spiritual vocabulary—about starseeds, Disclosure, and the fifth dimension. Neither woman had been doing anything like this prior to 2020. During the COVID shutdowns, each came to fully embrace this otherworldly religion, independently of one another, all on their own. This was something I also saw happening with several other women I had been tracking.

This chapter introduces their New Age belief system and shows how Yvonne and Tammy ended up embracing it. Tammy's starseed awakening took hold when she started following an online prophet with a large audience composed mostly of middle-aged white women. Yvonne's awakening followed a more winding path. As we have seen, Yvonne had already been on quite a spiritual journey since storming the Capitol. The pandemic had convinced her to leave evangelical Christianity and start a new journey that took her into Love Has Won and QAnon, both of which had led her to Washington, DC, on January 6. After the death of Love Has Won leader Amy Carlson in April 2021, Yvonne began moving into other realms of conspirituality. She began training with a mystic and ultimately decided that she was one herself: a Pleiadian healer here to help humanity awaken from its spiritual slumber before it's too late.

In November 2023, Yvonne reposted to Facebook a meme featuring a drawing of a girl looking directly at the viewer, with her hands cupped, holding some glowing, unseen light that washes her face in a rainbow of colors.

Her bangs part in the middle to reveal an opened third eye in the center of her forehead. The image is captioned "THE SILENT INVASION." Yvonne replies, "Yes! We are the Army (or in my case the Marines) of Consciousness. . . . You'll see soon enough."

Understanding this new alien invasion means taking a journey back in time to the late nineteenth century to meet the woman who started the New Age movement from which starseed theology emerged. Helena Blavatsky was a Russian immigrant who lived in late-nineteenth-century New York City. You may not have heard of her. But you probably recognize the names of some of her followers, which included a host of early-twentieth-century musicians, artists, and creative types, including the inventor Thomas Edison. You can see Blavatsky's ideas in the paintings of abstract artists Wassily Kandinsky and Piet Mondrian. You can hear them in the poetry of William Butler Yeats.

Blavatsky provided the basic framework for nearly all of today's New Age religions. And it all began with a belief system called theosophy.

✦ ✦ ✦

Helena Blavatsky was born to an aristocratic Russian family who liked to travel. Having toured the Russian Empire during her childhood, Blavatsky as an adult traveled across the world, where she was exposed to numerous world religions. Or so she claimed. Blavatsky said the key event in her life was meeting a Hindu saint from the thirteenth or fourteenth century named Morya, an entity she says she saw in visions going back to her childhood. She said Morya identified himself to her as one of the "Masters of the Ancient Wisdom." Over the years, Blavatsky told several different versions of the story of how she met Morya, changing the place, date, and circumstances. According to Blavatsky, Morya became her guru and introduced her to other spiritual Masters. She said she met even more of them through various world travels that may not have happened. For example, there is considerable doubt that she ever visited Tibet, let alone trained there for seven years as she claimed We do know that Blavatsky eventually settled in New York City to write about her alleged experiences and what she had learned.

Blavatsky taught that everyone has an "inner God," an eternal "higher self," and that the purpose of life is to find it and elevate its power so it can be liberated. Borrowing from Hinduism and Buddhism, she said that human beings were reincarnated endlessly so that they could evolve with each lifetime. She taught that the earth and cosmos were evolving, too. She said all this evolution was directed by a brotherhood of spiritual "Masters," who usually remain unseen.

The Masters are a star-studded spiritual roster, including Moses, Jesus, Buddha, and Confucius. The full list of Ascended Masters is long and growing, filled with most of the leading divine figures from across the world. The full lineup reads like the spiritual equivalent of one of the epic Marvel Avengers movies that features all the superheroes in a single film.

Theosophy has an unusual relationship with Christianity. In theosophy, Jesus Christ is a divine being, but he doesn't have the same theological status or role as the Christian Jesus. There are lots of other divine beings who hold roughly equal authority. It's less that there's a pantheon of gods than a league of mystical saints. Jesus is one of the leading spiritual figures, but you don't need to worship him exclusively. You might feel that your place in the organizational structure leads you to report directly to one of the other spiritual Masters. It's like a more extreme version of the Catholic idea of patron saints.

More to the point, it's like Hinduism, which Blavatsky was using as her base. Hinduism has a pantheon of gods, and Hindus dispute which one is the most powerful. One group believes it's Shiva, another thinks it's Vishnu, another says it's Brahma, and still others say someone else. Master Morya, who Helena Blavatsky claimed to have met, supposedly performed miracles with help from Ganesha. In theosophy, you can pick your own Master in whatever religious tradition you prefer. They can be Hindu, Christian, Buddhist, or Muslim. If there's not a name that appeals to you on the list, you can add a new Master to the mix

Theosophy became the basis for most New Age religions that followed. It took off in a minor way in the 1920s and '30s, peaking with forty thousand registered members. But theosophy's influence went far beyond its numbers, in part because of the influential thinkers and artists whose work incorporated it. There's also a more ominous side to the story of theosophy, one that relates to race and Naziism and that we will explore in the next chapter.

The most prominent offshoot was probably the I AM movement, founded by a Chicago couple, Guy and Edna Ballard, who drew over a million followers in the 1930s. The Ballards claimed to have had regular conversations with a group they started calling the "Ascended Masters." While hiking at Mount Shasta, California, they said they met Ascended Master Saint Germain, a European alchemist from the eighteenth century, who the French writer

Voltaire said was immortal. The Ballards said that Saint Germain wanted them to deliver his messages to the public.

The I AM movement, which is currently making a big comeback, spawned other groups that borrowed its traditions to build their own new theologies. The most influential of these was Elizabeth Clare Prophet, a woman who ran a version of I AM in the 1960s through to the 1990s that was closely aligned with far-right politics and preached an impending apocalypse based in nuclear Armageddon.

The starseed movement grew out of these offshoots that combined theosophy with ideas drawn from science fiction writers. Adherents of this branch of New Age spiritualism believe that aliens have long been on earth and are here to help lead humanity to a higher state of consciousness. In this version, the Ascended Masters are advanced beings from other dimensions and planets. There are many different versions of this faith. Some believe humanity's evolution is being directed through "The Galactic Federation of Light," a group of extraterrestrials from the Milky Way galaxy that work with Saint Germain and the Ascended Masters.

One of the more popular figures in New Age circles today is an angelic entity called "Kryon of the Magnetic Service." Kryon's followers believe that, for the shift to 5D to happen, the earth's magnetic field needs to be recalibrated and that Kryon is the project manager for that job. That belief originated with an audio technician from San Diego named Lee Carroll, who said that Kryon started channeling through him in 1989 to let humanity know it was time to start preparing for Ascension.

Probably the two most influential recent prophets of this kind of alien theology are science fiction authors Dolores Cannon and David Icke. Starting in the 1980s, Cannon popularized the idea of alien starseeds who would help save humanity by assuming human form. Cannon, who wrote books until her death in 2014, is also known for linking her extraterrestrial theology to many well-known conspiracy theories. Meanwhile, British science fiction author David Icke, writing in the 1990s through today, added the idea that humanity was endangered by an evil cabal of reptilian shape-shifting aliens who often took human form (and most of whom were Jewish). Icke claims the cabal is working through the Illuminati and the New World Order. In other words, David Icke provided the building blocks for many QAnon conspiracy theories.

The main takeaway here is that New Age religions are discordant and adaptable by design and evolution. There has always been a choose-your-own adventure quality to New Age faiths, which share common concepts but not much else. Adaptability has always been one of its most important traits. This makes New Age faiths deeply idiosyncratic and personalized. They survive by empowering followers to make the faith their own. People can manifest the religion they want by picking the parts that speak to them and ignoring what doesn't feel right. They can always trust their intuition to make the right choices.

There's also the expectation that your beliefs will change and evolve as you learn more hidden secrets. Things you didn't understand before will now suddenly make sense. Much is hidden and there's always something to be learned. If something doesn't make sense, it's probably because you don't yet have the right knowledge or context to understand its meaning. All will be cleared up in time and study. Expecting your faith to evolve as you learn new and shocking "truths" makes it easier to change spiritual directions when something doesn't work out.

It all feels very much inspired by Ganesha, the Hindu god followed by Helena Blavatsky's leading Ascended Master Morya. Ganesha places obstacles in the path of humans, or removes them, to teach particular lessons and direct instruction. Ganesha closes pathways when you are finished with one thing and need to move in a different direction. By adopting that approach, Blavatsky built New Age spiritualism in the footprints of Hinduism, where you progressed through it over lifetimes of obstacles and learning. The soul's path is not an unobstructed straight line in this belief system. It's a strange, winding journey of discovery and evolution.

Today's New Age spiritualism is a diverse and ever-evolving mixture of different kinds of beliefs. Almost all New Age spiritualists offer a mish-mash of belief systems that work together with an improvisational quality. Every new sect borrows from the ones before it, as well as from their own contemporaries, and everyone puts their own unique spin on it. Start with Helena Blavatsky, toss in something from the Ballards, and add heavy doses of Dolores Cannon, and then maybe some Elizabeth Clare Prophet to spice things up. That's the base. Then you can add to it what you want to make it your own. It might be new holy figures, twisting around the theology, or inventing new elements. It doesn't have to make logical sense. These theologies are almost entirely about belief and faith, feelings and belonging, personalized to make people feel like they have special knowledge and a direct line to a world beyond the veil.

This mix-and-match spiritualism—the ultimate theological consumerism—is becoming increasingly popular. A 2022 survey found that, among all adult Americans, 69 percent agreed with statements that "everything is interconnected" and "everything happens for a reason." About 65 percent of respondents believed "we create our own reality," around 55 percent believed in karma, and more than 50 percent agreed that "nothing is as it seems." Nearly 40 percent of Americans believed in extraterrestrials and UFOs. Meanwhile, about a quarter of Americans believed key New Age concepts like manifesting, reincarnation, astrology, parallel realities, telepathy, and mediums or channeling.

A disproportionate number of the New Age spiritualists are middle-aged and older women. A 2018 Pew Research survey found that a full 70 percent of women believed in one of the following New Age concepts: psychics, reincarnation, astrology, and the idea that spiritual energy can be found in objects. Just over half—55 percent—of men do too. Interestingly, about 60 percent of Christians also believe in at least one of those concepts. Likewise, the number of Americans who report becoming more spiritual over time (as opposed to more religious) are skewed heavily to middle age and older people.

All those believers also means that New Age spiritualism is a big moneymaker. The global wellness industry in 2023 was estimated to be worth $6.3 trillion. That's up substantially from 2020, when it was worth about $4.5 trillion. Most of that is health, nutrition, weight loss, physical activity, and personal care and beauty. One market research firm estimated the "Spiritual & Devotional Products Market" as being worth $3.6 billion in 2022 and estimates that it will rise to $8.3 billion by 2031. Spiritual services are an even bigger moneymaker, with one market research estimate projecting that "Spiritual Products and Services" combined were worth $165 billion in 2023. The conspirituality market has some unknown, fractional share of that total.

The New Age market is a huge, diverse pool of spiritualists. There are true believers, clout chasers, spiritual entrepreneurs who are "there for the right reasons," and grifters who are there to make a buck by fleecing vulnerable people—and everyone in between.

Although the conspirituality end of the market can seem sketchy to many people, especially those who can't imagine how anyone can believe these things in the first place, it's important not to dismiss it as a collection of manipulative scam artists. Certainly, spiritual hucksters abound, but the line between them and the true believers isn't clear or fixed.

I think much of the questionable appearance is the product of an extremely competitive market. Spend any time in New Age circles, especially among the more fringe believers, and it becomes clear that there are far more people trying to make a living as seers and mystics or selling candles and crystals than the market can sustain. With so many people selling supernatural services and products—and many more joining their ranks every day—the competition is often brutal.

It's crucial to note that this competition is not always economic, either: routinely, it is for attention alone. Many of the new online prophets and gurus don't seem to be in it for the money. For them, creating a social media platform is about gaining followers, influence, or adoration. Some of them simply want to feel important or have people listen to their message. They don't ask for money, and they hold out their lack of material motives as a sign of the pureness of their faith.

The extreme competition means that everyone is in sales mode, even if they aren't trying to make money. With so many people in New Age circles vying for attention, many of them have come to rely on practices that border on predatory. They play on insecurities and fears while appealing to utopian hopes. That is especially true when it comes to middle-aged women and conspirituality.

During the pandemic, the purveyors of the "alternative wellness community" hit a gold mine with conservative middle-aged white women and adjusted their messaging for the new audience. As a result, much of New Age spiritualism has now geared itself toward that target demographic, trying to get them to watch their videos, purchase services, and buy their stuff. The promises they extend include unlocking new abilities, changing fates, or learning how to fulfill destiny as starseeds.

Typically, that training isn't free. Nor are the different sacred items needed to activate your full starseed powers and ready yourself for Ascension. It's all quite involved and requires a series of classes, healing and channeling sessions, and the purchase of an assortment of items, elixirs, and ointments, each of which has a unique spiritual purpose.

You can see how all this works together with Love Has Won, the online spiritual group that Yvonne started following during the pandemic. Love Has Won is a descendant of theosophy, the I AM movement, alien religions, and several other New Age traditions. Its leader, Amy Carlson, picked and chose elements of all those versions of New Age faith and then added her own new elements, including parts of the QAnon conspiracy theories. She branded her spiritual product and then put it out on the internet, looking to recruit believers who would purchase spiritual items at the Love Has Won online store.

As strange and unique as Love Has Won may seem, it is completely consistent with larger New Age theologies. Recombining and recycling ideas into a unique mélange of belief and practice and product, Love Has Won quickly found its way into the affections of women like Yvonne.

✦

When Yvonne discovered Love Has Won, she felt like she had found people who understood her. The main website drew her right in, using the same tactics as the starseed checklists: appealing to people who were looking for something to explain why life wasn't working out like they had hoped it would.

"Feel Blocked, Drained, Fatigued, Restless, Nausea, Achy, Ready to Give Up? We Can Help!" the front page of the Love Has Won website announced. "We are preparing everyone for a Full Planetary Ascension and provide you with the tools and techniques to assist you Home into The Light."

Yvonne found a spirituality that was a mix of past New Age theologies. There were the Ascended Masters of theosophy, featuring the one the Ballards added: Saint Germain. Amy Carlson had added help from Kryon of the Magnetic Service, as well as a new Ascended Master with whom she claimed to work directly: deceased comedian and actor Robin Williams. They were all working for the "The Galactic Federation of Light." Carlson claimed to be supervising "Ground Teams" of aliens who are here to do the heavy lifting on the local level. She spoke of Ascension and Disclosure and the jump to 5D, quoted Dolores Cannon, and included ideas from David Icke and QAnon.

When Yvonne's Christian church closed, she was drawn to the Love Has Won live streams that were broadcasting over the internet all day, every day. Those live streams reassured her that heaven-on-earth was just a click away. "We can Assist You in Awakening into 5D Reality, where your experience is one of Constant Joy, Wholeness of Being, Whole Health, Balanced, Happy, and Abundant," their website promised.

Yvonne started following the path to Ascension that ran directly through Love Has Won's elaborate online store. In exchange for a "donation," she could receive the goods and services needed to get her there. Everything for sale carried an "angel number" price tag, the repeating digits being a sign of deep spiritual significance. It was the kind of numerology that Helena Blavatsky had fused into the New Age movement from its very start. At the Love Has Won store, a one-hour Spiritual Intuitive Ascension Session was $77.77. A thirty-minute Unity Consciousness Family Session was $99.99. A one-hour 5D Astrology Compatibility Session & Report was $88.88, which was the same price as thirty minutes of Quantum Warrior Numerology. An Intuitive Galactic Insights Tarot Reading was $33.33, the same price as a bottle of Gaia's Colloidal Silver in the Baby & Child Wellness section.

Yvonne found the store stocked with all kinds of tantalizing spiritual items. Each one was allegedly a "high vibrational" product designed by "Mother God" (the name that Amy Carlson took). They all promised "to heal her children in an integral way." There were healing eyedrops, sunscreens, salves, "plasma" sprays, incense, and essential oils. The crystals and candles promised to "create a field of energy to boost any environment" and "move pure unconditional love across the planet." During the pandemic, Love Has Won sold a whole line of colloidal silver elixirs (branded Colloidal Silver, Gold, Platinum, along with a variety pack and a Colloidal Cocktail Kit). All falsely promised to boost immunity against the COVID virus and to be a cure-all for every other ailment. These elixirs were all supposedly mixed specifically for each individual client. "The custom alchemy blend of colloidals will be created based on your unique energetics, ailments, sensitivities, & needs," the website claimed. Love Has Won promised the colloidal silver products "will replace all prescription medication and 3D medicine to create a 5D healing experience."

The store also featured a wide assortment of Love Has Won branded merchandise. There were car magnets, buttons, t-shirts, sweatshirts, blankets, and tarot cards. You could buy canvas-print photos of Amy Carlson. Ringtone recordings of Carlson's voice were marketed as "Our Beloved Mother of All Creation's Wake Up Call Alarm Tone Trio Pack." There were personalized caricatures of Mother God and the main Love Has Won personalities, all hand-drawn by artistic followers. For kids, there were Love Has Won onesies, jars of Gaia's Baby ButtButt Balm, and colloidal silver drops in child dosages.

The diversity of products for sale was rivaled only by the array of spiritual services. There were Higher Consciousness Transmutations, which seemed to be pre-recorded guided meditations. They offered a variety of Intuitive Sessions, which were various kinds of counseling, including overcoming addiction, family therapy, and something called The Whole Kit and Kaboodle

Session Package. The other categories of spiritual services included: Participation Sessions, Tarot Sessions, and Astrology Services. There were several diagnostic services where group members claimed to be able to use telepathy to figure out what was spiritually wrong with you. One was called a Metaphysics Assessment; another was called Gaia's Naturopathy Healing Review. Once they diagnosed the problems, you could buy different kinds of Etheric Surgeries, a procedure by which one of the group members (or for a higher price, Mother God herself) would "remove all inorganic material" from your body by remotely going into your psyche and cleaning it up.

Perhaps the most ambitious project was an entire Love Has Won home education system, which claimed that "home schooling through the Crystal School framework is the future of our planet." Carlson denounced "compulsory education," which she described as "breeding grounds for programming, fear, compliance, and belief systems" that trained children to be "robotic." She said public school children were "forced to test and rank themselves based on a scale that has no relation to the unique genius that lies inside them." The Crystal School was also a response to fallout from the "greatest technological and social media boom of all time" and parents who suffered from a mass "addiction to external validation," which caused them to develop "a fakeness that creates a further disconnect with their children of what is real and what is illusionary." Regular public schools were teaching children to live in "a world that is devoid of real human connections, compassion, and love," as kids were only "taught to focus on what others think and how they appear to society."

Carlson imagined her Crystal School as the educational tool of a revolutionary spiritual movement. She was training the generation that is "here to quash government, educational, and legal systems that lack integrity." Her school would develop in children their "warrior spirit" and encourage their "tempers and fiery determination," training them to "lead with a machete, cutting down anything that lacks integrity." Parents were encouraged to identify their children as special advanced beings of a particular kind and then purchase the appropriate curriculum for "Crystal Children," "Rainbow Children," or "Indigo Children." "They are here to show us the way," Carlson said, and to "take us to the next level in our evolution, and reveal our inner power and divinity." Her school would cultivate a group of "human angels" by developing their innate spiritual gifts, psychic abilities, and paranormal powers, including telepathy.

There would be no reading, writing, science, or arithmetic curricula offered through the Crystal School. Instead, students had classes called Water Wisdom, Crystal Cures, Mushroom Magic, Medicinal Metals, and Energy Medicine, where they learned "the basics of everything from chakras, to meditation, to astrology." The homeschooling system had different lesson plans for every age group available for monthly subscriptions, which ranged from $11.11 for "Tier 1–Love Muffins" to $55.55 for the "Rainbow Warrior Tier," which gave access to the full range of educational materials.

In less than a year, Yvonne had purchased several hundred dollars' worth of products and services from the Love Has Won store. She spent $88.88 for Etheric Surgery with Mother God, where Carlson allegedly performed a remote healing ritual that happened without Yvonne having any contact with her or anyone else in Love Has Won. After that she bought a Custom Crystal Pyramid candle and a chakra candle set. Then she donated a few hundred dollars for a secret project related to the jump to 5D.

Not long after this, Carlson died from alcoholism, anorexia, and colloidal silver poisoning. Her followers claimed she had ascended. Soon after, the business manager ran off with the Love Has Won bank account, worth a few hundred thousand dollars.

Carlson's death sent Yvonne searching for a new guide for her spiritual development. She found her new guru the same way Guy and Edna Ballard claimed to have met Saint Germain: hiking around Mount Shasta.

✦

Yvonne made her pilgrimage to the New Age mecca of Mount Shasta, California, in the summer of 2021. She and Troy were there for what is called the Lion's Gate Portal: the eighth day of the eighth month, a time when many New Age spiritualists believe the stars in the constellation Leo align in ways that open an interdimensional portal. Every August 8, New Age pilgrims of all kinds descend on Mount Shasta. So it wasn't surprising that Yvonne ran into a mystic looking for new followers: the place was crawling with them.

To Yvonne, finding Keia felt like a miracle. Yvonne posted to Facebook that she had traveled to Mount Shasta with Troy "hoping the Universe will spread even more magic in my life!" The area around Mount Shasta caters to New Age pilgrims. "Crystal shops are everywhere," Yvonne told me months later. To assist the magic, Yvonne and Troy took psychedelic mushrooms at their campsite. When the effects started to kick in, they were watching a group of about twenty people in the campsite below them holding a ceremony. It was mostly white women in their thirties and forties, wearing white, natural cotton skirts and dresses, accessorized with beaded necklaces, bracelets, and anklets. Several also wore scarves or head coverings.

Suddenly, Yvonne was struck with an urge to join them. "I'm watching and I'm like, 'they know something.'" So she walked down to get a closer look, with Troy trailing along.

At a break in the ceremony, the leader of the group introduced herself as Keia. She was a white woman with long brown hair who said she was a medicine woman from Reno, Nevada, and had been trained to do this ceremony by Lakota Indians. Keia explained that the people with her were students she was training to become shamans like her. She asked what had brought Yvonne to Mount Shasta, and Yvonne started sharing her story. Soon after, Yvonne started crying, her shoulders heaving. "As soon as I met her, I started weeping," Yvonne later told me. "I mean, it was so crazy. The energy around her was so wild."

The next morning, Keia was leading a toad poison ceremony and invited Yvonne to join them. "It's a form of psychedelics," Yvonne told me, in case I didn't know. Yvonne said she went into her psychedelic trip with the intention of purging family trauma. "I feel like our family has tons of ancestral trauma that needs to be released and repaired," she told me. The toad poison hit Yvonne so hard she started throwing up. "I don't remember any of the experience, but I purged all day long," she said, laughing. Keia said she was leading another ceremony the next day and invited Yvonne to try again.

Yvonne sees her second toad poison trip as her big spiritual breakthrough. "This one I do remember, and I definitely purged all trauma." Looking back on it, Yvonne says she was given a gift because, as she puts it, "I was open to the spiritual part, and I was open to all of it. . . . I had prayed, 'God, show me the truth.'" "You gotta go inside, because your truth is inside. . . ."

Yvonne stops talking in mid-sentence. "Oh, my God," she says like something important has happened. "It's 4:44 here in Idaho," she tells me excitedly, referring to the time on the clock. Yvonne knows I know about "angel numbers": the popular belief in New Age circles that every time you notice a clock with an angel number, it's a sign of encouragement from beyond the veil. The most sacred angel number on the clock is 11:11. Whether morning or evening, 11:11 is the ultimate time-stamped blessing.

Yvonne continues to tell me about how God answered her call during the toad poison ceremony by freeing her from all the bad things that had happened in her childhood, as well as other family trauma stretching back across lifetimes. It was transformative for her. She says the ceremony caused her to see her mother differently at a time when she was ready to cut off contact completely. Now Yvonne felt empathy. "She had no mom and dad. How could she know how to be a parent? Right?" Yvonne explains. "She's never known how to comfort us."

Yvonne says that the toad poison trip caused her to realize "that everyone is broken and . . . we all just do what we think we're supposed to."

Most of what Yvonne describes fits with what scientists are discovering about how psychedelics can assist in the treatment of trauma, depression, and addiction. Hallucinogens like toad poison and psilocybin mushrooms have been shown to rewire the brain, creating new neural pathways that allow many people to be able to stop drinking or smoking, or to get lasting relief from depression and anxiety without relying on prescription medications. Those pathways opening up feel to many people like God-ordained experiences, where they believe they gain profound insights about themselves and their lives. The research is still in its infancy, because these substances were illegal for so long that scientists were prevented from studying them. Yvonne and many other New Age believers see those bans as having been created by pharmaceutical industry executives, who thought cannabis and psychedelics would put them out of business.

Yvonne was so inspired at the end of her weekend at Mount Shasta that she posted a series of photos of her experiences to Facebook. "I met part of my amazing soul family. One of which is a medicine woman!" she captioned a group photo. Yvonne then posted a selfie with Troy, where they both look completely baked. One of Yvonne's eyes is swollen from all the vomiting. "Experienced my first ceremony and released thousands of years of ancestral trauma," she captioned the photo. "One thing I noticed is my anger is gone!" A friend wrote in the comment section, "Lay off the peyote."

Instead of laying off psychedelics, Yvonne embraced them as her pathway to God. "I have done like mushrooms probably seven times this year, and it's all been about Spirit," she told me at the end of November 2021, less than four months after meeting Keia. "All my intentions are like, 'I'm fucking going to remember who the fuck I am. And I'm going to be doing what I need to do because I believe there is new earth,'" she says emphatically. "Consciousness is evolving. Our DNA is evolving," she explains. "If we lean into love. . . . We change the world instantly."

"God is going to open the door," she says, gratitude filling her voice. "Sometimes I just wanna lay down and kiss the ground and cry because I'm so grateful to be alive."

Yvonne pauses, and her tone gets more serious. "For fifty-three years, I hated being alive. I was so, so many times like, what the fuck are we here for? This sucks. Yeah, this sucks," she says, like someone liberated from a bad place. She reflects on her spiritual journey up to that point, which began after finding Love Has Won during the pandemic. "And for a year and a half now, I have been the happiest I have ever been, and I am so grateful to be alive because I know that God is love, and we are going to know in our lifetime—and it's gonna be soon, sister!" she says to me enthusiastically.

✦

Yvonne went all in with Keia. She signed up herself and Troy for "7 Moons: The Spiritual Warrior Training," a seven-month program to become certified in "Usui Holy Fire II, Reiki Master, Psychic Development, and Vibrational Therapy." The cost of the full program was several thousand dollars.

Keia pitched the 7 Moons course as not only becoming certified in these practices but also showing you how to start your own New Age business. "Want a career in alternative and holistic arts?" the flyer for the training program read. "Do you want to hone your spiritual gifts? Are you a lightworker, empath, psychic, healer, or prayer warrior? Then you are reading this for a reason." Keia's promotional material pitched a "7 month, in-person, Group training and Certification Program designed to give you an incredibly transformative balanced training and lifelong career as a professional in the holistic arts."

Keia's own journey to the holistic arts had been grim. Her Facebook page talked about "a childhood of abandonment, chaos, abuse, foster homes, drugs." In a newspaper article in the *Reno Gazette-Journal* from 2006, Keia talked about having wild weight fluctuations as a kid and being diagnosed with severe depression at fifteen. She developed a drug addiction and was in and out of treatment centers for years. She attempted suicide several times. Keia was on the cover of the *Reno Gazette-Journal* again, when her nine-month-old child died in the care of a babysitter who fled to the Philippines before local authorities could press charges. In 2011, the thirty-one-year-old Keia was on the front page promoting a new nonprofit she had created in honor of her son to lobby lawmakers to strengthen the laws against child abusers. "I want this to be a difference maker. I want to be a voice for children," Keia told reporters.

In 2022, Keia was using those experiences to recruit followers. Her Facebook page discussed how she had gone through a series of "the most gut wrenching initiatory experiences" to unlock her spiritual powers: "near death heart failure, the murder of my youngest son, divorce, homelessness, poverty, pain, single parenthood, loss, grief, confusion and so much more. All in such a swift and powerful way. Nearly bringing me to leave this earth." Having risen from the darkness, Keia advertised that she would teach others the ceremonies and techniques "that helped me heal years of addictions, depression, pain, trauma, and so much more."

As Yvonne advanced in her training, her devotion to Keia eventually began to sour. It happened when they reached the part of the course about how to run a New Age faith-related business. Yvonne became disillusioned when she realized Keia "does all this Seven Moons because it's all about money."

"I'm throwing so much money at her right now, it's like, holy shit, I don't even have any money and I'm throwing money at you girl," she said in a discouraged voice, when I asked how her training was going. "I know she's so gifted, and I'm not even questioning that. I get that these people have had to do it," she said of Keia and others charging money for spiritual training. "And I'm not faulting them, nor am I judging them for it. I'm just saying. Times have changed, and I feel that this is my calling."

Yvonne couldn't understand how the people preparing the world for Ascension could be so focused on making money. At one point, Keia told Yvonne, "within three to four months, you could start charging for this." Yvonne reported that she had replied to Keia, "I have no intention. If I have a gift from God, I'm giving that gift freely. Why would I charge somebody for a gift? I will trust the universe to provide for me. I won't take from my fellow humans."

Yvonne started to think that Keia and the others who looked at spirituality as a business were taking the wrong path. She began to think that Ascension would depend on starseeds with purer motives. "I think other people will join that calling as humanity. The system is going to crumble," she insisted. "They don't realize that, and that's the part I don't get," Yvonne said, perplexed by how the woman who was training spiritual warriors for battle seemed to have forgotten what the war was all about.

There was a shift in Yvonne after this epiphany. She would go on to become her own guru. She would be self-taught and trained, studying everything she could about New Age beliefs so that she knew her stuff better than anyone else. Yvonne wanted to be a teacher of theology and a living embodiment of its beliefs and ideals.

In the process, Yvonne would increasingly isolate herself from nearly everyone in her life.

✦ ✦

Yvonne and Tammy have dramatically different ways of practicing their faith. Yvonne needs a belief system that she can commit to entirely. As she always says, she was the kid who took the bus to Pentecostal churches on Sundays. Yvonne didn't just buy into the belief system of the Marines; she was determined to become a Marine drill instructor, a "Gunny" (a master Gunnery Sergeant) who instilled the values in others. When Yvonne found evangelical Christianity, she formed her identity around it, becoming one of her church's main youth leaders. Then when Yvonne found Love Has Won during the pandemic, she didn't just follow from afar; she studied Amy Carlson's beliefs and practices, digging up old videos and watching them all. She learned its theology by heart, bought candles, had etheric surgery, and donated to the Ascension fund. Yvonne did the same thing with Keia: threw herself into learning and studying the healing beliefs and rituals, until the student felt she knew more than the master. Yvonne chooses to believe in one thing and to invest herself entirely in its practices and theology.

Tammy's approach to faith is entirely different. While Yvonne orders her religion from the *prix fixe* menu, Tammy orders à la carte. She draws from different traditions and belief systems, picking what she likes, what makes sense to her, and what feels right. Christianity might always be the basis, but Tammy's Christianity doesn't track along with the Bible very closely. There's plenty of room for angels, demons, spirits, Ouija boards, angel numbers, reptilian overlords disguised as humans, Ascended Masters, and starseeds. Her beliefs are similarly eclectic: She sticks with an idea when it works for her and then changes her beliefs if something feels off about it. She doesn't require dogma or consistency.

Part of the difference is the role that faith plays in their lives. Yvonne is looking for something to believe in with all her being. Tammy is looking for something to get her through the day, something to hope for. Faith makes Tammy feel something other than depressed or worried or frustrated or mad. It's something she can care deeply about that won't betray her, abuse her, or tell her she's a bad mom. Faith keeps her from being bored. It's friends and a community. It's something to help her family, other people, or the world. Faith inhabits the part of her mind where things are easier, and her problems have been solved. It's figuring out how to make Ascension arrive more quickly so she can finally get to the good part of life.

Tammy's à la carte approach to faith explains how she became a starseed. She is a serial reposter of memes. That practice is far more common on the political right than on the left. On the right, visual memes are *the* central feature of social media culture. Each meme can only present a short, simple idea. Tammy spends much of her time online reposting memes, endlessly clicking on and sharing the ideas she likes. Sometimes she adds a comment. But mostly she just clicks away. As a result, her feed is filled with a wide assortment of ideas Tammy likes but that don't hold together very well if you tried to make sense of them as a whole.

Tammy has increasingly added more conspirituality to her beliefs over time. There are big gaps in Tammy's social media history because her accounts would get banned for posting QAnon memes and public health misinformation related to COVID. Piecing together what survives shows change over time toward a New Age brand of faith mixed with conspiracism. Prior to COVID, nearly all of Tammy's online spiritual references were Christian. During COVID, if you were following Tammy on social media, you began to see her getting heavily into QAnon. She starts in the shallow end, with "save the children" and reposting fearmongering around masking and vaccines. Then she starts reposting about the new world order, and eventually its memes about reptilian people. Other alien beings soon enter the mix. Ideas appear that are straight from the I AM movement, Elizabeth Clare Prophet, David Icke, and her personal favorite, Dolores Cannon, the mother of the concept of starseeds. Now Tammy's feed has a heavy New Age element. She's still obsessed with the QAnon conspiracy theories, and she constantly reposts those memes. But now the conspiracies she likes usually fit clearly within New Age theology. Like Yvonne, Tammy has positioned herself online as a keyboard warrior, battling in a great spiritual war, one click at a time.

Building faith from a mix of New Age concepts and conspiracism has led to an army of new online prophets. That's what happens when you encourage people to believe they are advanced beings with hidden special powers in a do-it-yourself theology that presents faith as a choose-your-own adventure. Many people convince themselves that they are seers, mystics, and starseeds here to save the world. The new prophets use much of the same language, but they all have their own niche and gimmick. There's strong social media branding to their prophetic videos, with standard openings and a common structure for each episode, built around formulaic bits.

Months after January 6, Tammy started following one of these online prophets, a man in his sixties with a long graying beard. He always wears a knit cap pulled down over his forehead, and he refers to himself as "Wizard."

Wizard works in construction and belongs to a motorcycle club. He grew up in southern California but now resides in the northern part of the state. Prior to the pandemic, his wife was heavily into health and wellness and sold essential oils online. In 2021, she became a devoted QAnon follower. Sometime after that, Wizard started posting QAnon-themed videos to the social media platform Telegram. Then he started moving in a more religious direction that blended his own take on Christianity with New Age conspiracism.

Wizard's audience is almost exclusively middle-aged white conservative women like Tammy. He appeals directly to them, "love bombing" them throughout his short videos, which last anywhere from a few minutes to about twenty. He sits close to the camera, so you can better see the expressions on his face and get the full effect when he stares directly into your eyes. He always starts by telling his followers, "I love you" and "you're special," often giving shout-outs to specific regulars by name. Sometimes he sends birthday wishes. Throughout the longer videos, he periodically blurts out a random "I love you" or "You're special," typically using the phrases as a transition between parts of the broadcast.

Wizard ends most videos with words of support and encouragement. He finishes the longer ones by playing the Christian worship song "When You Speak," and doing an exaggerated upper-body dance of awkward moves while sitting in the chair. While chair dancing, he tells his followers how much he loves them and how proud he is of them. He gives words of affection and validation that many older women probably don't hear much anymore, if they ever did.

From a theological standpoint, Wizard is all over the place. Most episodes begin with him swearing in on a Christian Bible promising to tell the truth, finishing the oath with, "So help me Dad," rather than "So help me God." The clock on the wall behind him is perpetually at 11:11. He talks about 3D and the move into 5D. Wizard mentions Jesus in cryptic ways, often appearing to suggest that Wizard himself might be the Messiah. He'll post memes that have his profile next to Jesus to suggest that they look similar (he does the same thing with QAnon favorite John Kennedy Jr.). Wizard never makes the claim directly. It's all hinting and innuendo, another puzzle for his conspiracy-minded followers to figure out. Some of them thought Wizard took things too far when he posted a meme that morphed his face into the Shroud of Turin, believed by many to be the burial linen placed over the body of Jesus Christ that bears his facial impression. Wizard responded to the complaints by announcing, "I'm not saying I'm Jesus. I'm a close relative."

It's not all love and uplift. Most broadcasts feature a segment in which Wizard unleashes his anger and vengeance. The subject of his rage is always different. Sometimes it's QAnon themed, or it's COVID related, or he goes off on Democrats. He frequently yells at followers who question or criticize him. The intensity varies as well. Sometimes he's just mad; other times he rages, shouting at the camera, pointing his finger in a menacing way, often strongly suggesting the problem will be solved by violence in the end.

And then he brings himself back down, blurts out an "I love you very much," and it's on to the next segment or the chair dancing close. The way Wizard bookends his sudden angry rants with expressions of love reminds me of the Two Minutes Hate from George Orwell's dystopian novel *1984*, where the public is allowed to vent its rage by shouting about their enemies for two minutes before resuming their usual demeanor.

I started watching Wizard's videos after Tammy kept telling me about him in our conversations. I was concerned about the way Tammy was talking about him, as if she might have a crush. You could see it in the video she posted to Wizard's Telegram channel in September 2022, after Wizard's broadcast about the death of Queen Elizabeth II, who in QAnon lore is a leading reptilian in the cabal. "The Wicked Queen is finally announced dead!" Tammy says with jubilation in her voice. "That's awesome news! Awesome, awesome, awesome!" she says excitedly. "Never thought I'd be so happy about hearing about somebody's death. But here we are."

In the video, Tammy widens her eyes in a knowing way. "Awesome. What a great day to be alive. Especially for the kids, man. They're gonna have such an awesome, beautiful, wonderful life when this is all over and done." Tammy continues, "I got my seatbelt buckled, per Wizard. I'm not going nowhere. Just hanging on tight." She smiles, almost shyly. "Love you Wizard," she says. She speaks the next words slowly, pausing between each one for emphasis. "I love you so much. Thank you for everything you do. Thank you. You're awesome." She gets tongue-tied, smiles, and eventually just points her finger at the camera, intending her words for Wizard. "Yeah, you."

Tammy recorded a similar video the next day. "I'm not feeling very good today," she says as the video opens. "I'm hoping it's just Ascension symptoms. Woke up with a headache, nauseated, not feeling too good." "I just wanted to say hi again, and I love you guys," she says and pauses for a beat. "I love you, Wizard." She asks for prayers for a neighbor whose husband had passed away nine months earlier, a death she had just found out about. "Thanks, Wizard, for that," she says, referring to his personal prayers. "I love when you're all fired up like that," she says to Wizard directly. "You get me fired up. And I think we were all pretty fired up yesterday after hearing about, finally, the lizard dying," Tammy says referring the Queen's death.

"Can't wait to see what's next. Hopefully it's Biden dying," she says and scoffs. "Or the witch Hillary. One of them. All right, but love you guys. Can't wait to hear you later, Wizard. Love you."

Tammy recorded many videos that year for Wizard and the people she calls her "Wizard Fam." She always directs comments specifically to him and says, "I love you, Wizard" at least once. Many of these videos include responses to Wizard's "homework" assignments for his followers. The homework involves creating videos and answering questions about themselves. For example, one homework question was, "What is your superpower?" Tammy's answer was, "Love you, Wizard. Superpower: resilience."

In October 2022, Tammy recorded a "homework" just prior to leaving for a candlelight vigil after Sabrina's suicide. She is dressed in black with a leopard print headband across her forehead. The first question of the homework assignment was about her favorite color, the second asked what color she wore that made her feel pretty. The third question was: "When did you last go to church?"

Tammy says she last went to a church in 2019 hoping to make friends, but "Spirit inside told me something was wrong there. . . . Now, my church is here," she says, putting her hand over her heart. "Wizard, thanks for ordaining all of us. I'm glad that you baptized me." She smiles and almost bats her eyes at the camera. She speaks with confidence and seems almost giddy for a moment. "You gave us the confirmation, appreciate that, thank you." She gives a thumbs up, kisses her hand, blows a kiss and points her finger at the camera with an almost flirty smile on her face. "You're the best," she says to Wizard.

In December 2022, Tammy recorded a video for Wizard because, as she put it, "I just wanted to tell you how I'm feeling right now. First, I got water, so I'm feeling clean. I've been washed by the Holy Spirit, I do believe." She pauses and her tone changes, she starts smiling. "Remember what it was like, how you felt when you were falling in love?" Her smile widens, her eyes look down for a moment. "That's how I feel. I feel like I'm falling in love." Her tone changes. "I am in love," she says definitively. "When I look in the mirror, I'm half expecting to see somebody different. And actually I do see somebody totally different." She sighs. "I love you guys."

Tammy eventually stopped devoting herself to Wizard and his circle. She and some of the women she had met on his channel started to become more skeptical of him and his claims, especially as he portrayed himself as a Christ-like figure. The women distanced themselves from him as a group, and they have kept their online friendships with each other intact. They continued to post videos, now just for each other, so they could talk about their lives.

That group of women has gotten even more into New Age faith, searching and learning on their own, and rebranding themselves "Sistars," a combination of "sister" and "starseeds." Now it's Tammy and her friends leading their own spiritual awakening, based on what they read on the internet, the videos they watch, and the memes they repost. After following Wizard's belief system for about a year, Tammy is back to picking and choosing her beliefs on her own.

Tammy has decided her path is helping to lead the Ascension into 5D. A good part of Tammy's excitement about 5D is rooted in her belief that it will bring her wealth. Tammy is a believer in what is called the NESARA (National Economic Security and Recovery Act) conspiracy. It's a wild story that claims that Bill Clinton allegedly signed a law releasing trillions of dollars to the American people and that all the beneficiaries' information was contained on a computer housed in the World Trade Center. Most versions have George W. Bush ordering planes to fly into the buildings on September 11, 2001, an hour before the money was scheduled to be released to the public. The theory holds that Bush then started the Iraq War as a distraction.

What happens after that varies depending on the telling, but the gist of it is that the Ascended Masters, with Jesus and Saint Germain in command, will force through the release of the funds. All debts will be canceled, and everyone will get rich beyond their wildest dreams. Tammy thinks she's on the beneficiary list and that Ascension will bring her earthly prosperity and then transform her soul.

Not everyone is on that list, according to the NESARA conspiracy. Lots of people don't get the money. They don't make it through Ascension, either. In Tammy and Yvonne's world, most of these people are reptilians, and they will be defeated and perish. Many others will be left behind because they remain too spiritually asleep to save themselves. Others just aren't cut out for 5D.

This is one of the places where the bigoted underside of New Age theology raises its ugly head. As it turns out, many of the people who aren't cut out for 5D are the same kinds of people targeted by the right today. It's Jews, and people who aren't white (especially people who support Black Lives Matter), along with trans people, gay people, and those who support a woman's right to control her own reproductive health. As we will soon see, however, homosexuality and abortion support aren't deal breakers in conspirituality circles like they are in evangelical ones. And neither are trans rights.

In other words, it all gets pretty complicated, and unquestionably bizarre.

CHAPTER 7

Culture Wars

Yvonne and I arrived at Tammy's place a day after Yvonne was sentenced to two-and-half-years for her crimes on January 6. Tammy lives about twenty-five miles outside of Williamsport, Pennsylvania, near a remote village that is a stop along a winding road called the Appalachian Thruway. The township's population fell to under one thousand in the last census. Nearly 99 percent of the inhabitants are white. The roads to get here snake between stubby mountains. Driving around in the last days of summer feels like you're sinking into different shades of green and brown. Tammy's home at the time was a weathered trailer that her son rented, where she was staying while he was in prison on yet another parole violation.

Tammy and Yvonne had never met. Originally, I had no intention of bringing them together. I had planned to be in Washington, DC, for Yvonne's sentencing, and then I was going to rent a car and drive up to see Tammy. When I made the arrangements, I had assumed Yvonne would be flying home after her hearing.

Instead, about a month before I was going to fly out to DC from my home in California, Yvonne asked me if I would be willing to drive back with her to Idaho. Her daughter, who lived in northern Virginia, was moving back to Boise, and Yvonne was supposed to drive her car across country. But then her son who lived in Ohio went through a breakup and moved back home as well, leaving behind *another* car that needed to get to Boise. Yvonne asked if I would be willing to drive with her from Virginia to Ohio after her sentencing; then she could drive one car, and I could drive the other back to Idaho. I said I could do it, provided we built in time to stop at Tammy's place on the way.

Another twist brought a British filmmaker along for the ride. I had been doing research for a documentary company based in London, which was producing a transnational set of films about polarization in today's world. The director, Liz Smith, had become intrigued by the stories I had been sharing with her about the women of January 6, and she decided she wanted to focus the American segment of the film series on my research on women and conspiracy theories. She asked if I'd be willing to let her film me and whether I thought Tammy might consent to being on camera. Tammy was excited by the idea. When I told Yvonne about the documentary, she said she would participate, too.

So on a sunny day, still warm enough for short sleeves, the three of us—Yvonne, Liz, and I—pulled into Tammy's town late in the afternoon. I was driving the car and Liz sat next to me in the passenger seat. She had mounted a camera on the dashboard to record the conversations as we drove. Those mostly involved Yvonne leaning forward from the backseat and explaining the details of various conspiracy theories to Liz and me. She barely paused during the entire four-hour drive.

When we got to Tammy's place, I made introductions, and Yvonne and Tammy started conversing, knowing they were fellow conspiracists. Liz watched in fascination as they moved quickly into the language of conspirituality.

The first moment we were alone, Liz made an aside to me. "My God," she said with amazement, "they've just met—and they finish each other's sentences!" She was shocked by how Yvonne and Tammy knew the same stories by heart, used the same New Age words and phrases, and expressed the same beliefs on nearly every issue we discussed. The next day, when Liz filmed the two women sitting on lawn chairs in the field outside the trailer, they occasionally answered questions in unison. They had so thoroughly internalized a range of conspirituality concepts that they both responded reflexively.

Later, when we were filming inside the trailer, they expressed the same opinions when it came to culture-war topics like homosexuality, trans rights, and abortion. The conversations were revealing. At one point we were talking about Sabrina, Tammy's trans daughter. The film captures our conversation.

I ask Tammy how she felt when Sabrina had announced she was trans. "I felt confused. Bad. And angry," Tammy says candidly, taking time with each word. "But I knew it was either have a relationship with my son—" she pauses and corrects herself, "or daughter. I chose to accept it the best that I could," she says, a degree of resignation in her voice.

Yvonne interrupts her and speaks directly to me. "I love you," she says in a laudatory tone. "I feel like you so honor her by continuing to say 'Sabrina.' And I love that you are very aware of that even when she's not here."

Tammy then says to me, "*This* is the special thing that you were supposed to do." Tammy is referring to her belief that I had come into her life for a reason. She thinks that the reason may be related to Sabrina, a conviction based on events I'll discuss later in chapter 9.

"I know you sometimes say 'Wayne,'" I reply to Tammy. "I'm going to always say Sabrina."

Tammy says, "When he was alive, I called him Sabrina." After a beat, she adds, "For the most part. Like, sometimes I forgot and screwed up." She gets more animated. "And *believe me*, he'd let me know!" She catches herself again, "or *she'd* be like," Tammy mimics her daughter's voice, 'Maaaaah! *Sabrina!*'"

Yvonne chimes in again, and the conversation takes a turn. "I understand why you're honoring Sabrina," she says, clearly trying to be empathetic to Tammy's situation. I hold my breath. "But let's be real. Transitioning? You're fucking with God." Yvonne's tone becomes harder, more unyielding. "It wasn't meant to be. It wasn't natural. And that's where they got us. *They* are using the transgender movement!"

"Who's *they*?" I ask, concerned by how Tammy might react to the sudden shift in the conversation.

"The Illuminati!" Yvonne replies like I wasn't understanding something obvious. "The ones that created it, the ones that run Big Pharma." Yvonne shifts back to talking about trans people. "I doubt most of them would transition if they knew that it was going to kill them."

I was familiar with this conspiracy theory. Many people in QAnon and conspirituality circles believe that the hormones some trans people take eventually kill them. As with many conspiracies about minority social groups, this one about trans people gives followers a reason to oppose gender-affirming medical care without feeling like they are being bigots.

"You're talking about the hormones?" I ask Yvonne, knowing where this was going.

"Yes," she answers—and then goes back to using male pronouns when talking about Tammy's trans child. Yvonne veers next toward reincarnation as part of the explanation. "Of course, neither of us had the consciousness to say to him: 'You've done lifetimes as a woman; of course you're gonna feel like a woman. But you're here to learn the lessons as a man; you gotta do both. You need to understand both the feminine and the masculine.'"

"You wanna dress like a woman?" Yvonne says in a more demonstrative voice. "Go ahead, if that makes you feel good, then do whatever you feel like. I'm not trying to change who they are. But I am trying to say, you are in this body by choice. You *chose* to come as a man. Just because you feel like a woman, you need to understand, that's because you lived *lifetimes* as a woman."

Tammy nods in agreement. "That's right, I told him that. I told him, I said, 'You were probably a woman in maybe your last lifetime.'" Tammy's voice gets more animated. Tammy says she told Sabrina about her own past lifetimes. "I said, 'I *know*, I was a man. I know, for a *fact!*'"

"Yes!" Yvonne replies, like Tammy has just given definitive proof of the concept. "Look, God wouldn't have made you a male if you weren't intended to be a male in this life."

As the conversation continued, it was clear that conspirituality had also changed their thinking about homosexuality, something I already knew about Yvonne. The changes had been stark. At the height of Yvonne's evangelical Christianity, her nephew, who was in his twenties, came out to her. Steeped in conservative Christian dogma at the time, she advised him to speak to a pastor who considered homosexuality a sin. When Yvonne's own son announced he was gay, she was still with her evangelical church and had the same negative reaction, struggling with her son's sexuality.

All that changed with Yvonne's embrace of New Age spiritualism. You can read the results in the Facebook post Yvonne wrote to celebrate her son's twenty-first birthday in 2023. "I've learned so much from this amazing human being," Yvonne writes, calling her son "my child in this 3D Matrix but . . . so much more on the other side of the veil." He "was always different, he always beat to his own drum and Troy and I really tried to honor that even in our very limited consciousness," Yvonne writes with a tone of regret.

She blames the way her evangelical church had "programmed" her to see her son as sinful and says how grateful she is that "I was able to recognize and change mine." "We've all been given a whole lot of lies with very little truth sprinkled in," she writes. "There is a small group of people who have controlled this Earth and the narrative. They created the illusion of borders and separateness. They taught us division and lies and hate. We are born loving beings. Anything other than love is programmed into our being by all those around us," Yvonne says to a Facebook list that includes many evangelical Christians. "I had no idea the lessons and what I learned until I finally broke free from the beLIEf system I had bought into." She intentionally capitalized the "LIE" in belief to emphasize what she sees as false Christian programming.

Yvonne concludes by directing words to her son. "You . . . have taught me how to release so much of that programming and to see humans for who they are and how they love, not what belief system they buy into. Thank you for choosing me. Thank you for being an example and thank you for honoring love. You are a beautiful soul."

Yvonne underwent a similar spiritual conversion on the issue of abortion, although not quite as dramatic. "I had two abortions," she announces to me and Tammy during our conversation in Tammy's trailer, "so I was, because of those and the regrets, I was super pro-life." Yvonne has posted this same story on Facebook. She says she is still pro-life but no longer believes abortion is murder like she did prior to her New Age awakening in 2020. "What I learned later from Dolores Cannon is the soul doesn't come into the body until at birth," Yvonne explains. In her eyes, there is no soul involved in abortion, so there is no physical or spiritual crime. "There's no judgment. I get that now and I finally could forgive myself after all of that," she says before changing her tone again. "But to still be a spiritual being, I'm still going to be pro-life because that's what I want." Her voice fills with emotion, "To me, the fact that we kill our own kind is as low dimensional as you can fucking get!"

Tammy nods in agreement. "That's right," she says.

Yvonne then explains that her pro-life politics set her apart from her former guru, Keia, which was a factor in Yvonne turning away from her. The divide became apparent to Yvonne during the summer of 2022 when Yvonne was in Reno, Nevada doing the 7 Moons Spiritual Warrior training with Keia and her other students. During a break in training, someone looked at their phone and announced the Supreme Court's decision in Dobbs vs. Jackson Women's Health Organization, the ruling that overturned a woman's right to control her own reproductive health. "I thought for sure that they would all be pro-life because of the fight for life, and knowing what life means, and that's why we're here, and the spirituality," Yvonne said, as if there was a standard New Age doctrine on abortion. "But every single one of them were appalled that Roe v. Wade was taken away, and I thought, ohhhhh," she says with her voice trailing off, as if she's reliving the moment. Not long after that, Yvonne decided she had outgrown Keia and began training on her own.

What you can see in Yvonne and Tammy are the ways that New Age conspiracism has tempered their conservatism and made them, in many ways, more tolerant people. When scholars examine the role of women in right-wing movements, they typically focus on how women give cover for extreme far-right rhetoric. Women tend to phrase their views as an extension of their roles as mothers and caregivers, rather than as an expression of political ideology or bigotry. In some ways at least, conspirituality seems to be doing the opposite. Many conservative women who have adopted New Age beliefs like Yvonne and Tammy are softening and sometimes changing their traditional views. It's not a total liberalization of their beliefs—far from it, as we shall see. But New Age theologies seem to act as moderating forces with many women on the right. They have even caused some to adopt progressive-*ish* ideals on a range of issues—at least at first glance.

Using a broader lens, we could say that conservative women are returning New Age spiritualism to its late nineteenth-century origins. In fact, you might be surprised by how much today's conservative followers of conspirituality have in common with Helena Blavatsky, the founding mother of theosophy, the root of modern New Age religions.

✦

There are many photographs of Helena Blavatsky, and she isn't smiling in any of them. The photos show a serious and imposing figure. Blavatsky had a round, heavy-set face with large blue eyes. Her hair was typically parted in the middle and tied up in a bun. She dressed modestly, wore black or subtle colors, and was often pictured with a shawl draped around her shoulders or covering her neck. Her facial expression is nearly the same in every photo. It looks like she purposefully drained herself of all emotion before the photographer clicked. She always appears inscrutable, even bored. Looking at a photo of her, you would never know that this was an extremely charismatic person who sought to break society out of the rigidity of Victorian norms.

Blavatsky was a rebel in her own day, an early Progressive Era reformer. The Progressive Era wasn't all muckrakers exposing corporate malfeasance and the terrible working conditions at factories, or trustbusters creating the regulatory state. Blavatsky represented a different part of the Progressive

Era, one that engaged in social experimentation and developed new ways of thinking about sex and race. Some of what she stood for was quite democratic and forward-looking. Other parts of her worldview, especially when it came to questions of race, were not democratic at all. This was also true of most other white Progressive Era reformers.

Blavatsky's biggest social innovations came in the ways she elevated women and female spirituality. Blavatsky wasn't just the mother of New Age spiritualism; she made sure that women had a prominent role in every facet of it. She was a leader among nineteenth-century feminists, believing in the equality of the sexes, the "brotherhood of men and women," and tolerance for differences between them. She wanted to give women spiritual independence, power, and authority in theological matters as well as within earthly organizations. Although Blavatsky was married, she downplayed the importance of marriage and motherhood. She believed the demands of being a wife and mother prevented women from attaining the higher reaches of spiritual enlightenment, because women raising large broods of children were too focused on domestic duties. Who could concentrate on attaining enlightenment with all the constant distractions from kids?

Blavatsky thought that true enlightenment meant balancing the Divine Feminine and Masculine into an androgenous blend. She believed in reincarnation and taught that human enlightenment came after a person's soul cycled through all life experiences. In Blavatsky's theology, your current human form is just the most recent vessel your soul has occupied. If you're an "old soul," you've already progressed through many different human lifetimes—sometimes living as men, other times as women. The most advanced souls—the ones closest to true spiritual enlightenment—have attributes of both male and female. In her theology, the highest-level spiritual beings are ethereal and appear without gender.

This same theological worldview is what helps Tammy and Yvonne make sense of gender, homosexuality, and trans people, like Tammy's daughter Sabrina. They see homosexuality and trans identity as an issue of people being born into one sex who are experiencing echoes from their recent past lives. They believe homosexuality is what happens when a soul that has been living as a male for one or more lifetimes is reincarnated as female (or when a string of female lifetimes is followed by life in a male vessel). Following Blavatsky, they think that when the soul crosses from male to female (or female to male), it carries characteristics from the previous life into the new host body. To Yvonne and Tammy, homosexuality is the echo of a past life (or lives) lived as a different sex than the vessel into which they were born for this current lifetime.

To them, trans identity is just a more extreme form of Blavatsky's imagined switched-at-birth phenomenon. They think someone becomes trans when they were a different sex in their immediate past life. The soul might have no experience with the sex it is born into, so it feels like it's in the wrong body. That dysphoria might last for a few lifetimes. Perhaps the soul transitions into homosexuality before the memories of past lifetimes fade and the new sex and gender role become more familiar. Yvonne and Tammy both maintain their own versions of this belief, but the general concept is the same one Helena Blavatsky articulated.

They also share Blavatsky's views on abortion. Helena Blavatsky didn't believe abortion was murder in the conventional sense—but she didn't support it, either. She didn't think the soul enters a human vessel until after a baby is born. As she put it, "It is perfect nonsense to say the child has a soul and is a human being before it is born." Theosophists debated about when humanness happens. Some thought it occurred within the first seven months. Others thought it took more like seven years for a soul to be fully conscious in a new host.

While Blavatsky thought abortion might not kill a human with a soul, she opposed it anyway, because she thought it was compounding the sin of an unwanted pregnancy. She said an abortion was the "willful and sinful destruction of life, and interference with the operations of nature, hence—with KARMA." She believed abortion should be punished like a suicide attempt, which was often treated as a misdemeanor in the nineteenth century—except that, in this case, it was, as she put it, a "double suicide." To Blavatsky, abortion was still taking life or the potential for it—a view that is very much like what Yvonne and Tammy believe. When Yvonne calls abortion "as low dimensional as you can fucking get" she is paraphrasing Blavatsky, equating supporters of abortion with low-level souls in the enlightenment hierarchy.

In this way, Yvonne and Tammy have more in common with the original version of New Age theology than the liberal one espoused by Keia, Yvonne's former guru. Keia is a leader of New Age programs that focus on getting women in touch with the "Wild Woman archetype" and exploring their "wild and untamed heart." In New Age circles, the "Wild Woman" is innately sexual, and part of the training is drawing out latent sexuality as an expression of the Divine Feminine.

Helena Blavatsky would view Wild Woman trainings as the opposite of enlightenment, which was asexual in every sense of the word. Like many Progressive Era reformers, Blavatsky saw sexual self-control as the key to success in life, human evolution, and spiritual enlightenment. To advance as a race, species, or individual soul, people needed to observe strict discipline and carefully regulate their behavior, according to Blavatsky. She fell into a large group of Progressive reformers who thought the greatest impediment to human advancement was sexual lust. These reformers put great effort into developing strategies and techniques for reducing sexual urges. Most of them refused to drink alcohol or take drugs and were strict vegetarians, because they believed meat and dairy promoted lustful desires just like drugs and alcohol did. (The inventors of graham crackers and corn flakes developed those products specifically as part of a bland, vegetarian diet that inhibited sexual urges.) Helena Blavatsky portrayed herself as someone who had conquered her lusts. She even proudly declared that she had never had sex, despite being married.

This brings us back to those joyless photos of Blavatsky. Her constant dour appearance was likely the intentional pose of a woman trying to project asexuality and self-control. She was undoubtedly signaling her higher state of consciousness by portraying herself as androgynous, unfeminine, and devoid of the slightest trace of sensuality. The image Blavatsky projected put her closer to the genderless, ethereal beings whose souls had achieved true enlightenment.

Blavatsky's beliefs about sexual self-control also placed something else at the core of New Age theology: white supremacy. It doesn't take a lot of research to uncover the disturbing racist underpinnings of New Age spiritualism. It does, however, take us into an elaborate and bizarre world of submerged continents, angelic creatures, and advanced beings with a third eye.

✦

Helena Blavatsky believed that all humanity originated in genderless, ethereal beings. She claimed that, as the angelic creatures started to take human forms, different "Root Races" developed at each stage of human evolution. Over time, she contended, a hierarchy of races formed based on which groups could control their sexual lusts. The "higher races" were the ones that remained pure by only having sex for procreation with other humanoids.

According to Blavatsky, the most advanced beings lived on the continent of Atlantis. They had third eyes in the middle of their foreheads, which gave them great spiritual insight. Those psychic powers didn't save Atlantis from sinking in the great flood, which, in Blavatsky's alternative history of the world, also submerged the continent of Lemuria, a different civilization of advanced beings located in the Pacific Ocean. The highest remaining race after the flood, according to Blavatsky, were the Aryans, who retained supernatural powers by mating with the survivors of Atlantis.

Blavatsky claimed that the Aryans spread to Europe and India, making these the most advanced centers of spiritual enlightenment on the planet in the modern day. You can see where all of this is going, and how easily this notion was adapted to ideas of "race science" and the imagined "Aryan" past that fueled the Nazi movement. Branches of Nazism were steeped in occult beliefs just like this—beliefs that drew upon theosophy and other esoteric beliefs of the era.

In Blavatsky's system, the United States is the epicenter of the next great evolution in humanity. She believed the white Aryan descendants who had emigrated from Europe to America would develop into a new race that regained the lost supernatural powers of Atlantis as they evolved into a higher state of consciousness. She said the next evolution had already begun, making the United States the spiritual capital of the New Age and white Americans its chosen people—at least the ones who controlled their sexual urges and retained racial purity.

White people rose to the top of Blavatsky's hierarchy, and she believed that the "lower races" were destined to die off over time, just like previous "lesser races" she conjured in her imagination had done in the ancient past. Blavatsky believed that the "lesser races" were the ones whose ancestors didn't control their lusts and had sex for pleasure with the other creatures of ancient earth. She said their descendants—who she identified as Africans and Indigenous peoples—could not control their sexual lusts, and so they remained in spiritual and evolutionary stasis, unable to progress like the white "higher races" had done. Blavatsky added Jews to the list, because she saw them as a lesser hybrid race of nomadic peoples. According to Blavatsky, most of the earth's "lesser races" had died out long ago, which is the same eventual fate she projected for most non-white peoples in the modern world. In Blavatsky's words, the "lesser races" "were not ready . . . to occupy the form of men destined for incarnation in higher intellectual races." As a result, "the tide-wave" of human and spiritual evolution "has rolled past them to harvest experience in more developed and less senile stocks" of men.

This kind of racist thinking easily blended with more radical forms of white supremacy both then and now. Although modern theosophists downplay the links between Blavatsky's theology and racist extremism, there are clear connections. A Russian theosophist produced the *Protocols of the Elders of Zion*, a book from 1903 that the remains highly influential in extremist and antisemitic circles. It claims that a Jewish cabal is trying to rule the globe by creating a new world order. Blavatsky herself adopted the Hindu swastika as one of theosophy's primary symbols. Blavatsky did not advocate racial or religious genocide. But she was convinced the "lower races" were destined for a naturally occurring extinction.

Given the racist origins of New Age religions, it's not surprising that the followers of New Age beliefs, whether they identify as political liberals or conservatives, are almost exclusively white. A Pew Research survey from 2014 revealed that 91 percent of the followers of New Age religions were white people who were at least third-generation Americans. In other words, New Age beliefs are not attracting immigrants or their children. They appeal to white people whose European immigrant families long ago Americanized and blended into the general identifier of "white"—the demographic out of which many New Age spiritualists believe the next evolution in human consciousness will come.

Part of the turn to conspiracism among white people today is tied into that demographic reality. Studies show that racial groups that feel aggrieved or perceive a loss of their group's status relative to others are more likely to turn to conspiracism. We have long known that conspiracy theories are especially strong among racial minority groups that have experienced extreme prejudice and repression. In the United States, Black Americans have long been regarded as the most likely demographic to believe anti-government conspiracies, largely due to all the real and awful things the government has done to that population (such as the forced sterilization of Black women, the Tuskegee syphilis study, and a wide range of medical experiments performed on incarcerated Black men). Black conspiracism grows out of lived experiences and genuine horrors inflicted by governments and the medical establishment, which, for example, used to get most of its research cadavers by robbing Black graveyards.

White conspiracism seems more rooted in the perception of loss in social status, in part driven by the advances by non-white Americans as a result of the civil rights movements of the 1960s and '70s. Many white Americans experienced the end of segregation and government attempts to redress the effects of past racial discrimination as oppression against white people. Many white Americans became increasingly conscious of their own whiteness and their place as a social group. The rise in a sense of white grievance and victimization in recent decades has led to a steady rise in the willingness of white Americans—especially working-class whites—to believe in conspiracies that explain their feelings of decline.

All this helps explain why New Age spiritualism was so ripe for its recent right-wing turn and the rise of conspirituality. We are seeing the re-emergence of bigotry and antisemitism that have always been part of the theological substratum of the New Age movement. Many of today's New Age believers openly and actively denounce bigotry. But there is no denying that racism was part of its founding theology, and it remains central to some branches of this eclectic faith. Even when latent, those elements are not far below the surface, especially in the conspirituality embraced by white conservative women.

In some cases, conspirituality is expressed through outright bigotry. The more extreme social media accounts today repost New Age concepts in clear neo-Nazi themed memes and posts. The most overtly racist accounts appear to be run by far-right men who use New Age concepts in transparent attempts to mainstream racism, antisemitism, homophobia, and transphobia in that community.

Overall, however, the bigotry in New Age spiritualism takes more muted forms, thus allowing it to appear innocuous to white women first encountering its messaging. Mainstream conspirituality tends to act less like a theology in which the apocalypse ends in a white nationalist race war and more like bigotry-lite. Conspirituality is quite clearly a movement built on white identity, as is the liberal version of New Age spiritualism, and there are racist undertones to many of the beliefs that women express. But the flexibility in New Age theology—and its underlying assumptions that humans learn, and their beliefs evolve—creates more theological space for adherents to rethink social relations and make changes in their own "programming."

The results are often contradictory. Today's New Age spiritualism pushes its followers to think of themselves as open-minded, thoughtful, and tolerant advanced beings from a higher consciousness. But as we've seen, the faith's history is riddled with racism. By middle age, most conservative women seem able to move only so far beyond the beliefs and prejudices they grew up with. In the end, their faith is a complicated mix of aggrieved white identity and a hope for a New Age in which race, class, and gender don't matter. It's easy to question the commitment to earthy equality, however, given how strongly these same people oppose the policies that might create that world and how they demonize the people who champion them.

Tammy's beliefs perfectly capture the tensions and complexity of conspirituality when it comes to social and cultural issues. On one hand, Tammy is an online warrior fighting for the political right against imagined enemies on the left. On the other hand, her spiritual views have softened some of her own ideas—at least when it comes to her family members.

✦⋆✦
⋆✦⋆

The Mormon missionaries started visiting Tammy when she was living in her son's trailer, around the same time that Yvonne and I visited her. "Expecting Sisters from the Mormon church," she texted me one day in early September 2023.

"Mormon church?" I texted back, curious to know more.

Some missionaries had come to Sabrina's ex-wife's place while Tammy was babysitting her grandkids, and Tammy had given them her cell phone number when they asked for it. "Since I have no life, I said sure. Lol," she texted back. "I'll put out my tarot cards, they will think I'm a witch. Lol. Jk. But I figured why not."

After that, two Latter-Day Saints missionaries in their early twenties texted Tammy relentlessly, trying to schedule weekly visits to discuss the Book of Mormon. Nearly every day, Tammy woke up to a "good morning angel Tammy" text from the young women. They would send a scripture passage for Tammy to consider and ask if she had read the parts of the Book of Mormon that they had discussed the previous day. They visited her most weeks for discussion of previously assigned readings, which Tammy compared to her own spiritual views. Some weeks Tammy put them off by saying she had to take care of her grandkids or coming up with an excuse for why that week wouldn't work.

This connection between Tammy and the young Mormon women went on for about three months. But then Tammy read a section of the Book of

Mormon that made her call an abrupt halt to the visits. There are numerous passages in the Book of Mormon that refer to blackening skin as a punishment for sin, often comparing the dark skin of the sinful to the white skin of the righteous.

Tammy was incensed. She called me to express her outrage at what she saw as blatant racism. "I have Black grandkids!" she practically shouted into the phone. Both Tammy's daughters have children fathered by Black men. Tammy adores these kids. She is convinced she has a special spiritual bond with her youngest grandson. "I'm not going to have anything to do with a religion that sees them as cursed," she told me indignantly.

We talked about how she was going to respond when she saw the young Mormons again. "I'm going to tell them that I don't need to hear any more about their religion," she told me. "I'm not going to join a church that won't let my grandchildren into heaven."

When the Mormon sisters came to see her next, Tammy politely explained her disappointment at the bigotry in the Book of Mormon. She told them she had enjoyed their company and conversations, and she wished them well, but she no longer wanted them to visit or text.

At the same time, Tammy's social media feed was filled with memes and posts that could easily be identified as racist. At the very least, they are unquestionable expressions of white identity and victimization. "EVERYONE COMPLAINING ABOUT AUNT JEMIMA & UNCLE BEN," reads the top of one meme, over two pictures, one of a box of Aunt Jemima pancake mix and another a box of Uncle Ben's rice. "BUT CRACKER JACK IS OK" it says along the bottom, just beneath a picture of the white boy in a sailor suit on the cover of a box of Crack Jack caramel-coated popcorn and peanuts. Another meme proclaims, "PROUD TO BE A . . ." over a picture of a white saltine cracker. Tammy comments, "And I AM EXTRA SALTY." A third meme shows a picture of Al Sharpton beside a confederate "Stars and Bars" flag. The meme caption reads "One is a racist symbol . . . The other is a flag!!" The most telling example is a meme of a fabricated quote from a top official with the Centers for Disease Control, saying, "We'll just get rid of all whites in the United States who refuse vaccines." Tammy replies, "They want to exterminate the white race!"

There are other kinds of bigotry in Tammy's social media feed, as well, usually filtered through QAnon conspiracy theories. Antisemitism is rampant in QAnon and its overlap with conspirituality. It appears in all sorts of places, like a post spreading the fiction that McDonalds restaurants sell human meat in its hamburgers, depicted in a meme of the red-mouthed clown, Ronald McDonald, with the caption, "Mouth & nose covered in blood" and implying blood coats Ronald's big red clown shoes. Tammy adds a caption to her repost: "NAZIS = ZIONISTS = PEDOPHILE SATANISTS."

I was surprised to find Tammy's feed filling with anti-trans memes, even as her support for her own trans child, Sabrina, was growing stronger. Most of these memes identify famous people as secretly being transgender. Most of the trans people identified are Black women. One meme suggests Beyoncé, Michelle Obama, and Meghan Markle are all secretly trans. Tammy labels the image: "all are CIA Transgenders. Put through MK Ultra," by which she means a series of secret governmental experiments that conspiracists often use to denounce things that make them feel uncomfortable. Another meme has an image of Dr. Seuss's Cat in the Hat superimposed over a picture of Michelle Obama, who conspiracists often refer to as "Big Mike." The image has been altered to make it look like Michelle Obama has a large bugle protruding through her dress. The cat is pointing to the bulge and the caption reads, "There's a Dong in that Thong! By Dr. Seuss." Tammy reposts a meme of Barbara Bush and adds her own caption: "Big Mike wasn't the first First DUDE!" There's even a meme that claims Kyle Rittenhouse, the right-wing activist who killed two men who were protesting a police shooting of a Black motorist, is trans. The meme reads, "Kyle's real name is Wendy Rittenhouse Lewis and she in not 18 but 26 y.o. female to male transgender." Tammy believes that, although these anti-trans memes are intended to be humorous, they also describe reality.

Tammy even sometimes cheers on anti-trans activism. When *Sports Illustrated* put a trans athlete on the cover of its famous swimsuit edition, Tammy reposted a meme calling for a boycott. "If you haven't cancelled Sports Illustrated yet, it's time to," she wrote above her repost. "They put transgender (biological man) Kim Petras on the cover of their latest swimsuit edition." Another time, she reposted a meme of a goat-headed satanic god with women's breasts. It's captioned, "Once you understand their 'god' is transgender, you start to understand why they are indoctrinating your children." Tammy replies "Wake up!"

The contradictions in Tammy's beliefs and actions on race and trans issues are what happens when a polarized and heavily politicized white identity meets her more complicated, pluralistic lived reality. On social media and in her political views, she is loyal MAGA, following Donald Trump and her online communities on the right. When it comes to her family, she can be fiercely loyal and change her views to include the people she loves, like with Sabrina or her biracial grandchildren. You can see the same thing when I asked Tammy how she felt about Donald Trump's call to execute all drug dealers when three of her children had recently been convicted for selling drugs. Tammy was clearly uncomfortable with the question and didn't have a clear answer.

The persistence of Tammy's strong MAGA views reflects another trend in the New Age faith movement. Just as the liberal parts of New Age spirituality are pulling conservative women in more progressive directions, the recent entrance of so many conservative women into the New Age movement has pushed it much further right, giving new expression to many of the reactionary features that today's liberal spiritualists had pushed to the background. That influx is leading to conspirituality taking a central place in the New Age movement, gradually rebranding it in its own image.

I witnessed that transition firsthand when I attended one of the nation's oldest and largest New Age conventions and trade shows. Held each year since 2003 at the LAX Hilton Hotel in Los Angeles, the Conscious Life Expo has become a massive event, attracting thousands of people.

I went to the Expo in February 2023, as Yvonne was starting to head deeper into New Age spirituality, and I was watching other women doing the same. I wanted to understand the community and its appeal.

I had first heard about the Expo on the Facebook feed of the research account I used to monitor online conspiracism and conspirituality. There are things about the cultures of conspiratorial thinking and New Age belief that you can't understand unless you immerse yourself in them. Los Angeles is within driving distance of my home, so I decided to make a weekend of it. I didn't find enlightenment, but it was definitely enlightening.

✦

Walking into the lobby of the Hilton during the Conscious Life Expo is like astral traveling onto another planet. You are immediately greeted by New Age posters with psychedelic designs and paintings of Ascended Masters, Pleiadians, extraterrestrials, and depictions of life in Atlantis or the Fifth Dimension. There's a central stage in the lobby occupied by New Age artists playing mostly instrumental, ethereal music on a synthesizer, Native American flute, or digeridoo. Sometimes people dance. It's an older crowd, for the most part. There's lots of gray hair and sensible shoes.

People are typically dressed in ways that give off otherworldly vibes. Many Expo attendees wear natural cotton ensembles, which reminded me of my time in India. Women are often adorned in colorful, "boho" style silk skirts and dresses. Lots of this is designer clothing. The garb of other attendees gives off a sleek futuristic feel, like they walked out of the movie *2001: A Space Odessey* or a 1980s New Wave synthesizer band. Their main color schemes are whites and grays and silvers. Groups of younger people look like they're on their way to an audition for the latest *Riverdance* production or the new season of the Lord of the Rings television series: They're wearing cloaks and short pointy ankle boots, long jackets with a metallic sheen or paisley designs, and loose-fitting cardigans with oversized hoods that drape like shawls. The colors are calming and earthy: shades of green and lots of blues, with accents and embroidery in golds, browns, and purples.

Thumbing through the magazine-style program as I sit in the hotel lobby, I immediately know I am in the right place to help me understand Yvonne and Tammy and other women of January 6 who have traveled similar spiritual journeys. The Expo hosts around two hundred and fifty panels between Friday and Sunday, with about fifteen speakers presenting in the various ballrooms and meeting spaces during any given hour-and-half time slot. Nearly all the panel titles contain words and concepts drawn from Helena Blavatsky, Dolores Cannon, and other theologians of New Age spiritualism: *Ascension, shifting into 5D, Ascended Masters, Disclosure, raising vibrations, the Great Awakening, New Earth, channelings, The Matrix, past life regressions,* and *starseeds*. There are a dozen panels promising some kind of "activation," including multi-dimension consciousness activation, hypno-intuition activation, 5D soul mission activation, galactic star code activation, neo sapien body activation, and starseed mission activation. There's even something called massive orgasmic activation.

A few more panel titles raise my eyebrows. I'm not sure what to make of *How to Become a Jedi Master on Planet Earth*, a session on Ascension led by someone billing themselves as an "ET contactee, Galactic Historian, and Starseed Intuitive." I feel similarly confused about the session entitled *Speak to the Mantis Beings*, identified as "Praying-Mantis Beings from the Antares Stargate." But I am all over the one called *Starseed Awakening Through Your*

Cat, where you learn about "your galactic feline heritage" and "how cats are here to awaken us to our starseed mission."

Sitting in the lobby, I begin imagining what Yvonne and Tammy would be interested in attending if they were here with me. I'm pretty sure Tammy would go to the panels on using spiritualism to bring wealth. They have titles like *Nine Dimensions of Abundance*, *The Missing Key to Wealth*, *Unlocking the Codes of Abundance*, *Fifth Dimensional Economics*, and *Outrageous Prosperity*. Tammy loves to sing, so I have no doubt she would prioritize the *Sing Your Way to Success* panel, which introduced the audience to "a repository of songs that have been engineered to bring you success in the areas of finances."

I'm pretty sure Yvonne would be disappointed by all the panels focused on the business side of New Age spirituality. She would scoff at *Growing Social Media Consciously*, *Quantum Business* (hosted by the *Wealthy Living Academy*), and *Selling Your Mind, Body, & Spirit Product*. I end up sitting in on a few of these. The audiences for these panels are filled with ordinary people who say they feel emotionally dead in their current careers and who are desperate to figure out how make a living spreading their spiritual message. I would love to see Yvonne's reaction, I think to myself, when the panelists' answer to every searching question is "you need to believe it will happen and manifest it." The questioner would invariably follow up by asking about concrete steps they could take, and the reply always seemed to involve buying an educational package or signing up for one-on-one coaching sessions. Yvonne would lament the incredible waste of spiritual power and talent in the pursuit of wealth—which, she would remind me, was going to be worthless once Ascension happened.

When I see a panel featuring the channeling of Kryon of the Magnetic Service, I know I have to go. I had seen a channeling of Ascended Master Jesus Christ earlier and, frankly, it was disappointing. Jesus didn't have much to say of substance. He mostly spoke in generic self-help mantras and said that everyone should keep their faith through hard times and Ascension. I find myself hoping for something more detailed from Kryon—the angelic being preparing the earth for Ascension by shifting its magnetic poles.

So I attend the panel from a spiritualist who claims to be able to channel Kryon. More disappointment. It ends up being just another Ascended Master offering a word salad of New Age vocabulary, with nothing much original to say. It's the usual stuff: Disclosure is coming, raise your vibrational levels, feel the energy, trust your intuition, focus on healing yourself and the world around you, face your trauma and let it go. I can't help but feel like the Ascended Masters need to provide more specific guidance, given how close they say we are to the 5D shift. If we are on the cusp of Ascension, shouldn't we be getting a detailed list explaining what to do? Turns out I am not the only one with that question; many audience members are looking for more concrete guidelines. Maybe Kryon only does that for a fee.

After the Kryon panel ends, I head to the vendor area. Nearly all the vendors are also speakers, so there are about as many booths or tables selling New Age services and products as there are panels. This is the conference for you if you want your palm or aura read, have a sound bath, get an astrology chart, visit with a medium, seer, or channeler, or employ a starseed coach. You can also buy whatever crystals, amulets, balms, oils, and lotions you need, along with more elaborate (and expensive) items, like a copper pyramid enclosure or a personal infrared sauna unit. My forty-dollar aura reading appears to confirm Yvonne and Tammy's suspicion that I am a powerful spiritual being here to help. Watching a few other people get their readings, I get the distinct impression that the aura analysis machine tells everyone they have untapped supernatural abilities. Then again, maybe all the starseeds and psychics in attendance threw off the results?

The Conscious Life Expo is not the place for old-school, 1950s-esque UFO hunters. The guy with photocopied handouts proving the existence of alien encounters and who has collected testimonials of UFO abductees doesn't get much attention—and he probably hasn't for a while, at least not since the great online Starseed Awakening. Half the people at the Expo are claiming to be Pleiadeans, Lumerians, or some other kind of otherworldly being—or to have the ability to channel entities from other dimensions. People presenting themselves as extraterrestrials tend not to care about grainy photos of flying saucers and lurid abduction stories. The guy with the handouts is so clearly a relic of a different era that I feel sorry for him.

The other mystics of his generation have learned to change with the times. One thing you notice at panels and booths is that almost everyone looks older in person than they do in the program book—and by at least a decade. Some look decades older. A few appeared to be using headshots from the 1990s. There is a fascinating generational mix of New Agers. The older mystics often appear to have dyed hair, botox, fillers, and sometimes plastic surgery. They typically sell channeling sessions or various kinds of readings. The younger New Agers tend to be fit, attractive women who are into health and wellness spiritualism. They usually run the wealth, business, and starseed panels. The six starseeds on the two-hour *Starseed Light Activation* panel seem to be in their twenties and thirties and give off a distinct New Age popular-girl vibe.

The great number of starseed and Ascension panels are not the only big change from past conventions. The program announced a new feature this year: an entire lower floor of the Hilton dubbed "The Rabbit Hole." At the top of the escalator that leads down into the hole stands a human-sized cut-out of the white rabbit from Alice in Wonderland, who is warning that things were going to get strange. The Rabbit Hole is where the weirder panels are being held. It turns out that the Rabbit Hole is also where the more right-wing and conspiratorial events are located. The Rabbit Hole is a whole floor primarily dedicated to conspirituality and anti-government politics.

This represents a significant change from the past. You can see that change by reviewing the "Prior Years" section of the Expo's official website. For its first two decades, the Expo's spiritual politics seemed more in line with the earth-conscious, nutrition-focused, left-leaning hippie image traditionally associated with the "New Age" brand. Past Expos featured celebrity names on the left, like perennial presidential hopeful Marianne Williamson; Congressman Dennis Kucinich; *Huffington Post* founder Arianna Huffington; John Trudell, one of the founders of the American Indian Movement who was the spokesman for the Occupation of Alcatraz from 1969 to 1971; and Thom Hartman, a progressive media personality who used to host Bernie Sanders on a "Brunch with Bernie" segment of his radio show. Most of the celebrities were there to promote environmental, vegetarian, healthy living, or animal rights causes. Former NBA star John Salley spoke as a PETA and vegan activist, while singers and actresses Michelle Phillips from the band The Mamas and the Papas and Nia Peeples, best known for the television series *Pretty Little Liars*, were there promoting healthy lifestyles. If the early Expos contained any criticism of the government, it was usually that Congress was working for big corporations and not doing enough for the little guy.

That said, conspiracism has always had a place at the Expo. For example, civil rights icon and actor Dick Gregory and former Democratic Senator from Alaska Mike Gravel were on panels in consecutive years (2010, 2011) questioning George W. Bush's account of 9/11 and the fall of the World Trade Center towers. But back then, even the conspiracies leaned left.

In 2023, things have clearly changed. The Rabbit Hole represents some of the most extreme examples of conspiratorial thought leadership today. The

Expo has tried to be tongue-in-cheek about it, what with the name and the rabbit cut-out, but the conspiracism and far-right politics it is promoting are all too serious.

The changes reflect how the pandemic has remade the health and wellness and New Age spiritual communities. Now the Expo features some of the biggest names in anti-government, anti-mask, and anti-vaccination activism. People shell out fifty dollars a ticket to hear television and film producer Del Bigtree talk about his movie *Vaxxed: From Cover-Up to Catastrophe*. His session sold out quickly. Bigtree would go on to become Robert F. Kennedy Jr.'s 2024 presidential campaign spokesperson.

Audiences pay the same amount to hear British conspiracy guru Sacha Stone. Prior to the pandemic, Stone was a relatively benign wellness advocate. During the pandemic, Stone went hard into conspirituality when his anti-vaccination advocacy catapulted him to right-wing fame. Now Stone talks about how the Illuminati rule the earth and are trying to control humanity through vaccines that implant a soul-controlling nanochip with each injection. Like Del Bigtree, Sacha Stone is closely connected with Robert F. Kennedy Jr.

The closing event of the entire 2023 Expo is the world premiere of the film *Plandemic 3: The Great Awakening*, produced by anti-vaccination activist and conspiracy theory peddler Mikki Willis. The original plandemic film—*Plandemic: The Hidden Agenda Behind Covid-19*—went viral on social media after its release in May 2020, especially after being promoted by far-right conspiracy theorist Alex Jones. Despite being banned by mainstream social media platforms, it continued to spread online, becoming one of the most damaging sources of medical misinformation during the pandemic.

Prior to producing these films, Willis worked as a videographer for Bernie Sanders's 2016 presidential campaign and did the same for Tulsi Gabbard's 2020 presidential run. Robert F. Kennedy Jr. wrote the foreword for the book version of *Plandemic*, which was published in October 2021. Here's what Kennedy had to say: "Mikki Willis is the Paul Revere of the rebellion against the burgeoning totalitarianism of the Biosecurity State. Willis' incendiary film, *Plandemic*, sparked the seeds of revolution in a billion open minds and ignited the dangerous global conflagration of critical thinking." In 2024, Willis worked for Kennedy's presidential campaign and produced the video introducing him to voters.

To meet demand, the 2023 Expo added an entire day of panels on the Monday after the convention's official end devoted to discussion of Willis's film and steps people could take to "protect freedom." The program describes Willis's session like this: "For decades, scholars and survivors of totalitarianism have been warning us that America is under attack from within. We didn't listen. Now we are here." It continues, "The Great Awakening will reveal how the COVID industrial complex was used to advance a century old agenda to weaken & overtake America." The entry ends by announcing: "To maintain the control of all nations, all resources, and all people, they must keep the masses distracted, demoralized and dependent. The Great Awakening will offer cognitive immunization against the real pandemic: mass hypnosis."

Welcome to the *new* New Age. In this age, conspirituality is king, and many of its leading voices have a direct line to the White House. Here communities like those that gather at the Conscious Life Expo have a friend in the new United States Secretary of Health and Human Services: Robert F. Kennedy Jr., now the most powerful health official in the nation.

CHAPTER 8

A Method of Hope

Two months after her nephew died by suicide, Yvonne announced that she had received a message from him through Facebook. "I was watching a video on Facebook on my television when this popped up," Yvonne wrote in December 2021. The pop-up suggestion was a video for a song called "Scars in Heaven" by the Christian rock band Casting Crowns. The song's lyrics speak of how, when someone dies, all their earthly scars are washed away, along with their pain and suffering. Yvonne said the video recommendation was a message from her recently deceased nephew, letting her know he was okay now.

Yvonne forwarded the video to her sister and then wrote a reply to her nephew in Facebook, thanking him for reaching out to her. "Thank you for giving me a glimpse of the world through your eyes today," she wrote. "You were and will continue to be a world changer. I already see it in our family and I know the ripple will continue!" Yvonne then apologized for not having been more supportive when her nephew had come out to her years before. At the time, she had been an evangelical Christian and considered homosexuality a sin. "I wish I hadn't been under such a hypnotic spell of judgment from the lies of religion!" Yvonne confessed. "Everything in the Bible would lead people to believe you were condemned," she wrote her nephew in disgust, "but that's another lie straight from the man."

"I love you," Yvonne said in a heartfelt closing. "I will fight this side while you are sending us all your energy and light! I feel you in each present moment and I will use your light whenever the darkness rears its ugly head!"

Two months later, when Yvonne's mother died, Yvonne announced that the Facebook algorithm had once again sent her a message from beyond the veil. It was a meme with a quotation from her favorite New Age theologian, Dolores Cannon—the one who popularized the concept of starseeds. The quote reads: "As perfectly imperfect as they are, we chose our parents for a reason." The meme is a sentimental sepia-toned photo from the early twentieth century, with a mother kneeling down to comfort a child who looks to be about four or five years old. The mother tells the little girl: "I'm not going to heal and wake up to my truth in this lifetime, but you will. You have all the codes to make it all happen for your soul, and then you'll raise the frequency for the collective." Yvonne believed her mother had placed the meme in her feed to comfort her.

"Don't worry mom! I got this!" Yvonne replied back. "I love you and I won't let our ancestral lineage down! I feel you all! Thank you for your protection!"

Yvonne believes the algorithms also sent her a divine message days after her conviction on all her January 6 charges. Despite warnings from her attorneys to stay off social media, Yvonne had been posting constantly on Facebook and recording videos for TikTok. She also went on several right-wing podcasts, including the popular conservative vloggers Diamond and Silk. TikTok users had been hammering her in the comment section. Yvonne was rattled by the vitriol from people celebrating her going to prison and saying they hoped the judge threw the book at her for being so unrepentant. She was sinking into dark places. That's when Yvonne said she received a message from Spirit.

"I'm sitting alone and processing this morning's interview and all the hate on TikTok, wondering if I'm doing the right thing," Yvonne wrote on Facebook. "Feeling so alone and so sad that the same humans I am fighting for are the ones calling for my head. I'm not going to lie, the human in me, Yvonne is done."

Sometimes Yvonne writes about herself in the third person, like she is the soul speaking about her human vessel. "I feel like I'm in a dream. My entire world is collapsing, and all I can say is I want to go home, I don't want to play anymore. Every ounce of my humanness is ready to quit. So I pray, I meditate and I ask what do I do? Is it ever going to change. Will they ever see what I see? Then I received this."

Yvonne reposts a meme that announces: "On the surface of the world right now there is a war and violence, and things seem dark. But calmly and quietly, at the same time, something else is happening underground, an inner revolution is taking place and certain individuals are being called to a higher light. It is a silent revolution." This was the message she needed, right at the very moment she needed to hear it. The algorithms, like a good and caring god, had sent her words of comfort and encouragement.

Serendipity like this is the bread and butter of conspiracism and conspirituality. In this world, nothing happens by accident. Everything in life is scripted and planned, both by the "black hat" forces of evil and the "white hat" good guys. Coincidences don't exist. Correlation is causation. It's not just that conspiracists assume a connection between two or three seemingly unrelated events. They believe it all fits together in an elaborate fantastical story with a bunch of disjointed and even more far-fetched subplots. Followers are encouraged to trust their intuition more than their eyes. They are told to feel the truth and trust their gut, *especially* in the face of overwhelming evidence to the contrary.

This has always been the case with conspiratorial thinking, in its various iterations throughout history. But now we are in the internet age, when mass conspiracism can spread across the globe in an instant. The viral spread is boosted by social media influencers looking to build audiences by appealing to conspiratorial believers who think that everything is connected. Many videos, memes, or posts suggest they contain hidden truths. Others all but claim that their secret knowledge is divinely inspired.

And then there is the issue we see with Yvonne, which is what scholars call "algorithmic conspirituality." This is a phenomenon by which people become convinced that social media algorithms are the voice of God. Algorithmic conspirituality is more common than you might expect. It started on TikTok, where a new genre of video emerged of people sharing spooky tales of how the TikTok algorithms seemed to read their minds and detect their deepest desires.

Concerned researchers began studying this trend. They soon discovered that social media algorithms can create feelings of serendipity so intense that even skeptical users—those who understand that they are dealing with sophisticated mathematical programming—are still taken aback by the experience.

Most of these skeptical users understood that social media companies have spent billions of dollars creating and refining those algorithms to give users what they want so they stay on the site longer and come back for more. They knew that those algorithms were built by mathematicians, computer scientists, information systems engineers, psychologists, and social scientists, and that they were based on cutting-edge research. They knew that everything you click, view, or enter into a search engine is now likely attached to a cookie that provides a data point about your interests and preferences. Seemingly innocuous social media quizzes get you to reveal intimate things about yourself that are added to your data profile. The sum total—the combination of online searches, clicks, cookies, and data-mining apps—are algorithms that can predict your needs and anticipate your desires.

Which is the whole point. Impersonal social media companies want to know you inside and out so they can sell targeted advertising to clients who want you to buy their services, products, or ideas. And they are now doing it so well that even people who understand how algorithms work can feel like something is happening on a spiritual level.

To many users, the experience of serendipity makes them feel like the algorithms are something more than mathematical equations. How, otherwise, could the program know so much about them? Researchers also found that people who experienced trauma and anxiety were especially likely to see a divine presence in the algorithms, as were religious or spiritual people. In other words, Yvonne and Tammy profile as precisely the kinds of people who rely on "the algorithm as an all-knowing oracle or deity . . . as a form of comfort during uncertainty," as media scholar Kelley Cotter puts it.

These beliefs represent what anthropologists call a "method of hope." The idea was most clearly articulated by the anthropologist Hirokazu Miyazak, who was trying to understand why islanders on Fiji who had been stripped of their land by colonial rulers continued to ask for compensation every year despite the effort clearly being futile. He concluded that the ritual gave them hope, even if they knew that it was almost certain nothing would come of it. His finding points to how humans need something to hope for, especially in situations where they feel powerless. In circumstances with no clear or easy solutions, hope becomes an end, rather than a means to an end. It doesn't matter that the desired things never arrive. Hope is what keeps them going and gets them through each day.

I saw conspiracism working the same way for Yvonne and Tammy and others like them. They protect their fragile hopes by forming communities of like-minded people who offer reassurance and pick them up when they are feeling down or falling into despair. In the online cultures that Yvonne and Tammy inhabit, conspiracy theories and conspirituality have become a method of hope for millions of people.

The need for hope helps explain why conspiracism has such a powerful hold on so many people. On one hand, belief in conspiracism and conspirituality is often extremely isolating. The deeper people go into conspiratorial beliefs, the more likely they are to alienate themselves from friends and family. On the other hand, the online communities of conspiracism become new virtual friends and families that collectively sustain hope. When a particular prophecy doesn't pan out, disappointed conspiracists come together to develop explanations for why something didn't happen. Together they hatch and agree on new narratives that can keep the larger hope alive.

When friends and family members reject conspiracists, these online communities offer comfort and support. Groups of people who have experienced the same real-world isolation affirm each member's individual sense of alienation from real-life loved ones. As Yvonne and Tammy's experiences show, the results are mutually reinforcing. People who become alienated from their real lives increasingly rely on their online communities and conspiratorial beliefs to satisfy their emotional needs.

Yvonne and Tammy each reveal a different side of the process. Yvonne demonstrates how profoundly alienating conspiracism can be. Tammy shows the centrality and resilience of conspiratorial communities, how they can offer the sensation of belonging to people who feel alienated and alone. Taken together, their examples reveal that the great power of conspiracism as a method of hope comes from how its incentives all work in the same direction. Conspiracism encourages people to dig deeper down the rabbit hole rather than trying to find their way out.

✦

Yvonne announced her spiritual awakening on Facebook. She had already left the evangelical church publicly, revealing her exodus through social media. At first, her goal was to explain her beliefs and conversion experience to her friends and family. She repeated her awakening story so often, to so many different people, that by the time she told it to me, the telling seemed fairly rote, almost scripted. It's a narrative that hints at martyrdom.

"My sister says all the time, why do you have to be so honest on Facebook?" Yvonne tells me. "I said, 'I know it sucks. Trust me, I don't *want* to be this honest on Facebook. If I could just shut Facebook down and get off it, I would be happy. But . . . *who's* going to bring that consciousness? *Who's* going to be the example?'"

In 2022, Yvonne started a blog to explain her beliefs to friends and family members by directly answering their questions about her new theology. "What God do you pray to?" one post is titled. "This was a question asked to me today by someone close to me," Yvonne explained. "I get it, I sound like nothing most growing up around here have probably ever heard of . . . My response was I pray to the same God you do." And then Yvonne explained her basic belief about "the Creator of the Universe," past lives, and 5D.

In another post entitled "What I believe!" she explains the unfolding and evolving nature of belief, as human beings learn more about themselves and explore their spirituality in deeper ways. "I believe we are much more than just human. I believe we are different and have different soul purposes," Yvonne says. "I feel a very strong connection to the Pleiadians. I've been told I am of the angelic realm, I feel this but am not sure I comprehend it," she says honestly. "I think we really can't fathom in this 3D state who we truly are! Here are 4 videos that I feel on a soul level, so imagine it's a mix of these." Yvonne posts the links to the latest YouTube videos that best capture her current spiritual views.

She does this a lot. Yvonne learned much of her New Age spirituality not from Amy Carlson or Keia but by watching New Age videos on YouTube. When she finished one, the algorithms would bring a recommendation for another. Thinking this was a sign from Spirit, who she believed was guiding her self-training, Yvonne clicked and watched. And then another, and another, and another. When we traveled across the country filming the documentary, Yvonne would play us videos from the backseat. At hotels she would sit on the bed watching or rewatching YouTube until she went to sleep. She was watching videos like this right up to the day she entered prison in October 2023 for her January 6 crimes.

Yvonne doesn't really have an online community of fellow true believers. She has videos.

If Yvonne's real-life friends watched her video recommendations, they weren't persuaded. Instead, they continued to question her beliefs and actions. They told her she was hurting herself and her family and putting her soul at risk. Yvonne responded by trying to explain that, in her belief system, there were many different paths to God, and everyone had to follow their own journey. "I guess the one thing I would say to my friends who just don't get it. Ask yourself this. What do my actions show?" Yvonne asked rhetorically before providing her answer. "I am learning to love unconditionally. I am learning who I am at my very core and heart level. I pray about everything and am seeking truth always! I took an oath of no harm. I am willing to die for my Earth and the freedom of humanity without inflicting any pain on another being." "I love you even when you push me out," she added.

Yvonne explained that she was the same generous soul she had always been. "I would give away anything I have freely to anyone who needs it," she said. "I have opened my home to the homeless and look for any way I can be the vessel used to love humanity." Yvonne asked her friends to join her in taking a live-and-let-live approach to everyone's spiritual journeys. "I'm not trying to toot my own horn but I'm also not telling anyone else their journey or their God is wrong. I am telling you all the answers you seek are inside you! Your journey may include the church. As long as your heart is pure and your intentions are pure Creator is going to guide," she wrote in her blog.

Yvonne put her spiritual journey on full display through Facebook. When she felt she had discovered a new spiritual ability or reached a new plateau of learning, she would announce it on social media. "I am a channeler," she announced in 2022. "I get downloads, literally downloads of information. I have discernment. I know how to use my intuition and am learning to trust my inner guidance more and more each day."

In another, she posted a link about the mythical civilization of Atlantis and announces, "Good history lesson if you'd like to know who we really are! I am an angel!" Another post shared the "Synchronicities we experience on a daily basis." "I have so many stories and I am sure I will share more as we dive deeper," Yvonne told her friends. "For now I just want to keep it to current synchronicities. The little miracles, the ones that just make you do a little happy dance." "The Universe is always working to catch your attention," Yvonne said. "It does everything it can to help guide you. Little sharp pains, stomach aches, headaches, weird vibes that come out of nowhere. We are so enthralled with the outside world, we've shut off our inner world. We don't feel, we don't notice when our body is screaming for our attention. We don't listen to the gut feeling."

"It's not your fault. It's the programming," she told her friends who didn't understand her. "You will only allow yourself to receive what you are open to. If your mind is made up that we are absolutely alone in the Universe, this blog probably isn't for you. Nothing I say is probably going to penetrate until you are a bit more open minded." "This is a free will Universe," Yvonne said, "and you have to want the truth and be open to it."

Yvonne's search for truth started to have real-world consequences beyond straining her relationships with friends. Yvonne had quit her job the prior year. Troy was eventually fired from his. When they had moved back to Boise after getting drummed out of the Marines, they could only afford a trailer home. Now they lost that too. Thinking Disclosure was imminent, and money would be soon worthless, Yvonne and Troy had stopped paying their mortgage and were evicted. They moved into a camping trailer that Yvonne's sister loaned them the money to buy. They parked it on land next to the home of a friend, who rented them the space and the electric and water hookups.

Yvonne explained the loss as a gain. She even saw benefit in the pain and humiliation of having to send away her daughter and small grandchild who had been living with them. Yvonne now saw the separation as a necessary detachment:

> The hardest thing I think about losing my house for me was my kids. Because my daughter lived with us, and my grandson. But it worked out and I knew it would. I needed to step away. I needed to be unattached from my children somewhat, because I wouldn't do it otherwise. We can't have any attachments when we ascend. That's the one thing: you have to get to a place in this lifetime where you are unattached to all human beings.
>
> My kids probably don't see it the same way I do. My daughter would've never left home. She would've just stayed living with us. I do miss having her with me, but she needed to go on her own. Her leaving just finalized my plans for Disclosure, because I would've never been ready to leave for 5D if she was still living with us. I would have always felt like I was the place that had to stay open for my kids to come home to.

When money got tight, Yvonne found a job at a bar, but then she either quit or was let go. (She says it was a mutual decision.) When the algorithms sent Yvonne a meme in her Facebook feed saying to close all bank accounts because money would soon be worthless in Disclosure, she took it as a divine command. "I knew the systems were coming down last year on my own!" Yvonne proclaimed on Facebook, "and now they are all about to crumble! Friday I was shown close my bank account, guess what I'm doing tomorrow?

closing it down and trusting our Creator! It's time to wake up! Don't blame me I've warned you all."

Yvonne's family and friends were worried about her, and upset, but no one could get through. One by one they started to withdraw, giving up hope that they could change her views.

Conspiracy theories and conspirituality are stigmatizing in exactly these ways. Research on the topic shows that watching a loved one become obsessed with conspiracism produces a mix of extreme feelings of stress, anxiety, anger, sadness, and hopelessness. People try to talk the conspiracist out of their beliefs, reason with them, and use logic and evidence. When that doesn't work, friends and family members often distance themselves, hoping the cold-shoulder treatment will force their loved one to abandon conspiratorial thinking. That isolation tends to do the opposite by simply driving the person even deeper into conspiracy theories.

That's what happened with Yvonne—except in her case, the conflict with loved ones centered less on the conspiracy theories than it did on her New Age spiritual beliefs. Yvonne's rejection of Christianity and her adoption of conspirituality was what drew the real concern of friends and family members and caused her social ostracization. The strongest rejection came from conservative evangelical Christian friends, who saw Yvonne's New Age conversion as heretical and worried that when she died, she would go to hell. The friends she had made at the church where she had been a youth leader eventually turned their backs on her. And then some family members did as well.

Yvonne expressed her sense of betrayal on social media. It started with a meme she reposted on Facebook: "So you are having a spiritual awakening? You lost all your 'friends'? You can no longer work a 'regular' job and your family thinks you are crazy? Congratulations! You escaped the matrix."

Over the next two years, she periodically reposted memes created by other conspiracists and starseeds about losing friends and family. The comments Yvonne added to the reposts reveal the anguish she felt. "I found out a lot about a whole lot of people I called friends, honestly even family! We live with masks on! I've chose to live in complete authenticity with myself and refuse to be different than who I am all the time. I lost most of my friends and it's sad and hard but you know what? I love who I am and I'm ok with you not loving me. I am loved beyond measure and I am living in integrity and truth to myself which is the greatest gift you can give yourself."

When Yvonne's mother died, few of her friends reached out to provide comfort. She talked about facing "the hardest things I've ever had to" and feeling abandoned by friends and forced into "doing it alone." "We as humanity have been taught Conditional love! You know how I know? I'm a prime example," she wrote after the funeral. "I could tag all of you, you know my good friends that all of a sudden have disappeared. Even though my journey has been my journey and I didn't do anything to any of you!" Then tone got more confrontational. "Where you at ladies?! How's that conditional love working in your lives?" she said, reminding them she knew more than a few of the secrets about their lives and marriages. "Lucky for you, I love you unconditionally and I wouldn't do that because I've already forgiven you for what you do not know. I may however send it to each of you in messenger just so you know that you were never really my friends to begin with," she said with sad defiance.

Weeks later, Yvonne was calling out specific family members on Facebook. Eventually, Yvonne started attacking Christianity. She started calling Christianity a "system of enslavement" and announcing on Facebook that "my Christian friends" were "mostly a bunch of religious zealots that look to judge others." She went after her former church when they set a million-dollar goal for renovations to the church building. "This building is a fraud and honestly most of the people who attend are frauds too!" In response, more people cut her off. One of her daughters withheld access to her children, only allowing Yvonne to have supervised visits where she was prohibited from discussing her spirituality.

By the time Yvonne's January 6 trial came around in March 2023, she and Troy were isolated and alone, aside from a handful of mostly online friends who shared their New Age beliefs.

Yvonne's response was to cling to her faith and go all in. As her trial approached, Yvonne was convinced Ascension would happen before she went to court. "I am not going to lie. I have never ever been more uncomfortable," Yvonne wrote on the eve of her trial, worried because she was still in 3D. "I know bliss is waiting. It's the only thing that keeps me going." Two days before the start of the trial she wrote: "Protect yourself! Sheild yourself . . . Make a bubble around yourself. Put on the Full Armor of God! We are powerful."

Yvonne started to assume a confident bravado. "I identify as a conspiracy theorist," she announced on Facebook, "my pronouns are . . . Told/You/So." During the trial, she posted memes saying that ascension into "5D REALITY!"

was imminent. Yvonne said that, without that belief, "I would never have made it this far. I would have given up." "I don't know how this movie ends but I know it'll be one hell of a happy ending for me and humanity," she proclaimed confidently. "I have enough faith for all of us. Thank God I am not doing it alone and there are millions of light workers waking up."

After her conviction, I watched Yvonne slide deeper into isolation and con-spirituality as she awaited sentencing. Prior to this, when we spoke, Yvonne mostly told me about her adult children and grandkids, about things with Troy, or work, or what she was doing to keep busy. Now our conversations focused almost exclusively on conspiracies and Yvonne's growing belief that Ascension was imminent.

She was convinced the jump to 5D would happen before her sentencing hearing, and she started searching for new signs and portents—anything that would give her hope. "Won't be long now," Yvonne wrote above a meme about the hypothetical planet "Nibiru," which is at the center of a New Age conspiracy where it crashes into earth. Having failed to end life on earth several times already, Nibiru became part of new conspiracies about its role in an alien Ascension. "Troy even made contact last night and learned he's also a channeler!" Yvonne wrote of Nibiru's alleged alien landing, which she imagined would happen shortly before her sentencing hearing. "You all are missing out! We are living in exciting times."

Beneath the confidence, however, a bitterness sometimes surfaced, espe-cially when it was clear Ascension wasn't coming before her sentencing hear-ing. Near that date, she reposted a meme that said: "If a truth burns down a relationship, a family, a community, or a society, it was only ever held together by lies. And to that I say, let it burn. I never want to live in a world where our need for 'comfort' supersedes our need to stand on a foundation only the truth can provide."

Yvonne replied: "Let it all burn."

✦

I missed the phone call because I was walking the dogs. It was Tammy. Then came the text: "Wayne killed himself." I knew immediately she was talking about Sabrina. I called right back.

It was September 2022, and Sabrina had been in the Lycoming County Prison in Williamsport, Pennsylvania on a charge of selling methamphetamine. The county put Sabrina in the male prison. Sabrina told her family that the guards were harassing her and had denied her medications, including her hormones. No one had the money for bail. Sabrina became increasingly agitated and depressed, which led to her being isolated in solitary confinement. Soon after that she was put on suicide watch. Days later, Sabrina made a noose out of her prison clothes and hung herself from the cell bars.

I was the first person Tammy called after Sabrina's ex-wife had delivered the terrible news. Tammy said she didn't feel like she had anyone else to call. She later told me she didn't trust her family to help or care, not even her other children. She did not believe anyone in her life was capable, or willing, to step up in a moment of need. So she called me, a person from the internet she had only met two months earlier—someone she had not yet at that point seen in person, not even a picture. At that time we had only messaged on Facebook and spoken on the phone.

Tammy had been shocked when Sabrina was arrested. Just days before, she had told me that Sabrina was the only one of her kids who had stayed away from drugs. She had called me after Sabrina's arrest to vent. "You're not going to believe this . . . ," the conversation began.

Tammy had already informed me about the drug problems of her other children. Tammy has three children besides Sabrina: a son and two daughters. She said her youngest daughter had stopped using when she got pregnant, but her son and her oldest daughter were both struggling. Tammy's son had a long history of drug use. Her oldest daughter wasn't far behind. The two of them had been arrested the prior year for possession of a large amount drugs with intent to deliver. News reports indicated police recovered "cocaine, methamphetamine, psilocybin mushrooms and over a dozen bundles of heroin," along with a large bag of needles, white wax baggies, latex gloves, and a digital scale. All the drugs "were accessible to a 3-year-old and 7-year-old at the residence." The two children belonged to Tammy's daughter, and their presence added felony child endangerment charges for both.

Now it was Sabrina. Prior to Sabrina's arrest, Tammy had just been telling me how well she was doing, and how proud she was of Sabrina for getting her life together. Tammy told me Sabrina had started her own rideshare business and seemed to be heading in the right direction. Tammy was more angry than disappointed that Sabrina had joined her siblings as a drug offender.

"I got bad news," Tammy had started the phone call to me in August 2022. "Can't go one day without bad drama." She told me Sabrina was being held on $50,000 bail for possession with intent to deliver. Tammy said she found out because her five-year-old granddaughter had called her asking if she could come over because Sabrina had just been arrested. "Sick of these kids putting my grandchildren in jeopardy," Tammy said in disgust. "I want this nonsense to end."

"This was greed!" Tammy said emphatically. "Just looking for easy money at my grandchildren's expense. Sick of it." "Never ends," she said in exasperation, "so disappointed."

Tammy had to help figure out what was going to happen with those grandchildren. Sabrina had custody of three children, one of whom was her ex-wife's child from a prior relationship. In exasperation, Tammy blamed Sabrina's ex-wife for the problem. "She doesn't care," Tammy told me in disgust. "She doesn't want to be a mom." At the time, Tammy was living with her youngest daughter and her boyfriend, while looking after her grandson, and didn't have room to take them, but she was determined to find someone who would. "They will never go in the system," Tammy promised.

We talked almost daily during that time, as Tammy tried to find a place for the kids. Sabrina knew she was going to be doing some prison time and was desperate to avoid having any of the children placed in a foster home. Tammy said that after getting repeatedly molested while in foster care, Sabrina was obsessed with making sure the kids stayed with family members. Sabrina was especially worried about her stepson, because he had behavioral problems, and his mother was having difficulty controlling him. Sabrina went so far as to pay the rent on her apartment through the end of the year and told her ex to move in with the kids if no one else would take them, using the free place to stay as incentive.

Tammy was also stressing out because her January 6 sentencing hearing was coming up and her public defender attorneys told her she needed character reference letters. "They asked me to get character letters from at least fifteen people. I said I don't know fifteen people," she told me, worry and frustration filling her voice. "I told them all I have are my kids. I haven't worked in over ten years, I don't go anywhere, so I really don't have friends. I know my youngest daughter is going to write me a letter, but not too sure about the other ones."

Even the letter from her daughter ended up being a challenge. "She said, 'You write it,'" Tammy told me, shaking her head. "I said, 'you can't write one?' She said, 'I don't want to.' So, I said, 'whatever.'" The only family letter ended up being a handwritten note from her son with multiple recent felony convictions.

The other letters came from online friends Tammy had never met in person. She had met some of them in conspiracy groups on the right-wing social media platform Telegram. A few were from the community that formed around the online prophet calling himself Wizard.

Those same online conspiratorial communities became her support group when Sabrina killed herself. Wizard asked his followers to post videos in which they told him and each other about their lives. Tammy doesn't use the name "Sabrina" or tell them her child who committed suicide was trans. She uses the name "Wayne" and talks about her "son." Some of Tammy's closest Telegram friends know her child was trans, but it is clearly not something she feels comfortable sharing widely in these right-wing spaces.

In her videos, Tammy repeatedly thanks Wizard and her friends for their support. "Your strength gives me strength," she tells them. "Your hope gives me hope. And your faith helps give me faith. All of you all, all of you on this chat, on this channel are just amazing, awesome human beings, and I love you all." She gets choked up. "I thank you all again, and you know, 'where we go one, we go all,'" she says, repeating the QAnon slogan. "We're going to weather every storm together, personal storms, we're going to be together no matter what. So again, I just want to thank you all."

Tammy turned to her online conspirituality community for support again two months after Sabrina's death, when her son was arrested for a parole violation while Tammy was staying with him. "Drama filled day," Tammy announced at the start of the video. "Apparently my son had a warrant for his arrest for a probation violation. Police are knocking at the door in the morning. I went to the bathroom to put my teeth in before I opened the door. By the time I got done, the police kicked the door down," she says shaking her head. "Idiot son tried hiding. So, as he was hiding. The police cuffed me and his girlfriend and so we were on the porch freezing cold in my jammies. They brought him out. Then we had to sit and wait until they got a search warrant for the house because they only had a body warrant to get him," she tells her online friends. "We sat on the porch for four hours in cuffs, freezing. Finally, the cops did get blankets for us to wrap ourselves up in. Anyways, sat on the freezing cold porch, but they made us piss outside, like freaking animals."

While this was going on, Tammy's son's parole officer asked Tammy if she had recently been in the hospital. Tammy said no and wondered why the officer had asked. It turned out her son had tried to avoid the parole violation by telling his probation officer that Tammy had overdosed and was on the verge of death at the hospital and he missed the meeting because he was by her bedside. The officer said they were about to call her federal probation officer about it, because Tammy taking drugs would have been a parole violation on her January 6 charges. Now the officer knew Tammy's son had been lying to them, which would add to his penalties.

"Tell you, freaking kids," Tammy said with disdain to her online friends. "They're not even kids. They're adults, you know, and they make such stupid decisions . . . seeing everything I've gone through, everything they went through because of my decisions, you think they would learn, but they don't."

During this time I was concerned about how much time Tammy was spending alone, how she seemed to be relying almost entirely on her conspirituality beliefs and community for comfort. Researchers have found a strong connection between loneliness and beliefs in conspiracy theories. One major long-term study that tracked over two thousand people for three decades discovered that "people reporting high levels of loneliness in adolescence, and those who experience increasing loneliness over the life course, are more likely to endorse conspiracy worldviews in midlife." Tammy could have been one of their case studies.

She also began reporting more otherworldly experiences, like she was trying to convince herself things were okay. The videos she posted to social media frequently talked about how much trouble she was having dealing with Sabrina's suicide. Between Christmas and New Year's, she reported being visited by Sabrina's spirit, who let her know things were okay. "Now he can move on, and so can I," Tammy said. "I am just so happy. I'm so happy. I have never ever felt the way I feel right now."

At the end of January, Tammy went on a series of "Hobbit Hunts" in the woods near her house that she recorded on social media. Hobbits are mythical creatures invented by the author J. R. R. Tolkien in his *Lord of the Rings* books. Tammy imagined there were some hobbits in the neighborhood and took an offering of gifts she hoped might coax them out of their hole. The offering was a bouquet of dead flowers, some leftover chicken wings, a Pop Tart, and a bottle of soda. "I have a machete, just in case," she tells any friends who might be unsure if the hobbits would be friendly or hostile. "I know, I'm weird," she said. "But hey, this is how we manifest things."

When Tammy got closer to the hole, she announced loudly, "I come in peace! I have food, 7Up, and flowers for ya. The flowers are a little dead, but I don't know what you eat. I just wanted to show you that I'm peaceful, and I don't wish you any harm." She told the hobbits that she would leave her offering and come back later. "And if the soda bottle's not empty when I get back, I'm going to take it anyway. Because I don't want to leave any litter here, okay? So, I hope you enjoy it. And maybe sometime, after you get to know me, you'll come out and say hi. Alright, we love you. We want peace," she shouts to the hole.

The videos were a clear expression of Tammy's hope. In one of them, she tells her friends that she was so excited to see if the hobbits had taken her offering that she didn't even do her usual spiritual rituals. "My morning routine takes at least two hours," she says. "You know, my meditation, my prayers and stuff." "I'm excited that, you know, some of you guys are as excited as I am about this. It's fun," Tammy tells them. "You know what I'm saying? I sit in the house a lot, so what better way to get some exercise, you know? Too bad my grandkids weren't around. Maybe this is why they love me so much, because I'm like this."

The videos capture her disappointment when she proved unable to manifest some hobbits. In each one, she arrives at the hobbit hole to find the offerings still there. "Oh, aww. I'm disappointed," she says with her voice trailing off in dejection. "Now, I kind of figured it was still going to be here. But like I was hoping, it's all hope," she says, getting to the heart of the matter. "It would have been so cool." She pauses again, trying to recapture the feeling of hope. "All right, it was an adventure," she concludes. "Hey, it's good just get out, you know, this is good for me just get out of the house. Even if it seems silly to people, and I'm sure it does. I don't care. I don't care," she says her voice trailing off. Then after a beat, the optimism is back. "Maybe I'll catch a leprechaun next time," she says hopefully.

When the hobbit hunt didn't work out, Tammy turned back to hoping for Ascension to arrive. "Looking forward to this big event," she said in one of her videos to her friend group. "I keep telling people, 'Be ready, be ready,' and they keep laughing at me because I've been saying it for two years." She pauses. "I'm ready," she announces with more than a hint of impatience in her voice. "But anyway, I'm doing better than I expected I would be doing in some kind of tragedy like this," she says in a more somber tone. "I never thought this could be me being in the club of losing a son, losing a child. But here we are," she says with a deflated voice.

Tammy tries to pick herself back up by imagining another encounter with Sabrina. "You know, I had a visit from him the other day," she says in a video to her friends. "I saw a bluebird that made its presence known. And I saw the bluebird and I immediately thought it was Wayne," she said. "And then I remembered last wintertime, him and I were talking about if one of us dies, we're going to come back as a bird or something. And I said, 'well, let's not make it a cardinal, because everybody does that.' So we decided it would be a bluebird."

"It was him," Tammy says confidently. "It made my day. It made my couple days, actually."

As the winter dragged on, Tammy grew increasingly fearful and downtrodden about her impending prison sentence for entering the Capitol on January 6. She told her friends she was hoping Ascension would come before her prison sentence started. "I was thinking today about March 1st when I have to turn myself in," she says hesitantly. "So less than a month, I get to celebrate my 52nd birthday in jail. Yay me," she says with an uncomfortable laugh. "Well, I hope things start happening. Maybe, I mean, I still got a little less than a month to go. Who knows? Maybe shit will happen, and I won't have to go to jail for twenty days," she says hopefully.

Tammy's online friends had been assuring her that Ascension would happen, and she wouldn't have to go to jail. "They were insisting, 'You're not going to jail, you're not going to jail. This is part of the movie. You're part of the movie!'" Tammy told me, gesturing wildly and speaking in the exaggerated voice of friends trying to convince her. She was referencing the conspirituality belief that life is illusion like in the film *The Matrix*.

Tammy threw cold water on the idea. "I said, 'yeah, I am part of the movie, but I *am* going to jail.'" Tammy said she wanted to believe Ascension would arrive first, and her friends were persuasive, but she couldn't bring herself to think that it was real. "But, you know," she says, "they had me *almost* believing that I *might not* be going to jail." Her voice gets more emphatic, "They *almost* had me believing that *Mark* might be at the jail waiting and say, 'SURPRISE!!! We're all in the movie!'"

On some level, Tammy understands that her beliefs are a method of hope. She knows that many of these things she holds onto are unlikely or preposterous. In the end, she doesn't care. She finds her life boring, grim, and lonely. She has little reason to expect things will get better. Most situations in her life only tend to get worse. She doesn't want to live in the real world, but she doesn't want to leave it either, especially now that she has grandchildren. She wants to be there for them—to be the kind of grandmother who cares for and protects them.

It's telling that Tammy—and Yvonne—use conspiracism when talking about their present and future. They seldom use conspiracies to explain or rationalize the past. They almost always view the terrible parts of their life histories in realistic terms. I have found their understandings of the abuse they faced, the broken people and systems that have let them down, and their own bad choices to be largely devoid of otherworldly explanations. They speak of those events candidly, with little sentimentality and with remarkable self-awareness and perceptivity. By contrast, when they talk about today or the future, it's always fantastical conspiracies and interdimensional solutions that promise to bring instant relief and joy. The past is a cold reality, the future is a hopeful promise.

For Tammy, viewing the world this way is what gets her through life. The conspiracies give something to look forward to—something to get her through the day, and the winter, and the death of her child, and the fear of prison. Hope is what she most needs and wants. It's the one thing she refuses to lose. It's what she actively tries to cultivate. Conspiracies and conspirituality give her hope, and she will fight against any reality that promises to take that hope away.

CHAPTER 9

Soul Contract

How do you get conspiracy theorists to disengage from the conspiracies? Is there a way to convince starseeds to focus less on Ascension to 5D and more on life in the three-dimensional world? What's the best way to refocus true believers from fighting an imaginary global cabal of reptilian overlords to solving pressing real-world problems that directly affect them and their families?

Let me be clear: I'm not talking about getting people to abandon New Age spiritualism. Most of today's New Age spiritualists are focused on living more in tune with the environment and developing healthier mind and body practices. A great many reputable scientific studies have demonstrated the benefits of New Age–inspired meditation, yoga, and vegetarianism. Believers like Yvonne and Tammy were attracted to this kind of spiritualism because they genuinely want to pursue a path of love and light. Much of the core belief system—reincarnation, spiritual missions, divine intervention, some kind of impending apocalyptic event—isn't that different from more traditional religions, especially Hinduism and Buddhism, from which New Age spiritualism borrows heavily.

The problem with conspirituality is not the spirituality; it's the conspiracies. The danger lurks in radicalized conspiracism, in which large numbers of New Age believers lose trust in experts, science, and evidence-based reality and place their faith in conspiracy theories with little to no basis in empirical fact.

The downsides of conspiracism are numerous. Rejection of science and vaccines is causing the spread of preventable illnesses and the return of diseases like measles and polio, which universal vaccinations had all but eradicated. Growing distrust of government practically ensures mass casualties in the next big public health crisis or natural disaster. The nation faces a regular stream of conspiracy-inspired violence, mostly in the form of mass shootings. Conspiracism often promotes bigotry of all kinds (racism, white supremacy, homophobia, transphobia, etc.). It undermines democracy by distorting understanding of political policies and their effects. It elevates authoritarian political figures who can easily manipulate a cynical public that no longer engages in evidence-based critical thinking. Conspiratorial politics fuels today's polarized electorate, preventing Americans from seeing their shared values and views. By creating the perception of alternate realities, conspiracies make it nearly impossible to have rational political debates over any shared set of facts.

And while all this happens, conspiracism continues to rip apart friendships and families. In short, when it comes to creating social problems, New Age conspirituality is largely indistinguishable from conspiracism in general.

For Tammy and Yvonne, one of the central pillars holding up the conspiracy part of conspirituality is a concept called "the soul contract." It is essentially a belief in predetermination: that everything in life happens as part of a preordained, scripted plan. Many religious traditions have analogs to this concept; in the Calvinist stream of Christianity, for example, the idea of predestination maintains that some people are chosen to receive God's salvation. In the New Age version, each person's soul gets to choose the outcome prior to starting out each lifetime. Think of it as freewill predestination, where you choose your own adventure and then strap in for the ride. To really experience your choice—to fully learn the life lessons you have pre-selected for this go-round in the human experience—you enter your human vessel with no knowledge of your soul's past lives or of the path you chose for your soul's current human incarnation. You experience life in real time, as if you are fresh and new and this is the first life your soul has ever lived.

This brand of predetermination not only provides explanations for life's hardships; it essentially blames the victim. In a "soul contract," prior to starting out a new life, you agree to the main lessons you are going to learn and the hardships you are going to endure. You personally select the experiences. You go into life with the full knowledge of what you're signing up for. If you don't like something that has happened to you, the concept of a soul contract says, "too bad, you picked this path, deal with it." If things don't work out like you expected or hoped, the soul contract says, "your soul knew all this going into it." Disappointment, trauma, agony, injustice: all negative things that happen to you are all things you agreed to experience so you could learn some important soul lesson.

The idea of a soul contract helps to sustain conspirituality. For Yvonne, Tammy, and millions of others, soul contracts explain why the conspiracies mostly fail to come true and why the conspiracists find themselves alienated from friends and family. The soul contract says, "Don't question your beliefs. The frustration and confusion you feel is part of your soul lesson." It tells followers, "Your disappointment, the sense of alienation you experience, and the hardships you face are all lessons your soul chose for you to learn in this lifetime." The soul contract reminds them that their job is to stay on the path, to keep learning, to keep looking for the hidden meanings, and to keep working for Disclosure. "In time, all will be revealed," is one of its central mantras.

Part of a soul contract is patiently waiting for all the conspiracy theories to be exposed as true. As we will see with Yvonne and Tammy, that mindset makes it extremely difficult to dislodge the conspiracism from New Age spirituality.

So what can be done? Is it possible to return to some shared understanding of truth, facts, and reality? Can we dislodge conspiracies from spirituality?

Countering mass conspiracism is no easy task. The problem didn't develop overnight, and it won't be solved quickly either. Getting in was a process. Getting out will be a process, too. Undoubtedly an even tougher one. We'll talk about what that looks like and the strategies that researchers are finding most promising.

But first: halting the spread of conspiracy theories among the millions of people who believe in a New Age spiritualism rife with conspiratorial thinking will mean coming to terms with the concept of soul contracts.

✦

I had been avoiding watching the video for well over a year. Every now and then Yvonne would ask me if I had seen it and tell me that it was great and that I really needed to watch it. Of all the videos she consumes, this one is her favorite by far.

I always told her I would get to it, but I never did. I had found the text of the video on the internet long ago, and while I had read that, I hadn't watched the video. Yvonne brought the video up again while we were driving to Tammy's place after her sentencing hearing. She insisted I watch it the morning after our arrival, as we were getting ready to leave the hotel in Williamsport, Pennsylvania to head to Tammy's trailer to film the documentary. So I did.

Tammy knows this video, too, and has seen it many times. So have millions of other New Age spiritualists. There are different versions on YouTube and other social media platforms, but it's basically the same thing. It's a narration of a children's book, *The Little Soul and the Sun: A Children's Parable*, by New Age author Neale Donald Walsch. The book introduces the concept of soul contracts in an easy-to-understand way.

Neale Donald Walsch first made national headlines starting in 1996, when his book *Conversations with God* hit the *New York Times* bestseller list and stayed there for the next two and a half years, selling seven million copies. The book grew out of Walsch's unstable adulthood. He went through three divorces and frequently changed careers, holding down jobs as a newspaper reporter and editor and a radio station program director; he even created his own advertising and marketing business. Eventually it all went bad, and Walsch fell into despair.

"I was homeless with a broken neck, living in a park," Walsch explained in publicity interviews. "I spent my days collecting cans to sell for 5 cents each just to have enough money to eat." Angered by his fall, Walsch says he wrote a letter to God and that, to his great surprise, God answered back. According to Walsch, what followed was a series of conversations with God that Walsch recorded in forty separate books, several of which became *New York Times* bestsellers. His children's book, *The Little Soul*, takes the concept of a soul contract from *Conversations with God* and reframes it as a bedtime story.

In that story, a character called the Little Soul speaks in the voice of a child and tells God that it wants to understand darkness. God says that it's important for all souls to understand both light and darkness. The two of them make arrangements for the Little Soul to go down to earth and be put into a human vessel to experience darkness directly. Before the trip, God gives the Little Soul some advice. "When you are surrounded with darkness, do not shake your fist and raise your voice and curse the darkness," God tells the Little Soul. "Rather, be a light unto the darkness and don't be mad about it . . . Let your light shine so that everyone will know how special you are."

The Little Soul says that it specifically wants to learn how to be forgiving. God thinks that's a great lesson to learn. To help, a Friendly Soul volunteers to go down to earth with the Little Soul to teach it how to be forgiving by doing a "bad thing" to the Little Soul. "I will do something really terrible," says the Friendly Soul. "And then you can experience yourself as the one who forgives." "I would do it because I love you," says the Friendly Soul. The Little Soul asks the Friendly Soul what it would do that would be so terrible. "'Oh,' replies the Friendly Soul with a twinkle. 'We'll think of something.'"

"And so, the agreement was made," the story ends. "The Little Soul went forth into a new lifetime, excited to be the light, which was very special. And excited to be the part of 'special' called 'forgiveness.' And the Little Soul waited anxiously to be able to experience itself as 'forgiveness,' and to thank whatever other soul made it possible."

In a spiritual system based on the idea of a soul contract, the bad things that happen to you are a blessing. They are part of a divine lesson that you agreed to learn prior to being born in a human body. No matter what that lesson may be, no matter how awful the thing that happens—whether it is betrayal, divorce, abuse, poverty, rape, murder, genocide—it is all divinely inspired.

Ironically, the same day I finally watched the video, the concept of soul contracts came up in conversation with Yvonne and Tammy while we were filming the documentary. The discussion started with trauma, and then it turned to abortion and when it was okay to terminate a pregnancy. Earlier, Tammy had spoken about being raped by a family member. I asked Yvonne whether abortion would have been okay if eleven-year-old Tammy had gotten pregnant. Yvonne said no, because Tammy's baby would have made a soul contract to be born in those circumstances. Being the product of rape was "that baby's choice," as Yvonne put it. She said the baby had signed a soul contract to understand the experience of living as a child born from rape. The soul that entered the baby had consented to that experience.

"You don't understand," she continued, probably when she saw the skeptical look on my face (I had heard this kind of thing from Yvonne before, so I wasn't shocked by the idea). She explained that "when they come in" to the new human body, souls have already agreed to all the trauma they will experience in that human vessel. "Like my friend that died of ALS," Yvonne said, offering an example. "He had a soul contract. Just like I chose *this* contract. That's why I will never feel sorry for myself. *I* chose this!"

This is how Yvonne views most everything that happens in life. "It's a soul contract, and it's for a lesson," Yvonne said again. Tammy nodded in agreement.

When Yvonne's mother died, she interpreted both her grief and her anger at her mother through the concept of a soul contract. "So many hard lessons came from her," Yvonne posted to Facebook, as she started to explain the trauma of her childhood, like she was the Little Soul who thanks the Friendly Soul for teaching her about forgiveness. "We continue to blame others for all our pain and suffering not realizing at any time we can break these chains," Yvonne wrote. "We can realize we aren't the trauma life has thrown at us. We are beings here to experience this trauma and realize it has no power over us." "Wake up and see the illusion!" Yvonne told her friends. "GROW and let go! It's beautiful and forgiveness is the ultimate FREEDOM! No one is responsible for your joy! You have to just remember you are the joy using a vessel to express it in this world."

Yvonne interprets her growing isolation from friends and family as part of the same soul contract. She believes every soul is on their own journey and that only the truly enlightened will make the jump to 5D. Since non-believers will be left behind, Yvonne thinks she has to prepare for the emotional separation. "I needed to unattach from my children somewhat," she told me in 2022. "We can't have any attachments. That's the one thing you have to get to a place in this lifetime, in this world where you are unattached to all human beings." Whenever she feels rejected by people she cares about based on her spiritual beliefs, Yvonne repeats the phrase "No attachments!"

That message is continually reinforced by New Age influencers. "The more spiritually attuned you become, the more sensitive you are to energy in general," spiritualist Dolores Cannon used to tell her followers. "Keep your circles pure, sacred and small." After posting that quote in a meme, Yvonne replied, "It's why I'm ok being solo! I definitely feel energy and know who my energy suckers are!"

On that trip across the country with Yvonne, I found her to be more focused on conspiracies and Ascension than ever. She was convinced the jump to 5D would happen before she would have to serve any of her two-and-a-half-year prison sentence. When filmmaker Liz Smith shot footage of Tammy and Yvonne sitting outside Tammy's trailer for her documentary, Yvonne expressed certainty that Ascension was going to happen at any time. "You can put this on camera: I will be shocked if I spend one day in jail," she proclaimed to Liz. "I believe the truth will come to this world before that letter and my report date. There's so much breaking right now."

"I hope that your documentary comes out in time," she added. "But to be truthful, I think the shift will come before then. And maybe this trip is just meant to help you raise your consciousness."

Later, when the filmmaker, Liz, and I were alone at a rest stop in Nebraska, she wanted to talk about Yvonne's certainty about not going to prison. "She actually thinks Disclosure is going to come really soon, so she's not going to have to go to jail," Liz said, surprise brimming in her voice.

I told Liz about how this was part of a pattern. Last spring, Yvonne was convinced she'd never actually go to trial. Last summer, she thought Disclosure would happen before her sentencing hearing. When the judge rescheduled that hearing from June to September, Yvonne took it as a sign that Ascension was starting. She held that belief right up until the judge gave her two and a half years. Now she was saying the same thing about ascending before her incarceration.

Liz commented on how Yvonne never stopped talking about Ascension and all kinds of conspiracies. I reiterated that, in the past, Yvonne and I had had lots of great conversations that had nothing to do with conspiracies. "But it feels like that's changed now," Liz observed. "Since I've been on this trip with you, which is now six days, there's not one single conversation which isn't about a conspiracy theory."

Liz wasn't wrong. Our conversations on the trip had consisted almost entirely of Yvonne sharing conspiracy theories with us. Most of it was about Ascension and Disclosure. "That's where she's at right now," I said to Liz. "She's in another huge trauma space. She just got sentenced to two and a half years in federal prison."

Days later, back at Yvonne's camping trailer in Boise, on the last day of filming before I flew back home, Yvonne was still talking about Disclosure. "I really don't believe that there will be jail time," she said. "But if there is, it's not going to be that bad. It's going to be as bad as I make it." Her voice gets more hopeful, "I mean, think of all the souls I'll get to meet and all the people I will get to experience that I wouldn't if I didn't. And there will be *beautiful* souls in there that will have stories."

Yvonne didn't think the women in prison would be resistant to her message of 5D heaven on earth. "I mean, some of them will be resistant, just because it's so different. But the truth is, they're probably the people that want healing the most."

When Yvonne finally had to surrender herself to the federal women's prison in Waseca, Minnesota, in October 2023, that, too, became part of her soul contract. In a few candid moments, she admitted how frightened she was by the prospect. But mostly she fit it into her spiritual journey. She said that if they stuck her in solitary confinement, she would just "astral travel" to connect with helpful souls. She talked about teaching other women once inside. A few days after Yvonne entered the Minnesota prison, Troy reported in a Facebook live stream that she already found a disciple. "The inmates have been very supportive of her and one girl is looking for a spiritual teacher to help her grow," Troy said with strong emotion in his voice. "She's been praying that somebody shows up at prison to help her. And her prayers have been answered."

Rather than prison shaking Yvonne out of her conspiratorial beliefs, the experience has only pushed her deeper into them. Unable to watch YouTube videos or access social media, Yvonne went to the prison library and devoured books on spiritualism, self-help, and science fiction. She pored over them, looking for life lessons and clues to her divine purpose. She also had her sister send her a copy of *Little Soul and the Sun* and passed it around to the other prisoners so they could learn about soul contracts.

With each month, Yvonne's beliefs seemed to grow stronger as she relied on them to get her through. After serving for six months, Yvonne was admitted to a special program that provided counseling and allowed for early release. Yvonne saw it as a sign that she was making spiritual progress and Spirit needed her on the outside.

When Yvonne got out of prison, one of the first things she did was watch the video of *Little Soul and the Sun*, posting to Facebook how much she had missed hearing it. She included a link and urged her friends and family to give it a listen.

Yvonne is a very good teacher. I know because, in many ways, she has been mine. I don't share most of her spiritual beliefs. I reject the conspiracies. I oppose her politics. But Yvonne taught me an array of New Age spiritual concepts with skill and passion, answering all my questions patiently and enthusiastically. She has always treated me with kindness and genuine concern. We don't share the same set of facts, but Yvonne has been more honest and candid with me than most people in my life are. She is extremely bright and well spoken. She is also charismatic and pushy as hell.

We are all part of Yvonne's soul contract. Even you, who are reading these words. Yvonne knows I'm writing this book and that she will be featured in it.

She wanted to tell her story, so her example could teach others, so that there are more souls on the side of light when Disclosure finally comes. Now that she has been released from prison, the former Marine drill instructor, with years of experience in public relations, is excited to start her new calling.

On January 20, 2025, the day of Donald Trump's inauguration, he issued blanket commutations and pardons for nearly all the 1,500 January 6 defendants. The proclamation ended what Trump called the "grave national injustice" of punishing those who stormed the Capitol. The pardons would usher in a "process of national reconciliation." The order included commutations of the sentences of individuals like Stewart Rhodes, founder of the far-right militia group the Oath Keepers, and Enrique Tarrio, leader of the Proud Boys. Trump ordered the Attorney General to dismiss "all pending indictments against individuals for their conduct related to the events at or near the United States Capitol on January 6, 2021."

The pardons came just weeks after Yvonne had been released from prison. Yvonne was thrilled, and she saw the executive order as Trump having her back. It increased her loyalty to him and her belief that he is a "white hat," working on the side of the light. It reconfirmed her beliefs in the QAnon conspiracy theories, a common reaction I have seen across online conspiratorial communities.

And the January 6 pardons have convinced Yvonne that the truth is finally being revealed. More and more people are waking up. She is more convinced than ever that Disclosure is imminent. Yvonne is eager to get to work.

✴

When it comes to figuring out what to do about conspiracism like this—which is still spreading on a mass scale—it is much easier to talk about what *doesn't* work than what does. Research by scholars of conspiracism is unfolding quickly, and it is illuminating the contours of conspiracist communities and the way conspiracy theories spread and evolve. But most of what experts have learned so far about exit strategies primarily identifies the ones to avoid. Here's what doesn't work (or is far less effective than you might expect).

Fact-checking: Conspiracists don't trust established experts of any kind. If you show them the latest academic scholarship or a government study or a Pew Research survey, they will tell you that they don't believe those kinds of sources. They identify mainstream expertise as fatally biased. They will say things like, "Well, those are your facts; I have my own." Whatever you say, no matter how definitive your evidence or ironclad your logic, they will tell you why you are wrong and why their view is the correct one.

A caveat: Fact-checking *is* useful in preventing people from sliding into conspiracism in the first place. And it's also helpful for those who have already decided, for other reasons, to get out of the rabbit hole. But presenting facts and logic to a currently convinced conspiracist isn't likely to change their mind. If they are already a believer and not yet a skeptic, giving them facts won't do much.

Shaming, ridiculing, and isolating don't work either. You will not end conspiracism by laughing at conspiracists, dunking on them online, or refusing to invite them to Thanksgiving dinner. All that might make you feel better, let you work off some frustration, or keep the holiday season a bit more pleasant. But it's not going to shake conspiracy theorists out of their belief that a cabal of pedophile Satanist celebrities is running the world. None of this has an effect on their certainty that the truth is being ignored, and the mainstream media is covering it all up. If you won't talk to them, their conspiracy "family" will. Or as Yvonne has done, they will lament the loss but consider it a blessing in disguise—because "there are no attachments in 5D," so they were going to need to break off emotional connections before Ascension anyway.

It's the same with pointing out to conspiracists that their conspiracies keep failing. While the failure of a prophecy can be an event that triggers a conspiracist to question their beliefs, it's far from a certain pathway out. Conspiracists always have a way to rationalize failure or when real-life events seem to go in the opposite direction of what they predicted.

Take the case of the Los Angeles wildfires in January 2025. Online conspiracists had no problem dealing with the inconvenient fact that the fires consumed the homes and neighborhoods of the elite celebrities that they view as among most powerful players in the globalist cabal. That was clear when Tammy texted me shortly after the fires started to ravage Pacific Palisades and destroy beachfront homes in Malibu. Tammy texted me to ask if I was okay, since she knows I live in southern California. Trying to help, she told me that the celebrities had deliberately set fire to their own homes.

"Why would they do that?" I asked.

"They are destroying the underground tunnel networks they use for trafficking children," she told me in a matter-of-fact way. "They needed to get rid of the evidence before Trump gets in office and he exposes them."

This is how it goes. World events, calamities, or unexpected political developments will not end conspiracism. The conspiracists merely twist the new realities into their existing conspiracies, or they call an unexpected event a "psy-op" or a "false flag" by the bad guys. Many just ignore reality altogether and keep their faith in "the plan" or Ascension or the Great Awakening or whatever they currently call their version of the endgame.

So, what *does* work when it comes to getting conspiracists to disengage from conspiracism?

Unfortunately, as of this writing, there are a limited number of proven strategies. In part that's because it's hard to get people out of conspiracism for all the reasons described in this book. There's also not much research yet on exiting conspiracism. The field is still relatively new, and the recent wave of scholarship has focused almost exclusively on identifying what draws people into conspiracy theories, not what gets them out.

That said, this scholarship suggests there are many roads out. Sometimes exiting conspiracy-laden worlds is a process that happens over time. In other cases, a trigger event makes the conspiracist question a central pillar of their belief system. It's all hard to predict. Exiting could be inspired by observing a failed prophecy, noticing that two conspiracies are contradictory, or having a new conspiracy challenge a deeply held personal belief. It could be learning about the dishonesty of a trusted conspiratorial source, observing objectionable behavior by fellow believers, or finally being persuaded by friends or family members that life is better outside the world constructed by conspiracism. Sometimes pure emotional exhaustion prompts an exit. There is no magic formula. Given the powerful ability of conspiracists to rationalize away evidence and logic, it's not the kind of thing that can be planned or orchestrated. Disillusionment has to happen naturally.

I have met some former conspiracists who can give us a better sense of how the process works. For Erica, a former QAnon follower and Trump supporter, the break started when these two trusted sources collided. "It was a combination of the conspiracies surrounding the COVID vaccine that QAnon was pushing and Trump's robust cheering for the COVID vaccine," she told me. "The combination of the two couldn't make sense in my head as the QAnon influencers were so adamant that the COVID vaccine was a depopulation tool."

Contradictions around COVID were also the exit factor for Rich Logis, a former leader of the Florida MAGA community. Logis began questioning his faith in the conspiracies spread by Donald Trump due to Trump's COVID response, his lies about the 2020 presidential election being stolen, and the January 6 insurrection. That set the stage for his eventual break. "My epiphany happened gradually, and then suddenly, all at once," he says of what happened next. Logis explains that "the accelerant was [Florida's Republican governor] Ron DeSantis inviting anti-vaxxers to his press conferences in Summer/early Fall 2021." "I was not anti-vaccine," Logis reports, "and DeSantis doing this confused me. This was when my doubts really commenced."

For Stephanie Kemmerer, the catalyst was hearing the truth from a trusted friend. Kemmerer is a former conspiracist who believed the downing of the World Trade Center towers was an inside job and that the Sandy Hook Elementary School shooting was a staged event. She got her "wake up call," she says, when she was "shockingly confronted by a very close friend who told me they worked with a Sandy Hook parent."

"I felt relief," Kemmerer says of the incident that triggered her exit. "'Thank God someone stopped this' was the weird thought that flashed through my mind." Although Kemmerer quickly abandoned all the conspiracy theories she had embraced, she cautions people against thinking that there's some cognitive on-off switch for conspiracism. Because conspiracy theories are not just abstract beliefs but, as we have seen, narratives by which people find purpose and meaning and hope, "just getting rid of them doesn't magically fix you." She explains that "conspiracy theories attach to and attract scared, lonely, uninformed people who feel unimportant and cast aside. They also infuse the believer with a sense of righteousness and smugness."

Kemmerer credits an emotionally supportive partner as the most important factor in her post-conspiracy theory healing. Her case echoes what the research shows: When destabilizing moments like these come, the key to a successful exit, rather than retrenchment, is having a trusted person or group to turn to for support and resources. Usually that's a friend or family member who remained on good terms when everyone else abandoned the conspiracist. Sometimes those who draw someone out of conspiracy theories are new people they have just met in person or even online. Since it's impossible to predict what might cause a conspiracist to question their beliefs and when that might happen, we can make ourselves ready and available to both loved ones and strangers who are showing signs of doubt in previously held conspiracies. The key is maintaining a lifeline and connection to conspiracists we know—and perhaps sometimes just being the right person, in the right place, at the right time.

The essential ingredient in the process of helping someone exit conspiracism, research suggests, seems to be empathy. Treating conspiracists with kindness, patience, and understanding appears to be a precondition for a successful exit. Wavering conspiracists need someone they can trust—someone with whom they can talk through their feelings and doubts without being shamed or ridiculed. In other words, they need a compassionate friend.

That kind of connection is crucial because conspiracist communities are notorious for trying to claw back members who try to leave. "People tried to get me to come back for a very long time," Erica reports about her QAnon community. "I had to stop communicating with almost everyone that I had stayed in contact with after I left. It was a lot of manipulation, using the conspiracy theories I used to believe in to try to make me change my mind, arguing with me and saying that I'd been brainwashed by the Democrats I was talking with."

Erica tells me she was sometimes tempted to go back rather than face the truth about herself and her past beliefs. "It was easier to be lost in the conspiracies than finding out how wrong I had been, the cruel things that QAnon stood for, and the underlying violence and hate of the movement. It certainly would have been easier to be lost in delusions than to watch the horror unfold." Erica says she was also sad about losing her QAnon friends. "I miss the people I thought were my friends and community, but they are still lost," she concludes.

The key for Erica, Rich, and Stephanie was finding new online communities that gave them a place to land—especially ones populated by other former conspiracists. Open online spaces created by "formers" are proving crucial in efforts to draw others out of conspiratorial thinking. These are open-access forums and live-chat spaces (on platforms like X and Facebook) organized around exiting conspiracism, where former believers share their experiences. The spaces often include friends and family members of conspiracists, as well as a wide range of concerned individuals hoping to help stop the spread of conspiracism. I met Erica, Rich, and Stephanie in spaces exactly like this, where I have spent considerable time over the past four years.

Research suggests that these kinds of online spaces and communities offer the best hope for bringing people out of conspiracism. Researchers note that the existing communities are too scattered and isolated to address a global problem that spans multiple cultures and age cohorts. They identify the need for targeted messaging and diverse support networks armed with the resources and attention to make them widely accessible.

What the experts are describing regarding a strategy for helping people exit is a mass, crowd-sourced solution. Rich Logis is trying to move in exactly this direction with a nonprofit that he founded. The organization, called Leaving MAGA, is focused on providing a community for former Trump supporters. Since so many Trump supporters buy into a variety of conspiracy theories, Logis's work focuses a great deal on helping people dislodge conspiracism from their thinking patterns and try to find community and support outside conspiratorial networks.

Any mass strategy for countering conspiracism also means adopting a new mindset, one based in empathy and curiosity. One reason the digital age is rife with conspiracism is that people live in isolated cultural groups and information silos. We don't trust each other, and we see the other side as hostile and fundamentally opposed to our values. Surveys continue to show that we still have a lot in common. But surveys are rarely convincing in a badly polarized society in desperate need of trust and understanding. To maintain—or rebuild—a modern democracy will require that we figure out how to reestablish trust. How can we repair the damaged social fabric of our communities and nation? Is it possible to renew our confidence in our neighbors, to restore the social contract?

I've started to think a lot about a new "soul contract," of sorts—to borrow a term from Tammy and Yvonne's world. I wonder whether we might yet forge a different kind of soul contract—one rooted not in a choice made in a past life but a connection forged in a current one. While I am not convinced by the notion that, before we are born, we consent to all the bad things that will happen to us, I do wonder whether there's a version of a soul contract that focuses on belonging and community. Renewing this kind of soul contract would mean seeing other people not as enemies to be vanquished but as members of a shared community—neighbors whose common interests are yet to be discovered.

That goal doesn't require sacrificing core beliefs or values. It means taking a different approach to the other side, one based in patience and empathy. That means more online places directed toward those trying to exit conspiracism, populated with supportive voices willing to welcome back the disillusioned. It means non-conspiracists reconnecting with the conspiracists in their lives, perhaps with a different outlook, goal, and lowered expectations this time around. Given the current epidemic of conspiracism, halting the spread is going to take a lot of people making a contract, of sorts, with conspiratorial thinking friends and neighbors—one rooted in persistent care for and curiosity about them. And as I've found in my relationships with the women of January 6, sometimes that soul contract needs to be with ourselves: a commitment to the humanity of others, a self-reminder that we need to be patient and empathetic in the face of constant frustration.

That kind resolve will be necessary, because the other best path forward is unlikely to happen in the current political environment: addressing the underlying causes that drove the person to conspiracism in the first place. The problem, of course, is that there are no easy solutions for the vast array of trauma and hardship at the root of most conspiracism. And rather than improving, the situation only promises to get worse in the short term. With the social safety net facing steep funding cuts and reductions in services, more people are going to find themselves in the kind of precarious situations that give rise to conspiratorial thinking. The road ahead is likely to produce conditions in which conspiracy theories thrive—on both sides of the political aisle.

Unfortunately, given the circumstances, rebuilding trust through a new kind of soul contract might be the only path forward that doesn't involve some kind of destructive and protracted conflict. We are in this together, whether we like it or not. Reengagement is essential and inevitable. By taking that first step, you might not change a conspiracist's mind. You can't alter someone else's lived circumstances or reverse or suddenly heal their past traumas. But you can start rebuilding the connections and trust that might make a difference.

Sometimes all you can do is try to get the conspiracist to focus on the real world and spend less time online. Researchers have shown that activities and goals that give conspiracists a real-world focus can help to break the spell. When conspiracists are focused on real-life objectives, outside their online circles, those groups and conspiracies begin to matter less to them. Most people prefer relationships in the 3D world, rather than virtual or interdimensional ones. Giving conspiracists a reason to stay engaged with reality—with neighbors, and family, and the community in which they live—gives them fewer reasons to jump online. That strategy might not pull someone out of conspiracism. But it's a necessary first step.

It's a step I'd like to think I had a small part in helping Tammy make—even though she's as much a conspiracist as ever.

✳

The moment Tammy called to tell me Sabrina had hung herself, I knew my graduate thesis could no longer happen. I was already precariously close to breaching academic impartiality by reaching out to her over Mark Angst's suicide. In the two months that followed, I had learned a great deal more than I already knew about Tammy's tragic past. I was also witnessing new, serious traumas hitting Tammy in real time, right before my eyes, on a near daily basis. It had all left me wondering how to navigate the muddle of academic inquiry and my increasing investment in Tammy's life.

Now, as I heard the agony in her voice on the phone after Sabrina's death, and talked her through the shock, I knew I couldn't sit back and observe. Regardless of what Tammy believed or had done and the great differences between us, she was in crisis. Helping a person deal with a child's suicide was more important to me than academic rules. I wasn't going to put my graduate project ahead of a distraught woman who told me she was calling because she didn't know where else to turn. Ignoring one another's humanity is what got us into this mess as a society, I decided. I had come to feel strongly that showing humility and compassion would be the only way out.

So I asked her what she needed and I tried to help. We talked and texted almost daily as she processed Sabrina's suicide and her feelings about it. I suggested she reach out to a therapist. Tammy tried, but like in the past, the therapists who took Medicaid were either not accepting new patients or the first available appointment was months away. I listened and offered advice when she asked for it or when I thought it might help.

Tammy quickly focused her despair into getting justice for her child. Sabrina had told family members that the prison guards had tormented her for being trans and had withheld her medications. Tammy blamed the prison and the guards for pushing Sabrina over the edge. We talked about steps she might take to get what Tammy was now calling "justice for Sabrina."

I asked Tammy if it would be okay if I made a few phone calls to see if I could use my limited connections to get her some quality legal help. She was grateful for any assistance. I called a friend who is well connected in the world of social justice. She made a few calls on my behalf, and several days later I was on the phone with a lawyer from a boutique Philadelphia law firm that had handled high-profile sexual abuse cases against the Catholic Church, the Boy Scouts, and Jerry Sandusky, the disgraced Penn State coach who had molested young boys. I explained the situation to the lawyer, including my involvement in it. He wasn't sure what to make of the whole thing, but he asked for Tammy's number. He spoke to her for a while, and then Tammy called me back, saying the lawyer said he was going take the case pro bono.

When the legal preparation started to move forward, Tammy allowed herself some hope that she might actually get a measure of justice for all the government systems that had harmed Sabrina in the past. It wouldn't make up for being sexually abused in foster care for two years or being wrongly incarcerated in juvenile detention in the Kids for Cash scandal. But it was something.

Tammy allowed herself to hope that any money from a settlement or jury verdict could stop her family's downward slide. She dreamed of grandchildren getting the kind of education that could bring middle-class security. More than anything, she wanted something positive to come out of Sabrina's tragic life and all the wrongful treatment by the very systems that were supposed to have protected her.

That impulse contributed to me writing this book. At one point when we were talking about what justice for Sabrina might look like, Tammy said to me, "You should write a book." At the time, we had been discussing the connections between Sabrina's story and what had happened to Tammy growing up and how the cycles of trauma were linked. I told Tammy about the concept of generational trauma. It resonated with her. She immediately saw her own family as a clear example of how generational trauma worked. Tammy told me she was determined to break those cycles. She said having me write a book about them might help.

"I want my story told," she told me then, and many times after. "I want to show people the truth about how things are, share all I've been through, so they understand that this is how many people live. I want everyone to know how unfair things are for people like me, what we go through. I take responsibility for my mistakes. I have made many bad choices. But my mistakes aren't the only reason I ended up like this or why my kids are the way they are. We had a lot of help getting here, and I want people to know about all of it." "I'll tell you whatever you want to know," she said earnestly. "I'm an open book. I have nothing to hide."

I told her I'd think about it. When I decided to move forward, I determined the core project wouldn't change. I was still trying to understand Tammy, not transform her politics or convince her to abandon conspiracism. But the project also took on new meaning. Our relationship altered the story and affected the outcome. I wasn't just recording her story; I was participating in it.

Tammy has told me many times that our conversations have made a difference for her. She had bottled up so much pain over her lifetime that she needed to let it out. Early on, she would continually tell me how good it felt to share her experiences and feelings with someone. She was always surprised by how much lighter her burdens felt when she knew someone else knew about them.

Tammy likes to express gratitude, in part because she has received so little of it in her own life. When I first began complimenting her on something, or applauding her for making a good choice, or pointing out one of her positive attributes, she would get choked up or express surprise that she was blushing. She wasn't used to hearing anyone say good things about her or give her praise. Tammy would tell me that people never focused on her good qualities, so she wasn't sure how to handle it when someone did.

Aside from listening, I mostly talked with her about things she could do to reduce tension and conflict in her life. In those days, Tammy was staying with her daughter, her daughter's boyfriend, and her grandson. But the setup was draining her. Tammy and her daughter had always had a volatile relationship, but the intensity of their fights increased after Sabrina's suicide. Tammy told me she was worried that things would get out of control.

Tammy also felt resentful. She was paying rent, cleaning, babysitting, and cooking, while her daughter worked long hours and her daughter's boyfriend lounged on the couch. Tammy felt stuck. She worried about the constant fighting in the household and its effect on her grandson. Tammy was also concerned that he spent too much time inside with his eyes on a screen and not enough playing outdoors.

Being Tammy's age, I understood the minefield of living with an adult child—I'd been navigating that off and on for years. You're not supposed to parent, but you're still the parent, a role weighed down by expectations, especially if you're a woman. Tammy and I talked about how relying on others can leave you feeling powerless.

As a result of our conversations, she began setting goals, little things she could do to improve her daily life situations. Tammy decided she was going to stop reacting to her daughter's provocations the way she always had. We discussed taking a pause, a breath—something she was already practicing as part of her spiritual journey. We talked about removing herself from the situation and going for a walk and approaching her daughter about the issue when they were both calm. I suggested getting out of the house and maybe taking her grandson with her to get away from the yelling. Tammy said that sounded like good advice.

A few days later, Tammy texted me, saying she was proud of herself. The night before, when her daughter tried to start a fight, Tammy went for a walk instead of engaging. She felt good about breaking the pattern and being a better role model for her grandson. Not long after, she posted a photo to social media of her and the little boy at a local farmer's market.

By November 2022, two months after Sabrina's death, Tammy decided she'd had enough and needed to find a new place to live. The conflict at her daughter's house had grown unbearable. Without an income of her own beyond disability, she moved into a trailer rented by her oldest son, where he lived with his most recent girlfriend.

The trailer was badly in need of repair, but Tammy loved it. It had white aluminum siding covered in green algae. The front porch was filled with an apartment's worth of stuff from her son's girlfriend that couldn't fit inside when she moved in, combined with debris left from the previous renter. A roof leak had destroyed the ceiling tiles in a large corner of the living room, exposing the rafters and old, dirty insulation. The landlord had yet to fix it, and the clear plastic sheeting over the insulation looked like had been there a while and was sagging in places.

But Tammy called the rent a "great deal," despite the landlord's hollow promises to fix it up. It was a deal to her because the rent was low enough to fit within her disability income, which was less than $1,000 a month. She also liked that the trailer was in the country, surrounded by trees, hiking trails, and a stream. Tammy, who says she spends "99 percent" of her time alone, found the outdoors to be an escape and an adventure—like that hobbit hunt she'd imagined for herself to pass the time. Listening to her describe the natural world around her, it wasn't hard to envision her as the kid who won the "best camper" award all those years ago.

The location was idyllic to Tammy, but the isolation also came at a price. The problem became a crisis when Tammy's son went back to prison on another parole violation, meaning she no longer had access to a car and had to cover more of the rent, sometimes all of it. There were no buses or other kinds of public transportation in her area. Without a car, basic tasks like grocery shopping were nearly impossible, and she couldn't get a job even though she desperately needed one. Remote work wasn't an option in Tammy's world, where utility shut-offs happen frequently, and her phone was unreliable and the only device she often had for getting online.

We agreed she needed a car. But how do you make car payments without a job? And what kind of job can you get in your fifties after a decade of unemployment?

A new set of worries arose when Tammy needed a way to get to prison in March 2023 for her twenty-day January 6 sentence. She was concerned about relying on her children and had no one else to drive her three hours to Philadelphia so she could turn herself in. We were both concerned enough that I offered to change the date of a trip to the East Coast I had planned that spring, which was going to include a visit to see her (this was prior to the trip for the documentary). The original plan was to get together after Tammy got out of prison to talk about the experience for the book. I told her I would reschedule the visit around her surrender date, telling her we could celebrate her birthday since she would be spending it in prison, and then I would drive her to Philadelphia myself.

The bigger problem turned out to be getting her back home from Philadelphia when her sentence was up. Tammy's son's girlfriend had promised to pick her up when she was released at 8 a.m. On the designated day, Tammy waited outside the prison, but the son's girlfriend didn't show. So there stood Tammy, wearing the standard prison release outfit of canvas slip-on tennis shoes, khaki prison pants, and a navy-blue sweatshirt. She had no money, no identification, and no cellphone. (Prisoners have to leave cellphones, wallets, or purses with whomever drops them off, so they don't have those items with them when they get out.) It was March, and the ground was covered in slushy snow, which quickly soaked through the cheap canvas shoes. She had also exited the building with what she called "prison braids." The tradition in her cellblock was that whoever was about to get out would give five dollars from their commissary fund to a woman who cornrowed hair.

Now on the street outside the prison not knowing what to do, this fifty-two-year-old white woman—with her long hair in tight prison braids, wet shoes, and no ride—wandered her way into a Dunkin' Donuts. She asked another customer if she could borrow a phone. Tammy called me to help her figure out how to get home. She asked me to contact her son's girlfriend and one of the "Sistars" she had met through Wizard's Telegram channel, a middle-aged woman from West Virginia who is a caregiver for elderly parents with Alzheimer's and who, like Tammy, is deeply into conspirituality. The Sistar and I coordinated plans to get Tammy a hotel room in case she had to stay the night. Meanwhile, I started making calls to see about getting her a ride home. I finally reached Tammy's son's girlfriend, who eventually picked her up.

Once Tammy was back home, we started brainstorming how she could get a job. The biggest obstacle was a car. I suggested she appeal to the J6 community for support. Unlike many January 6 defendants, Tammy had never crowdsourced funds. She had a public defender and never set up a GiveSendGo fund, as many others had. I suggested reaching out to one of the groups assisting January 6 defendants with legal fees and support. Tammy explained to them that she'd served her time and needed a car to regain independence. One group gave her $1,500. A week or so later, she posted a photo of "Larry," her new red 2002 Ford Focus.

Now, with transportation, she found a job as a temporary part-time caregiver for an elderly woman. When that job ended, she found employment as a clerk at a convenience store. She asked me to serve as a reference on her applications.

Not long after, I texted Tammy, thinking she was home from work. She said she couldn't talk—she was trying out a dance class downtown. A few weeks later, Tammy texted to say she had run into the Mormon sisters at one of the open dance sessions. She'd told them she had enjoyed their conversations even though she had no interest in joining their church.

With a car and a part-time job, Tammy's world began to open up. She spent less time online and became more engaged in real life. There was a confidence now that hadn't been there when we first met in July 2022. She was taking her grandchildren hiking, organizing hobbit hunts for them, and seeing them whenever she wanted. For the first time in years, she didn't have to rely on anyone for rides.

Tammy started living her life on her own terms more than she could ever remember. Even disappointing news didn't dampen her hopes to the same extent as in the past. The Philadelphia law firm delivered bad news; after a year of trying to secure video footage and records from the prison, they could not get enough hard evidence to bring a case. For a year, that lawsuit had served Tammy as a method of hope. Now it was gone, and she was disappointed for her grandkids and for Sabrina. The sadness passed fairly quickly, however, as Tammy saw the lawsuit as one road closed, not an end to the goal of getting justice for Sabrina. "Maybe that's what the book is for," she told me about the story I was writing.

Tammy also took on serious new challenges. Several of Sabrina's kids, who were living with their mother in Sabrina's old apartment, told Tammy things that convinced her they were being sexually abused by one of the men who hung out there. She was also concerned about open drug use around her grandkids. Despite Tammy's own fraught history with Children and Youth Services, she didn't hesitate. She met with a social worker and filed a report. The social worker warned her not to get her hopes up, explaining how hard it is to get justice when young children are the only witnesses. Tammy knew she was fighting a broken system—but she fought anyway.

And this time, she won. That man, and another one, ended up in prison. The social worker began weekly visits with Sabrina's ex to work with her on parenting skills. When Tammy told me all this, I credited her determination for making it happen. In the past, she might have given up. But not this time. "You did this," I told her.

"Yes I did!" she replied with pride. "So glad I did. They would still be being abused if I wasn't persistent."

"Look what I accomplished in the last few months," Tammy said to me as we reflected on how her life had changed and the better path she was on now. "Got a car, got my own place, helped to catch a predator, got a drug addict off the streets."

Although Tammy has come a long way, she's still a conspiracist. Like Yvonne, Tammy saw Donald Trump's election and his pardon of the J6ers as a sign that Ascension had started and the global cabal was about to be exposed and defeated. She still reposts QAnon and conspirituality memes. She spends less time online, but her conspiracy communities remain a place to fight off loneliness and to find belonging. Her real life is still difficult, as are the lives of her surviving children. Conspiracies continue to be a method of hope to get through it all. One friendship with a woman who lives across the country isn't going to completely alter the path her life has followed since childhood. It will not suddenly reweave the social fabric that has come unraveled. These things move slowly. And sometimes, despite our best efforts, they do not move at all.

But I am proud of Tammy and the things she has done for herself in the years since we first spoke on the phone. She is heading in a better direction and is more engaged with offline relationships and pursuits. She is a loving and stable presence in the lives of her grandchildren, dedicated to breaking the cycle of generational trauma that has played such a destructive role in her family. If she is ever ready to leave the conspiracies behind, and she needs a friend to help her out of that world, I will be there for her, just as I know she would be there for me if I ever asked for her help.

Tammy doesn't need me to remind her of her good qualities quite as often these days. She has developed enough confidence that she can see them for herself. "I'm a very good grandma," she tells me. It's not an insecure brag, or Tammy trying to convince herself of something she's unsure about. It's a statement of truth—a realization that she can be good at something important.

Tammy's grandkids have a new name for her. She was so proud of it that she told all her online friends. One of her Sistars, the woman from West Virginia caring for parents with Alzheimer's, gave Tammy a keychain as a birthday present to symbolize it. On the end of the ring is a brass dragon, with detailed scales, outstretched wings, and a long tail. It perfectly captures the blend of fantasy and reality that makes Tammy who she is.

The grandkids call her "Dragon Slayer Grandma." And Tammy is determined to live up to the name.

Acknowledgments

Dr. Harjant Gill—for introducing me to anthropology and, more importantly, to ethnographic storytelling. Turns out I *could* do something with my degree. Dr. Caroline Heldman—for seeing something in this project before I did and insisting it was a book. And for believing that a former stay-at-home mom could pull it off. Dr. Amy Cooter—for one of the first conversations that made me think, *maybe this is a book*, and for reading the final manuscript with the sharp eye it deserved. Valerie Weaver-Zercher—for recognizing the value of this work early on and pulling it into focus. Your editorial instincts didn't just shape the book; they sharpened its impact.

Dr. Christine Sarteschi—for supporting my project, being accessible, and patiently answering my many questions when the conspiracists dabbled in "sovereignty." Liz Smith—for your sense of adventure, for seeing something in my work, and for taking an unexpected cross-country road trip with me that turned into a documentary film. Kim Halliday—for writing music and sending it my way, feeding my creative process at moments when I thought I had nothing left to give.

Chantelle De Carvalho and the Page 75 Productions team—for backing this story and helping bring it to life on screen. Travis View—for his expertise and generous suggestions to improve my depictions of QAnon and Helena Blavatsky. Rich Logis, Stephanie Kemmerer, and Erica R.—for sharing your experiences as "formers" and for your friendship and insight. #BallsGang—for the support, the niche expertise, and the community. You made the long, isolating process of writing this book less isolating—and much funnier. Tammy and Yvonne—for trusting me with your stories, and for the unlikely friendships that followed.

And finally, my family. Four years of this research have reminded me just how fortunate I was to grow up with love and support. Each of you has brought so much into my life. My husband, Terry Bouton—without him, this book wouldn't exist. His patience while I figured it out, his support while I worked unpaid, and his editorial brilliance gave me the space I needed to make this book happen. I could not have done any of this without you. Thank you for believing I could be a writer. Deanne, my mother—for instilling in me the concept of the greater good and raising me to think critically. My aunt Rhonda—for being a steady, calming presence and one of my biggest cheerleaders. My children and their partners—Andrew (and Bradon), Patrick (and Quinn), and Claire—for their patience when my time became scarce and for tolerating the endless stories I wanted to share. The second half of life brought me a book and a documentary film, but being your mom will always be my greatest pride.

Notes

CHAPTER 1: CAPITOL CONSPIRACIES

2 ***"It only takes one heart to change":*** All quotations from Yvonne in the book come from court transcripts, conversations with the author, emails, and social media posts. For the court testimony referenced in this chapter, see United States v. ST CYR, 1:22-cr-00185, (D.D.C. May 11, 2023) ECF No. 101 at https://www.courtlistener.com/docket/63339778/101/united-states-v-st-cyr/ and United States v. ST CYR, 1:22-cr-00185, (D.D.C. May 11, 2023) ECF No. 102 at https://www.courtlistener.com/docket/63339778/102/united-states-v-st-cyr/.

2 ***Trump had announced the protest would be "wild":*** Jarret Bencks, "Trump and the Language of Insurrection," *BrandeisNOW*, January 12, 2021, https://www.brandeis.edu/now/2021/january/trump-language-capitol-riot-mcintosh.html.

5 ***"we will bring this system down":*** *The Conspiracists*, directed by Liz Smith, 2024, https://theconspiracistsfilm.com.

6 ***"a broad politico-spiritual philosophy based on two core convictions":*** Charlotte Ward and David Voas, "The Emergence of Conspirituality," *Journal of Contemporary Religion* 26, no. 1 (2011): 103–121, https://doi.org/10.1080/13537903.2011.539846.

9 ***"When women get involved, a movement becomes a serious threat":*** Cynthia Miller-Idriss, "Women Among the Jan. 6 Attackers Are the New Normal of Right-Wing Extremism," *MSNBC*, January 8, 2022, https://www.msnbc.com/opinion/women-among-jan-6-attackers-are-new-normal-right-wing-n1287163.

10 ***believe that Joe Biden had stolen the 2020 election:*** "Republican Loyalty to Trump, Rioters Climbs in 3 Years After Jan. 6 Attack," *Washington Post*, January 2, 2024. https://www.washingtonpost.com/dc-md-va/2024/01/02/jan-6-poll-post-trump/.

10 ***"conspiracy-based coalition that brings far-right and mainstream operators together":*** "Conspiracy and the Masses," Political Research Associates, January 29, 2021, https://politicalresearch.org/2021/01/29/conspiracy-masses.

10 ***"a belief in widespread government corruption as justification for violence":*** Program on Extremism at George Washington University, "Into the Abyss: QAnon and the Militia Sphere in the 2020 Election" (Program on Extremism at George Washington University, March 2023), https://extremism.gwu.edu/sites/g/files/zaxdzs5746/files/2023-03/into-the-abyss-final.pdf.

10 ***we have likely underestimated the potential for women to express their conspiracism through violence:*** See, for example, Erin C. Cassese, Christina E. Farhart, and Joanne, M. Miller, "Gender Differences in COVID-19 Conspiracy Theory Beliefs," *Politics & Gender* 16, no. 4 (2020): 1009–1018; Ira Frejborg and Katarina Pettersson,

"Red-Pilled Mama Bears and Enlightened Power Goddesses: Discursive Constructions of Female Identities in a Conspiracy Theory Space," *British Journal of Social Psychology* 63 (2024): 1037–1052.

11 *one among many new conspiracies:* Jeanine Santucci, "QAnon Supporters Gather in Dallas to Witness Return of JFK Jr., Who Died in 1999," *USA Today*, November 2, 2021, https://www.usatoday.com/story/news/nation/2021/11/02/texas-qanon-believers-back-theory-trump-reinstated/6255234001/.

18 *conspiracy theories become what some anthropologists call a "method of hope":* Hirokazu Miyazak, *The Method of Hope: Anthropology, Philosophy, and Fijian Knowledge* (Stanford University Press, 2004).

CHAPTER 2: TRAUMA

21 *a massive 2023 study of "The Conspiratorial Mind" by the American Psychological Association:* S. M. Bowes, T. H. Costello, and A. Tasimi, "The Conspiratorial Mind: A Meta-Analytic Review of Motivational and Personological Correlates," *Psychological Bulletin* 149, no. 5–6 (2023): 259–293, https://doi.org/10.1037/bul0000392.

22 *most scholarship on conspiracism:* For a short and useful overview of the research on conspiracism, see Helen Hendy and Pamela Black, *Conspiracy Belief as Coping Behavior: Life Stressors, Powerlessness, and Extreme Beliefs* (Lexington Books, 2023).

23 *embracing conspiracy theories "may in some way offer them relief from their stressors":* Hendy and Black, *Conspiracy Belief as Coping Behavior*, 19.

28 *researchers have linked ACEs to nine out of ten of the top causes of death:* These findings and other helpful data and resources relating to ACEs can be found at, "ACE Fundamentals," *ACEs Aware*, accessed March 1, 2025, https://www.acesaware.org/ace-fundamentals/.

28 *far more children experience ACEs than you might expect:* "Adverse Childhood Experiences (ACEs)," US Centers for Disease Control and Prevention, accessed March 1, 2025, https://www.cdc.gov/aces/about/index.html.

33 *"black holes" in memory are common among the survivors of childhood sexual abuse":* Molly R. Wolf and Thomas H. Nochajski, "'Black Holes' in Memory: Childhood Autobiographical Memory Loss in Adult Survivors of Child Sexual Abuse," *European Journal of Trauma & Dissociation* 6, 100234 (February 2022).

36 *like many women, Tammy experienced intimate partner violence at the hands of multiple men:* These statistics come from studies cited by National Domestic Violence Hotline, which has provided tools and support for domestic violence victims for the last twenty-five years. "National Domestic Violence Statistics," National Domestic Violence Hotline, accessed March 1, 2025, https://www.thehotline.org/stakeholders/domestic-violence-statistics/.

CHAPTER 3: SOMETHING TO BELIEVE IN

44 *people who put faith in their own intuition above verifiable facts:* Evita March and Jordan Springer, "Belief in Conspiracy Theories: The Predictive Role of Schizotypy, Machiavellianism, and Primary Psychopathy," *PLOS ONE* 14, no. 12 (2019): e0225964, https://doi.org/10.1371/journal.pone.0225964.

45 *the fastest growing organized faith movement in the world:* Heiko Beyer and Niklas Herrberg, "The Revelations of Q: Dissemination and Resonance of the QAnon Conspiracy Theory Among US Evangelical Christians and the Role of the Covid-19 Crisis," *Zeitschrift für Religion, Gesellschaft und Politik* (March 1, 2023): 1–19, https://doi.org/10.1007/s41682-023-00147-2.

51 *the Illuminati serves as a stand-in for every real and imagined secret society:* Juan Antonio Roche Cárcel, "The Religious Genesis of Conspiracy Theories and Their Consequences for Democracy and Religion: The Case of QAnon," *Religions* 14, no. 6 (2023).

51 *the standard-enemies list also includes Hollywood elites, public health officials, and members of the Democratic Party:* "Conspiracy and the Masses," Political Research Associates, January 29, 2021, https://politicalresearch.org/2021/01/29/conspiracy-masses.

52 *Trump's dire language about "American carnage" in his 2017 inaugural address:* Donald J. Trump, "The Inaugural Address," Trump White House Archives, January 20, 2017, https://trumpwhitehouse.archives.gov/briefings-statements/the-inaugural-address/.

53 *a positive, civic-boosting scene that includes historical figures in little tableaux:* "Inspiration Lycoming County," Pilato Murals, accessed December 29, 2024, https://pilatomurals.com/murals/inspiration-lycoming-county/.

CHAPTER 4: PANDEMIC

60 *the pandemic ultimately served as a superspreader of conspiracy theories:* Hans W. A. Hanley, Deepak Kumar, and Zakir Durumeric, "A Golden Age: Conspiracy Theories' Relationship with Misinformation Outlets, News Media, and the Wider Internet," *Proceedings of the ACM on Human-Computer Interaction* 7, no. CSCW2, article 252 (October 2023); Michael Christensen and Ashli Au, "The Great Reset and the Cultural Boundaries of Conspiracy Theory," *International Journal of Communication* 17 (2023): 2348–2366.

61 *many spiritualists and life coaches . . . were now aligning themselves with right-wing conspiracy theories:* Stephanie Alice Baker, "Alt. Health Influencers: How Wellness Culture and Web Culture Have Been Weaponized to Promote Conspiracy Theories and Far-Right Extremism During the COVID-19 Pandemic," *European Journal of Cultural Studies* 25, no. 1 (2022): 3–24.

62 *blending of health and wellness/New Age spirituality and right-wing conspiracism fueled the conspirituality movement:* Charlotte War and David Voas, "The Emergence of Conspirituality," *Journal of Contemporary Religion* 26, no. 1 (January 2011): 103–121; Giovanna Parmigiani, "Magic and Politics: Conspirituality and COVID-19," *Journal of the American Academy of Religion* 89, no. 2 (June 2021): 506–529; Tristan Sturm and Tom Albrecht, "Constituent Covid-19 Apocalypses: Contagious Conspiracism, 5G, and Viral Vaccinations," *Anthropology & Medicine* 28, no. 1 (Nov. 2020): 122–139; Mar Griera, "Conspirituality in COVID-19 Times: A Mixed-Method Study of Anti-Vaccine Movements in Spain," *Journal for the Academic Study of Religion* 35, no. 2 (2022), 192.

64 *Love Has Won has been the subject of multiple documentary films, news reports, and podcasts:* For an overview of Love Has Won, see Christopher Moyer, "From

'Mother God' to Mummified Corpse: Inside the Fringe Spiritual Sect 'Love Has Won,'" *Rolling Stone Magazine*, November 26, 2021; and David G. Bromley and Katie Toomey, "Love Has Won," World Religions and Spirituality Project, September 30, 2022, https://wrldrels.org/2022/08/27/love-has-won/.

68 ***one thing they have in common is the need to tear down the current American system and global order:*** Brian Hughes and Cynthia Miller-Idriss, "Uniting for Total Collapse: The January 6 Boost to Accelerationism," *CTC Sentinel* 14, no. 4 (April/May 2021). https://ctc.westpoint.edu/uniting-for-total-collapse-the-january-6-boost-to-accelerationism/. Matthew D. Taylor, *The Violent Take It by Force: The Christian Movement That Is Threatening Our Democracy* (Broadleaf Books, 2024). Ari Breland, "Meet the Silicon Valley CEOs Who Insist That Greed is Good, Even if 'Effective Accelerationism' Kills Us All," *Mother Jones*, January-February 2024. https://www.motherjones.com/politics/2023/12/effective-accelerationism/.

70 ***distrust of conventional news sources is a hallmark of conspiracism:*** Edward H. Miller, "Today's Right-Wing Conspiracy Theory Mentality Can be Traced Back to the John Birch Society," *Los Angeles Times*, January 9, 2022; "COVID-19 Conspiracy Beliefs Increased Among Users of Conservative and Social Media," Annenberg Public Policy Center, May 3, 2021, https://www.annenbergpublicpolicycenter.org/covid-19-conspiracy-beliefs-increased-among-users-of-conservative-and-social-media/.

76 ***concepts taken from the Sovereign Citizen movement:*** Christine Sarteshi, "How Sovereign Citizens Threaten the Rule of Law," FlaglerLive.com, July 2, 2024, https://flaglerlive.com/sovereign-citizens/.

CHAPTER 5: MAMA BEARS

81 ***Biden's commutation received widespread criticism:*** "'Kids for Cash' Judge Among Biden's Pardons for Wrongfully Convicted and Nonviolent Offenders," *The Guardian*, December 14, 2024. https://www.theguardian.com/us-news/2024/dec/14/kids-for-cash-judge-biden-pardon; "Biden Commutes Sentence of Judge Who Took Kickbacks for Sending Kids to For-Profit Juvenile Detention," *National Review*, December 14, 2024. https://www.nationalreview.com/news/biden-commutes-sentence-of-judge-who-took-kickbacks-for-sending-kids-to-for-profit-juvenile-detention/.

81 ***Conahan was PARDONED by Biden:*** "Clemency Recipient List," The White House, December 12, 2024, https://bidenwhitehouse.archives.gov/briefing-room/statements-releases/2024/12/12/clemency-recipient-list-7/.

82 ***two of Tammy's own children were victims of the Kids for Cash scandal:*** The basic facts of the scandal related here, including the statistics cited, can be found on the website of the organization that broke the story. See "Luzerne County 'Kids for Cash' Scandal," *Juvenile Law Center*, accessed December 29, 2024, https://jlc.org/luzerne-kids-cash-scandal.

85 ***women were the online superspreaders of the QAnon conspiracy theories:*** "Key Misinformation Superspreaders on Twitter: Older Women," *Ars Technica*, May 2024, https://arstechnica.com/science/2024/05/key-misinformation-superspreaders-on-twitter-older-women/; Sophia Moskalenko, Tomislav Pavlović, and Brett Burton, "QAnon Beliefs, Political Radicalization and Support for January 6th Insurrection: A Gendered Perspective," *Terrorism and Political Violence* 36, no. 7 (2023): 962–981.

85 **they took different paths and followed different conspiracies:** Erin C. Cassese, Christina E. Farhart, and Joanne M. Miller, "Gender Differences in COVID-19 Conspiracy Theory Beliefs," *Politics & Gender* 16, no. 4 (July 2020): 1–12.

85 **QAnon gave that basic truth a wild conspiratorial backstory:** Frankie Mastrangelo and Gina Marie Longo, "Downlining Disinformation: How MLM Distributors Use Gendered Strategies for Recruitment and Pastel QAnon Indoctrination," *Social Media + Society* 10, no. 1 (2024): 1–12; Ira Frejborg and Katarina Pettersson, "Red-Pilled Mama Bears and Enlightened Power Godesses: Discursive Constructions of Female Identities in a Conspiracy Theory Space," *British Journal of Social Psychology* 63 (2024): 1037–1052; Lorna Bracewell, "Gender, Populism, and the QAnon Conspiracy Movement," *Frontiers in Sociology* 5 (January 2021): 1–4.

86 **"you don't need to be a mom to be a mama bear":** Frejborg and Pettersson, "Red-Pilled Mama Bears and Enlightened Power Goddesses." For how women in right-wing movement soften and mainstream extreme beliefs, see Seyward Darby, *Sisters in Hate: American Women on the Front Lines of White Supremacy* (Little, Brown, 2020).

87 **conservative women framed their activism as being frontline protectors of families and children:** Melissa Gira Grant, "Mothers of Oppression," *New Republic*, September 1, 2023, 38–45; Allen G. Breed, "'The Lost Cause': The Women's Group Fighting for Confederate Monuments," *The Guardian*, August 10, 2018, https://www.theguardian.com/us-news/2018/aug/10/united-daughters-of-the-confederacy-statues-lawsuit; Alice Herman and Karen Goll, "'Mama Bears are Rising Up': The Rightwing Christian Entrepreneur Aiming for a Takeover of Local US Government," *The Guardian*, December 16, 2024.

93 **a tradwife is a woman who embraces an idealized image of womanhood from the past:** Harmeet Kaur, "Tradwives' Promote a Lifestyle that Evokes the 1950s. But Their Nostalgia is Not Without Controversy," *CNN*, December 27, 2022, https://www.cnn.com/2022/12/27/us/tradwife-1950s-nostalgia-tiktok-cec/index.html; Alina Kim, "The Troubling Framework of the 'Neo-Nazi's girl-friend,'" *The Objective*, May 18, 2023, https://objectivejournalism.org/2023/05/the-troubling-framework-of-the-neo-nazis-girlfriend/.

94 **conspirituality has grown significantly as a faith movement:** Helen L. Murphey, "Contemporary Conspirituality: Centering Gender in the Field of Conspiracy Theory Research," *Feminist Media Studies* 23, no. 6 (May 2023): 3080–3083.

94 **age-related slights, like when Vice President JD Vance agreed with a podcast host:** Beth Allison Barr, *The Making of Biblical Womanhood: How the Subjugation of Women Became Gospel Truth* (Brazos Press, 2021). "J.D. Vance's Weird Thoughts on Older Women Exposed in New Audio," *The New Republic*, December 28, 2024, https://newrepublic.com/post/184888/jd-vance-weird-thoughts-older-women-postmenopausal-female-audio.

95 **liberal feminist concern often stops at menopause:** R. Thwaites, "Making a Choice or Taking a Stand? Choice Feminism, Political Engagement and the Contemporary Feminist Movement," *Feminist Theory* 18, no. 1 (2017), 55–68; Rebecca L. Jones, "Imagining Feminist Old Age: Moving Beyond 'Successful' Ageing?" *Journal of Aging Studies* 63 (December 2022): 100950.

95 **a 2014 Pew Research survey revealed the typical follower of New Age spirituality:** "2023–24 US Religious Landscape Study Interactive Database," Pew Research Center, 2025, https://www.pewresearch.org/religious-landscape-study/.

97 *support for Democrats dropped by 7 percent among middle-aged women:* Amanda Becker, "Harris Lost Support from Women Overall—But not Women over 65," *The Fulcrum*, November 26, 2024, https://thefulcrum.us/election-2024/ women-over-65-kamala-harris.

CHAPTER 6: STARSEED AWAKENING

99 *there are now thousands, and probably more like millions, of starseeds out there:* Ken Drinkwater, Andrew Denovan, and Neil Dagnall, "Starseeds: Psychologists on Why Some People Think They're Aliens Living on Earth," *The Conversation*, March 13, 2023, https://theconversation.com/starseeds-psychologists-on-why-some-people-think-theyre-aliens-living-on-earth-197291. For a broad view of starseeds and conspirituality, see Beth Daviess, "A Wolf in New Age Clothing: Starseed Beliefs, Conspirituality, and a Soft Pathway to Radicalization," *Center on Terrorism, Extremism and Counterterrorism*, Middlebury Institute of International Studies. Occasional paper (June 2024). https://drive.google.com/file/d/1L185wGY07SFmH6p5g2SQIyd PNCQ6rhsf/view.

102 *it all began with a belief system called theosophy:* My understanding of theosophy is drawn primarily from Bruce F. Campbell, *Ancient Wisdom Revived: A History of the Theosophical Movement* (University of California Press, 1980) and Olav Hammer and Mikael Rothstein, *Handbook of Theosophical Current* (Brill, 2013).

106 *about a quarter of Americans believed key New Age concepts:* Taylor Orth, "Most Americans Endorse at Least Some Aspects of the New-Age Spiritual Movement," YouGov, November 29, 2022, https://today.yougov.com/health/ articles/44581-most-americans-hold-some-new-age-beliefs-poll.

106 *"about 60 percent of Christians also believe in at least one of those concepts":* Claire Gecewicz, "'New Age' Beliefs Common Among Both Religious and Nonreligious Americans," *Pew Research Center*, October 1, 2018, https:// www.pewresearch.org/short-reads/2018/10/01/new-age-beliefs-common-among-both-religious-and-nonreligious-americans/.

106 *"the number of Americans who report becoming more spiritual over time":* Asta Kallo, "Around 4 in 10 Americans Have Become More Spiritual Over Time; Fewer Have Become More Religious," *Pew Research Center*, January 17, 2024, https://www. pewresearch.org/short-reads/2024/01/17/around-4-in-10-americans-have-become-more-spiritual-over-time-fewer-have-become-more-religious/.

106 *"the global wellness industry in 2023 was estimated to be worth $6.3 trillion":* "Wellness Economy Statistics and Facts," *Global Wellness Institute*, accessed March 1, 2025, https://globalwellnessinstitute.org/press-room/statistics-and-facts/.

106 *"'Spiritual Products and Services' combined were worth $165 billion in 2023":* Transparency Market Research, "Spiritual & Devotional Products Market to Reach Worth of US$ 8.3 billion in 2031, Expanding at a CAGR of 8.7%: TMR Report," Yahoo!Finance, June 12, 2023, https://finance.yahoo.com/news/spiritual-devotional-products-market-reach-133800628.html.

113 *"how psychedelics can assist in the treatment of trauma, depression, and addiction":* Sharon Reynolds, "How Psychedelic Drugs May Help with Depression," *NIH*

Research Matters, National Institute of Health, March 14, 2023, https://www.nih.gov/news-events/nih-research-matters/how-psychedelic-drugs-may-help-depression.

CHAPTER 7: CULTURE WARS

128 *"New Age theologies seem to act as moderating forces"*: Reactionary politics often contains progressive elements. That is even true of the politics espoused by the Women's KKK. See Emily Cataneo, "A Brief History of the Women's KKK," *JSTOR Daily*, October 14, 2020, https://daily.jstor.org/a-brief-history-of-the-womens-kkk/.

128 *"Helena Blavatsky, the founding mother of theosophy"*: My understanding of Helena Blavatsky is shaped by the essays in Olav Hammer and Mikael Rothstein, *Handbook of Theosophical Current* (Brill, 2013), especially Siv Ellen Kraft's essay "Theosophy, Gender, and the 'New Woman'" and Isaac Lubelsky's "Mythological and Real Race Issues in Theosophy."

130 *"she didn't think the soul enters a human vessel until after a baby is born"*: Helena Blavatsky, *The Secret Doctrine Commentaries*, ed. Michael Gomes (ISIS Foundation, 2010), 575.

130 *"she believed abortion should be punished like a suicide attempt"*: Helena Blavatsky, "Is Foeticide a Crime?" (1883), https://theosophytrust.org/444-is-foeticide-a-crime.

133 *"91 percent of the followers of New Age religions were white people"*: Pew Research Center, "2023–2024 US Religious Landscape Study Interactive Database," Pew Research Center, 2025, https://www.pewresearch.org/religious-landscape-study/database/religious-family/new-age/racial-and-ethnic-composition/#demographic-information.

133 *"Black conspiracism grows out of lived experiences and genuine horrors inflicted by governments"*: Amy Cooter, et al., "Cultural Change and Conspiracism: How Conspiracy Theory Trends Reflect Threat and Anxiety," in eds. Marc-André Argentino and Amarnath Amarasingam, *Far-Right Culture: the Art, Music, and Everyday Practices of Violent Extremists* (Forthcoming). Sociologist Amy Cooter observes that older studies identifying Black Americans as the most conspiratorial racial group were based on faulty survey questions that asked about government actions against "urban".

134 *"white conspiracism seems more rooted in the perception of loss in social status"*: Emily Bazelon, "White People Are Noticing Something New: Their Own Whiteness," *New York Times Magazine*, June 13, 2018, https://www.nytimes.com/2018/06/13/magazine/white-people-are-noticing-something-new-their-own-whiteness.html; Adam Enders et al., "The Sociodemographic Correlates of Conspiracism," *Scientific Reports* 14, 14184 (June 20, 2024), https://doi.org/10.1038/s41598-024-64098-1.

136 *"numerous passages in the Book of Mormon that refer to blackening skin as a punishment for sin"*: The most commonly cited passages in Book of Mormon that identify dark skin as a curse are: 2 Nephi 30:6, cf. 1 Nephi 12:23, 13:15, 2 Nephi 5:21, Jacob 3:8–9, 3 Nephi 2:14–15, and Moses 7:8, 12, 22.

138 *"conspirituality taking a central place in the New Age movement"*: Baker, "Alt. Health Influencers."

142 *"you can see that change by reviewing the "Prior Years" section of the Expo's offi-cial website"*: "Prior Years," Conscious Life Expo, accessed March 1, 2025, https://consciouslifeexpo.com/prior-years/.

143 *"the Rabbit Hole represents some of the most extreme examples of con-spiratorial thought leadership today"*: For more about the change, see Anna Merlan, "America's Biggest New Age Expo Welcomes Conspiracy Theories Back In," *Vice*, January 31, 2023, https://www.vice.com/en/article/americas-biggest-new-age-expo-welcomes-conspiracy-theories-back-in/.

143 *"Willis worked as a videographer for Bernie Sanders's 2016 presidential cam-paign"*: Josh Rottenberg and Stacy Perman, "Meet the Oja Dad Who Made the Most Notorious Piece of Coronavirus Disinformation Yet," *Los Angeles Times*, March 13, 2020, https://www.latimes.com/entertainment-arts/movies/story/2020-05-13/plandemic-coronavirus-documentary-director-mikki-willis-mikovits.

CHAPTER 8: A METHOD OF HOPE

147 *"phenomenon by which people become convinced that social media algorithms are the voice of God"*: The discussion of algorithmic conspirituality is based on the fascinating article by Kelley Cotter et al., "If You're Reading This, It's Meant for You: The Reflexive Ambivalence of Algorithmic Conspirituality," *Convergence: The International Journal of Research into New Media Technologies* 30, no. 6 (2024): 1893–1918.

148 *"what anthropologists call a 'method of hope'"*: Hirokazu Miyazak, *The Method of Hope: Anthropology, Philosophy, and Fijian Knowledge* (Stanford University Press, 2004). I found Miyazak's ideas about how hope is at the center of various cultural forms of knowledge production to be particularly useful in understanding cultures of conspiracism and conspirituality.

153 *"hoping the cold-shoulder treatment will force their loved one to abandon con-spiratorial thinking"*: Meggan M. Jordan and Jennifer Marie Whitmer, "'I Would Give Anything to Talk About Aliens Now': QAnon Conspiracy Theories and the Creation of Cognitive Deviance," *Sociological Perspectives* 66, no 6. (2023): 992–1014; Lauren Mastroni and Robyn Mooney, "'I One-Hundred Thousand Percent Blame It on QAnon': The Impact of QAnon Belief on Interpersonal Relationships," *Journal of Social and Personal Relationships* 4, no. 9 (2024): 2478–2499.

159 *"strong connection between loneliness and beliefs in conspiracy theories"*: Kinga Bierwiaczonek et al., "Loneliness Trajectories over Three Decades Are Associated with Conspiracist Worldviews in Midlife," *Nature Communications* 15, 3629 (2024), https://doi.org/10.1038/s41467-024-47113-x.

CHAPTER 9: SOUL CONTRACT

164 *"New Age conspirituality is largely indistinguishable from conspiracism in gen-eral"*: For the negative effects of conspiracism, see: Daniel Jolley, Matthew Marques, and Darel Cookson, "Shining a Spotlight on the Dangerous Consequences of Con-spiracy Theories," *Current Opinion in Psychology* 47, 101263 (October 2022), https://doi.org/10.1016/j.copsyc.2022.101363; K. M. Douglas, "Are Conspiracy Theories

Harmless?" *Spanish Journal of Psychology* 24, no. 13 (February 2022); T. Winter et al., "Conspiracy Beliefs and Distrust of Science Predicts Reluctance of Vaccine Uptake of Politically Right-Wing Citizens," *Vaccine* 40, no. 12 (February 2022): 1896–1903; Bastiaan T. Rutjens, "Conspiracy Beliefs and Science Rejection," *Current Opinion in Psychology* 46, 10139 (April 2022); Julia Ainsley, "One Quarter of Mass Attackers Driven by Conspiracy Theories or Hateful Ideologies, Secret Service Report Says," *NBC News*, January 25, 2023, https://www.nbcnews.com/news/us-news/one-quarter-mass-attackers-conspiracy-theories-hate-rcna67298; Jesselyn Cook, *The Quiet Damage: QAnon and the Destruction of the American Family* (Crown, 2024).

166 *"a narration of a children's book, The Little Soul and the Sun: A Children's Parable"*: This is a link to the version of the video Yvonne prefers: https://www.youtube.com/watch?v=YhHICGso8qk. You can find this particular video reposted by numerous New Age influencers and followers.

166 *"'I was homeless with a broken neck, living in a park'..."*: Lois Malcolm, "God as Best Seller: Deepak Chopra, Neal Walsch and New Age Theology," *The Christian Century*, September 20, 2003, 31–35; Borys Kit, "Walsch's 'God' Getting Spiritual," *Hollywood Reporter* 387, no. 21 (January 12, 2005).

171 *"the day of Donald Trump's inauguration, he issued blanket commutations and pardons for nearly all of the 1,500 January 6 defendants"*: White House website, "Presidential Actions," January 20, 2025, https://www.whitehouse.gov/presidential-actions/2025/01/granting-pardons-and-commutation-of-sentences-for-certain-offenses-relating-to-the-events-at-or-near-the-united-states-capitol-on-january-6-2021/.

171 *"figuring out what to do about conspiracism"*: The following discussion is based heavily on Emily Booth et al., "Conspiracy, Misinformation, Radicalisation: Understanding the Online Pathway to Indoctrination and Opportunities for Intervention," *Journal of Sociology* 60, no. 2 (2024): 440–457; Kristen Engel et al., "Learning from the Ex-Believers: Individuals' Journeys In and Out of Conspiracy Theories Online," *Proceedings of the ACM on Human-Computer Interaction* 7, 285 (October 2023): 1–37; Sijia Xiao, et al., "Sensemaking and the Chemtrail Conspiracy on the Internet: Insights from Believers and Ex-Believers," *Proceedings of the ACM on Human-Computer Interaction* 5, 454 (October 2021): 1–28; and Helen Hendy and Pamela Black, *Conspiracy Belief as Coping Behavior: Life Stressors, Powerlessness, and Extreme Beliefs* (Lexington Books, 2023), 139–143.

173 *"exiting conspiracy-laden worlds is a process that happens over time"*: For understanding the process of conspiracism and the kinds of interventions that might work at each stage of the process, see Booth et al., "Conspiracy, Misinformation, and Radicalisation."

175 *"the essential ingredient in the process of helping someone exit conspiracism, research suggests, seems to be empathy"*: Engel et al., "Learning from the Ex-Believers." The scholarship on political polarization is relevant here as well. See for example, Luiza A. Santos et al., "Belief in the Utility of Cross-Partisan Empathy Reduces Partisan Animosity and Facilitates Political Persuasion," *Psychological Science* 33, no. 9 (2022): 1557–1573.